CAN
YOU
STILL
TRUST
GOD?

OTHER BOOKS BY CHARLES STANLEY

CAN YOU STILL TRUST GOD?

WHAT HAPPENS WHEN YOU CHOOSE TO BELIEVE

CHARLES F. STANLEY

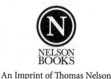

NELSON BOOKS

An Imprint of Thomas Nelson

Published in Nashville, Tennessee, by Nelson Books, an imprint of Thomas Nelson. Nelson Books and Thomas Nelson are registered trademarks of HarperCollins Christian Publishing, Inc.

Published in association with the literary agency of William Morris Endeavor Entertainment, LLC, c/o Mel Berger, 11 Madison Avenue, New York, New York 10010.

Thomas Nelson titles may be purchased in bulk for educational, business, fundraising, or sales promotional use. For information, please e-mail SpecialMarkets@ThomasNelson.com.

Unless otherwise noted, Scripture quotations are taken from the New American Standard Bible® (NASB). Copyright © 1960, 1962, 1963, 1968, 1971, 1972, 1973, 1975, 1977, 1995 by The Lockman Foundation. Used by permission. www.lockman.org

Scripture quotations marked NKJV are taken from the New King James Version®. Copyright © 1982 by Thomas Nelson. Used by permission. All rights reserved.

Any internet addresses, phone numbers, or company or product information printed in this book are offered as a resource and are not intended in any way to be or to imply an endorsement by Thomas Nelson, nor does Thomas Nelson vouch for the existence, content, or services of these sites, phone numbers, companies, or products beyond the life of this book.

ISBN 978-0-7852-4753-1 (Jacketed Hardcover)
ISBN 978-0-7852-5289-4 (ITPE)
ISBN 978-0-7852-4757-9 (eBook)

Library of Congress Control Number: 2020947346

Printed in the United States of America
21 22 23 24 25   LSC   10 9 8 7 6 5 4 3 2

CONTENTS

CONTENTS

PART 4: GOD PROVIDES A WAY THROUGH PAIN AND SUFFERING

PART 5: GOD REVEALS A PLAN FOR YOUR LIFE

INTRODUCTION

During this tumultuous era in our history, I've been struck by the anxiety and disheartenment I have seen as I've talked to friends and loved ones. It is understandable. We are facing uncertain times and significant challenges. Whether it is the pandemic, the economic decline, the social unrest, the global political maneuverings, or what have you—it seems there is more to think about than we can possibly wrap our minds around. And the truth of the matter is, we can overthink the issues that assail us until we are utterly obsessed with and confounded by them. We can't sleep. We cannot get away from them. We turn on the television, and there is more to baffle us. We are constantly praying about it all—but with fear about the problems rather than with faith that God is at work through all of it.

Pretty soon, every thought and every conversation are devoured by questions about what will happen. It is then we can become confused and overwhelmed with fear and pain to the point that we no longer trust the One who is truly in control of all things.

Perhaps you can identify with these feelings of helplessness and instability. You go to sleep imploring the Lord for help and wake up feeling unsettled, useless, and insecure. At the back of your mind may be the nagging question, *Can I really trust God through all of this?*

When things are going our way, trusting the Lord is easy. But when painful trials, unmet needs, or lost hopes assail us, the pain may cause us to ask, *Can I still trust God?* We may be tempted to question why a truly caring Father would allow sorrow and difficulty to touch His children's lives. We may even doubt whether He is *willing* to do anything about our circumstances.

But God assured His people, "Call upon Me in the day of trouble; I shall rescue you" (Ps. 50:15). Can we truly rely upon Him to do that? Followers of Jesus Christ need to understand that He is not only able but also willing to fulfill every single promise in Scripture. Even when we cannot understand why God would allow certain situations to occur, understanding His ways always leads to understanding that He will act in a manner that brings about eternal blessings for His children. It is what you *believe* that makes it possible to ask the right questions in the face of a tragedy or great needs in your life.

So whether you have picked up this book because of the turmoil in the world, the unwise actions of others, or because of profound personal trials, please be assured that you have come to the right place. You are not alone. Your life matters to God. He cares for you. And yes, you can still trust Him.

Likewise, through the years I have discovered three essential beliefs for maintaining my faith in God that I will share with you now. Even when you lack understanding about your circumstances, these beliefs can form a solid foundation for trusting Him. Therefore, I challenge you to take a long, hard look at what you believe about Him. Your ability to receive the blessings God has for you is determined by the degree to which these wise truths are embedded in your soul.

BELIEF #1: GOD IS PERFECT IN HIS LOVE

In other words, God *always* does what is best for us. If we really believe this, we will trust Him even in our most difficult trials. Satan, who works to undermine our trust, often takes advantage of adversity by calling the Father's motives into question. He whispers, "If the Lord really loved you, He would not have allowed this to happen"—he wants us to associate the sting of spiritual discipline with a lack of divine caring. However, the exact opposite is true. Hebrews 12:6 tells us, "Those whom the Lord loves He disciplines, and He scourges every son whom He receives." So, while natural thinking says peace and happiness are tokens of God's love, the Bible says difficulty and discipline are actually evidence of our membership in His family. The reason is clear: God cares for us so much that He will not allow us to stay as we are. Instead, He wants to transform us into the likeness of His Son.

We can depend on God's love because of His character—it is His very nature to love (1 John 4:8). The Bible says, "In Him there is no darkness at all" (1 John 1:5); in other words, He is absolutely holy, righteous, and perfect and therefore could never mistreat one of His children. He will always do what is positive and caring in our lives. *Calvary* is positive proof of God's profound love for mankind. All of us were in dire need of forgiveness and rescue from the penalty of sin, but we could not save ourselves—our debt could be satisfied only by the payment of a perfect life (Deut. 17:1). The heavenly Father made our salvation possible by sending His Son, Jesus, to die on the cross as our substitute, which is indisputable evidence of His sacrificial, infinite love for humanity (Rom. 5:8). God's love is also revealed in the covenant expressing His intention to make us His children (Jer. 31:33). Once we trusted Jesus Christ as our personal Savior, we became members of God's family. Our perfect heavenly Father is patient, loving, and kind toward us; He understands that we are children learning to live in this life.

God loves us flawlessly. Every action He performs or permits in our lives is an expression of His love, even though He allows some situations that we think could not possibly be for our good. Always remember that God is omniscient—He sees the end from the beginning and knows exactly what fruit will come from our pain and challenges. Although we may not understand His reason for allowing certain hardships, our difficulties in no way indicate He is anything but a good God and worthy of our trust.

BELIEF #2: GOD IS INFINITE IN WISDOM

The Lord never has to poll the angelic host—or anyone else—to get a consensus about the wisest action to take. In His unlimited knowledge, He always knows what is in our very best interest and acts accordingly. Regardless of what our circumstances look like, we must remember that God knows the optimal course of action in every situation and will only benefit His children.

Sometimes we look at difficulties facing us and think, *Well now, Lord, I know You are infinitely wise, but I think You've forgotten something.* Be assured He has not overlooked a single factor. In our limited understanding and reasoning, we simply do not see things from God's perspective. We may have all the information that is humanly possible to gather, but God is aware of *everything* influencing the situation as well as all the potential consequences for you and others. He alone comprehends the totality of every single decision. And because He is infinitely wise, He simply cannot make a mistake (Prov. 3:5–6).

While He completely understands every situation, He is under no obligation whatsoever to inform us of the rationale for His actions or decisions. For example, God did not make clear why He let Joseph languish unjustly in prison for thirteen years before elevating him to the position of prime minister (Gen. 39–41). Nor did He spell out why the Israelites had to live more than four centuries in Egyptian bondage before He miraculously rescued them and made them into a nation (Ex. 12:41).

Probably one of the hardest things for me is to see some of the most wonderful, godly people I know stricken with malignant cancer. No matter how much you pray and trust God, they sometimes die. The outcome looks grim, but I can't do anything about it. I feel completely helpless.

In the ministry, I see a lot of sick people. Young and old alike are stricken with diseases that weaken their bodies and disable them. I think of the war veterans I have known; some of them are in wheelchairs unable to walk or even feed themselves. It seems those with physical afflictions have the frailest bodies but the sweetest spirits. I think, *God, I've been physically blessed all my life, while others have suffered all of theirs.* There are just some things I don't understand—I never boast of understanding. I just have to say, *God, You're in control. You see the end result. If I could see the end result in that person's life, or if I could see what You're doing worldwide, then I'm sure I would agree with You. But at this point I don't know how I can do anything except trust that in Your wisdom You know what the best thing is to do.*

While we have no right to fully know God's reasons, our lack of such information is the very thing that creates our feelings of frustration, anxiety, and doubt. Consider the irony of the situation. If we in our limited human wisdom *could* comprehend God's motives and actions, that in itself would be cause to doubt Him, since His thinking would be no better than our own! But because

God's logic vastly exceeds our own (Isa. 55:8–9), we *can* trust Him—we have no legitimate cause for doubting because He is an infinite, all-wise God who knows the best action to take in our lives.

BELIEF #3: GOD IS ABSOLUTELY SOVEREIGN

The Lord has absolute authority over everything in creation. In other words, if even one tiny event in the universe happened outside God's power and control, we could no longer trust Him—in that case, we couldn't have certainty that He would work every situation for our best interest. But we can trust Him because He *is* sovereign and therefore has perfect, complete control over every last detail of life.

When Pilate asked Jesus, "Do You not know that I have authority to release You, and I have authority to crucify You?" the Lord answered him, "You would have no authority over Me, unless it had been given you from above" (John 19:10–11). Earlier, Jesus reassured His disciples that not even a common sparrow—worth only half a penny—could fall to the ground apart from the Father's will (Matt. 10:29). In other words, whether the circumstance is large or small, God is in absolute control.

Some might ask, "Then what about terrorist attacks or pandemics? Where is God in all that?" He is still in total control, though this is a perplexing idea for the human mind to reconcile. Some people find comfort in the idea of luck, fate, and chance, because trusting God can seem difficult when tragedy strikes or our basic needs are not being met. But what happens to God's perfect love, infinite wisdom, and total sovereignty if luck, fate, and chance play a role? These words shouldn't even be in the believer's vocabulary—we would never be able to trust God if events could take place outside His control.

I always go back to Psalm 103:19: "The Lord has established His throne in the heavens, and His sovereignty rules over all." I don't know why God allowed the Holocaust or a global pandemic to occur. Or why a tsunami killed more than 170,000 people in some of the poorest countries on the face of the earth. But I have come to the conclusion that there are some things I'm not going to understand on this side of eternity. Whether its purpose was to awaken the world to the reality of evil or to make us aware of the uncertainty of life, I do not know. I just have to trust God—in some way, in some fashion, He will turn these things to good.

We live in a wicked, vile, disease-filled world. Many circumstances are not God's perfect will, but He allows them through His permissive will, despite the pain they cause. In His omniscience, God knows what is ultimately best, including the long-term consequences of tragedies that seem heartless and inexplicable. We should not doubt God or abandon our trust when we lack understanding. Instead, we should surrender our lives to Him, accepting by faith that He is good and worthy of our full trust.

Our lives belong to our sovereign, all-knowing, loving God, and nothing can touch us except what He allows. Sometimes that includes hardship and suffering, which leave us wondering, *How can this possibly be good?* And yet many people who have gone through tremendous trials later look back and say, "I hated the difficulty while I was going through it and wondered if God had deserted me. But now, on this side of it, I can see why He allowed it." Not everyone fully understands the spiritual insight, yet it happens frequently enough that we can take comfort, realizing that God has His purposes and with perfect timing will bring blessing from our trials (Rom. 8:28).

So when you face struggles, remind yourself that God has your best interest in mind. He wants you to trust Him as your personal Savior and surrender your life to Him. There is no reason to doubt Him, because He is perfect in His love, infinite in His wisdom, and sovereign in His control of the entire universe. Why should believers ever fret, when even in the deepest, darkest valleys, there can be abiding joy and confidence? No matter what befalls you, our all-loving, all-wise, all-powerful heavenly Father has you in the cradle of His hand.

WHY SUCH AN EMPHASIS ON WHAT YOU BELIEVE ABOUT GOD?

Why am I placing such great importance on what you believe about God? Because if you don't hold on to the fact that the Lord is sovereign . . .

If you don't embrace that the Father considers you to be worthy and lovable . . .

If you don't believe God knows the best action to take in your life . . .

Then you are never going to trust Him in the ways He wants to lead you. You are never going to have faith that He will reveal His will for your life. And that means you are never going to put yourself in a position to receive all the joy and blessings He desires to pour out upon you.

It is critical that you pick up, embrace fully, and become firmly committed to the truth about God and His relationship with you. Because when you do so, it will birth within you a deeper trust in Him that will enable Him to lead you to His blessings.

I do not have space to even begin to compile a list of the ways God can bless you. They are as numerous and diverse as there are people on this earth. However, I will address five major blessings that God promises to give you in response to your trust in Him—how He meets your needs, communicates with you, frees you from fear and anxiety, leads you victoriously through adversity, and has an important plan for your life. I will also discuss how you can embrace each of these blessings fully and, in doing so, discover the extraordinary life He has purposed for you.

It all begins with trust in the all-powerful, loving God who has your very best in mind—always. Once you place your faith in Him and obey Him, nothing can hold you back from gaining the peace and power that He desires to give you. My question to you is this: Are you ready to take the first step in believing in a loving, wise, sovereign Father? Don't miss another moment that could be spent enjoying the blessings He has promised you.

THE MOST IMPORTANT BELIEF IN TRUSTING GOD

Let's begin with the most important question you will ever answer: *What do you really believe about Jesus?*

Do you believe Christ was merely a good man who gave us an example of how to live? Or do you believe that Jesus is God incarnate and that His sacrifice on the cross defeated sin and death, opening the way for you to know Him? This one belief about Christ makes all the difference in your life. Because it is when you receive Him as your Savior and Lord that He indwells you with His Holy Spirit and empowers you to know and truly trust Him.

So what do you really believe about Jesus? Have you ever received the salvation that He offers? Have you placed your faith in Him as the only One who can forgive your sins, provide you with a relationship with God, and give you eternal life?

It is not difficult. All you must do is tell Him that you want His life to be yours and accept His death on the cross as sufficient payment for your sins. In so doing, you agree with Him that there is nothing you can do in your own strength to redeem yourself—that it is only through faith in His name that you are saved (Rom. 10:9–11; Eph. 2:8–9).

I hope that if you've never taken this step of faith, you will. Because it is when you receive Christ as your Savior that you can exchange your old way of living for a new, victorious life. This is when you become able to embrace all He has for you. So commit your desires, hopes, and dreams to God, and you will be amazed at the way He works everything together for your good and His glory.

PART ONE

GOD MEETS YOUR EVERY NEED

ONE

THE PROMISE MAKER

Do you truly believe that God is capable of meeting your needs and that He desires to meet *all* of your needs?

Some people ask, "If God is all-powerful and all-knowing, and if He loves me with an infinite and unconditional love—and therefore, He not only is capable of meeting all my needs but also desires to meet my needs—why doesn't God just meet all my needs right now? Why do I still have needs? When the apostle Paul wrote from a prison cell, 'My God will supply all your needs' why do I still have a lack of supply?" (Phil. 4:19).

Others say, "I know God is capable of meeting my needs, but since I still have needs, God must not want to meet them."

Still others question sincerely, "Why didn't God meet all my needs the moment I accepted Jesus Christ as my Savior?"

These are excellent questions, worthy of close examination.

At the outset of our discussion about these questions, let me assure you again that God is committed to meeting all your needs according to His riches in glory by Christ Jesus. A commitment is a pledge, a statement of a sure promise. The value of any commitment is based upon two things:

1. The *ability* of the promise maker to fulfill the promise.
2. The *integrity* of the promise maker, which might also be stated as the character to follow through on what has been said and do what has been promised.

God certainly qualifies as One who will stand behind His commitments on both accounts. He has all the wisdom, power, and ability necessary to fulfill His promises to us. He also has proven integrity—God has always done what He has said He would do. God is utterly faithful to His Word. He is holy and immutable; He is unchanging. His character is impeccable.

There are those who say, "Well, the Bible's promises are fine for the people back then, but Paul was writing to the Philippians, not to me. Times are different now. Things have changed."

Friend, all of God's Word is for you, right now, right where you are. It all applies to you. Why is this so? Because the Author of the Bible hasn't changed. The Scriptures are true today because the Author still stands by His Word! His commandments, statutes, and promises have not changed; they reflect our unchanging God. He is the same "yesterday, today, and forever" (Heb. 13:8 NKJV). The only times in God's Word in which God has not done what He said He was going to do are times when God's promises were conditional and man's behavior was an intervening factor.

WHAT IS THE NATURE OF THE PROMISE?

The better we know God—the more intimate our fellowship is with Him— the more we will trust God to do what He has said He will do. And the more we know about a promise in the Bible, the more we understand our role in bringing a promise to fulfillment.

As we study the Bible, we must ask several questions anytime we come to a promise in the Scriptures:

- To whom is the promise given?
- Who is making the promise?
- What is God really saying?
- What does God desire for me to do?
- How does God desire to act on my behalf?

- What is the end goal or the purpose for the promise?
- What is God's motivation in making this promise?

The more we know about the promise, the more we understand whether it is a conditional or unconditional promise.

Two Categories of Promises

All of God's promises fall into one of two categories: unconditional or conditional. As we read, memorize, and quote God's Word, we must be very careful to discern clearly the difference between these two categories.

Unconditional promises. In an unconditional promise, God states that He will do something regardless of man's behavior. In other words, God is going to do what He desires to do with or without any input or response from mankind. Nothing will interfere with or keep God from doing what He has said He will do.

An example is the promise of Jesus to His disciples that He is going to return one day. Absolutely nothing that man does or does not do can keep Jesus from fulfilling this promise in the fullness of God's timing and according to God's plans and purposes. Christ *will* come again.

Another unconditional promise is the promise of Jesus that He would never leave or forsake His disciples. Regardless of what people do or don't do, regardless of circumstances or situations that may arise, regardless of any mediating or intervening factors, Jesus will not forsake those who have put their trust in Him. That unconditional promise stands for all disciples at all times in all places and in all situations.

Conditional promises. In a conditional promise, God's actions are based in part on man's responses to God's commands. What man does, therefore, influences God's fulfillment of a promise.

Too often, people take some of God's *conditional* promises as being *unconditional.* That is a very dangerous error to make, and it can lead to frustration, disappointment, disillusionment, and even doubt about the goodness of God. How so? Well, if a person regards a promise of God as being unconditional when it is actually a conditional promise, he may very well fail to meet the conditions associated with the promise because he isn't looking for any conditions. He assumes that God is going to do everything and he is required to do nothing. In his failure to meet the conditions, of course, he negates the promise. Not realizing this, however, he begins to wonder why God is taking so long to meet his need. He begins to doubt whether God really meant what He said. Soon he doubts whether God cares or whether God is truly to be trusted on any matter.

Consider a situation in which a father says to his son, "I will buy you a new car when you finish college." The son is very excited—so excited that he fails to hear the full meaning of his father's statement. The boy goes to college for two years and decides that he has had enough of college. He gets a job and starts wondering when Dad is going to provide the new car he promised. The fact is, the boy did not finish college in the sense of completing a college degree. He just finished college from the standpoint that he stopped attending classes! The promise was a conditional one, and the error occurred because the son defined the conditions in a way the father had not defined them.

Too many people make this same mistake when it comes to our heavenly Father. They decide when the conditions are met rather than trust God with that determination. The results are failure and disappointment. We must be very careful in reading God's promises to determine precisely what the conditions of a conditional promise may be.

Look again at Philippians 4:19: "My God shall supply all your need according to His riches in glory by Christ Jesus" (NKJV).

Ask yourself, Is this a conditional promise of God, or is this an unconditional promise? This passage happens to be a conditional promise. How is it conditional?

First, Paul said, "My God." If a person cannot say, "My God"—in other words, if a personal relationship has not been established with Jesus as Savior—then this promise is not in effect.

Second, Paul said that needs will be met "by Christ Jesus." If a person looks to any other person or source to meet his needs, the promise is not in effect.

This promise is based upon a relationship between Christ Jesus and those who follow Him. We might call this a family promise. It is in effect only for the family of God. It is not a promise for the unbeliever or the person who does not trust Jesus as Lord of his life.

Note that I did not say that this promise is limited to a particular church, denomination, or group of believers within the body of Christ. God has only one family—people who confess Jesus Christ as Savior and seek to follow Jesus as Lord.

What about the Christian who doesn't have all his needs met?

The first place you need to look when a need is not being met is not at God or at His Son, Christ Jesus, but at yourself. You err greatly when you ask, Why hasn't God lived up to His promise? You are wise to ask instead, What am I doing that is keeping God from fulfilling this promise in my life?

You may respond, "Well, I'm not doing anything to keep this promise from being fulfilled! If you knew my circumstances or my situation. . . ." Let me assure you that no circumstance or situation is going to keep God from acting on your behalf. Nothing is too great or too powerful to stand in the way if God chooses to act. The real question remains, What are you doing in the midst of your circumstances or situation?

Do you already have a preconceived idea about how God should act to meet your needs or whom God may use to meet your needs?

I have encountered a number of people who have said to me, "Well, if he would just do such and such and she would agree to do so-and-so, then my need would be met." Or they have said, "Well, I did such and such and therefore God must do this and that."

Those who make such statements are not trusting God to be their Need Meeter. Rather, they are asking God to exert His power on behalf of their wishes and commands. We are called by God to trust Him, and Him alone, to meet our needs and to be our total source of supply. Furthermore, God requires that we obey Him as a part of our trusting Him. We have the situation completely backward any time we start expecting God to trust us to know what is right and to obey our commands so that He might prove His love for us.

Our position is one of standing before God, declaring, "I trust You completely to meet my needs in Your timing and according to Your methods."

Anyone who takes the stance before almighty God, "You must do things *my* way," is presumptuous and foolish.

GOD'S MOTIVATIONS FOR MEETING OUR NEEDS

What's in it for God?

Why does God give to us?

What are His motivations for meeting our needs?

Motivated by Love

God's foremost motivation for meeting all your needs is this: He loves you. Yes, He loves you, loves you, loves you, loves you. I would repeat it a thousand times and more if I could. There is no bottom to His divine heart.

Why, then, must we do certain things in conditional promises? Why doesn't God just pour out to us all that we need?

Because ultimately God is about building a loving relationship with us.

Obedience to His conditions is part of having a loving relationship with God. Obedience is evidence that we are trusting God to be the source of our lives. He wants to be the One on whom we depend for provision, the One to whom we look for wise counsel, the One on whom we rely for protection.

Obedience in fulfilling God's conditions is also related to our growth and development as Christian believers. We've all heard the old song that says, "I know that you know that I know that you know . . ." That's what happens when we obey. We know we are obeying, and our obedience creates in us a greater strength to ask for what we desire and to act more quickly when God directs us.

Conformity to Christ

Often we come to a promise in the Word of God and we know it is true in our minds, but we have difficulty believing it to be true in our hearts, and especially we have difficulty believing that the promise is true for us. One of the reasons we find it difficult to claim God's promises as true in our personal lives is that we do not fully understand what God is seeking to do in our lives.

We must understand that God's primary purpose in our lives is not to meet our needs but to conform us into the likeness of His Son. Many people make God out to be some kind of a Santa Claus, always ready and willing to give them precisely what they crave at any particular moment. They see God as the wish fulfiller, the One who turns all our dreams into reality, the ultimate fairy godfather, the One who makes all things just the way we desire for them to be. While it is true that God is our Father and our Provider, and while it is equally true that God desires only the best for us for all eternity, God is not present in our lives to do things our way. He is present in our lives so that we might desire and choose to do things His way.

God does not exist for our pleasure. We exist for His pleasure.

God does not exist to make all our personal human and often shortsighted dreams come true. We exist so that we might have a part in His plan and purpose for the ages.

We do not make God and then tell Him what to do for us. God made us, and He is the One who orders and directs our lives.

When we approach the promises of God, we must always keep in mind that God's ultimate purpose in our lives is to conform us into the image of Jesus Christ. God desires for us the same relationship He had with Jesus—a close intimacy so that we do only what the Father directs us to do and all that we do is for His glory. Jesus was 100 percent obedient to the will of God the Father in all things. He relied exclusively upon God the Father for direction, wisdom, sustenance, provision, and power. Jesus drew His identity solely from God the Father—everything about the character of Jesus was identical to the character of God the Father.

Like Jesus. That is what the Father has in mind for you and for me. He is creating in us the character of Christ. He is molding us to be obedient to His plan for us and for an intimate loving relationship with Him.

God meets our needs always in the context of making us more like Jesus.

A Fresh and Daily Relationship

An important Hebrew name for God is El Shaddai—the all-powerful, all-sufficient God who protects and provides. El Shaddai was a living presence to the Israelites, the God who guided them in a pillar of cloud by day and a pillar of fire by night, the God who gave them manna every morning, the God who provided water from solid rock, the God who protected them from Pharaoh's armies, the God who met with Moses face-to-face. El Shaddai was the Provider—their only Provider.

The Israelites knew from their experiences in the wilderness that El Shaddai provided their daily needs. Jesus spoke of this also when He taught His disciples to pray, "Give us this day our daily bread" (Matt. 6:11).

The prophet Jeremiah wrote,

> This I recall to my mind,
> Therefore I have hope.
>
> Through the LORD's mercies we are not consumed,
> Because His compassions fail not.
> They are new every morning;
> Great is Your faithfulness.
> "The LORD is my portion," says my soul,
> "therefore I hope in Him!"
>
> (LAM. 3:21–24 NKJV)

The One who meets our needs is fresh and new in His supply every day. He doesn't give us stale leftovers. His supply is precisely what we need in the moment we need it. Everything He gives us is fresh, new, alive, vibrant, powerful.

We cannot awaken on any given morning and be without God's mercies and His compassions. Regardless of what we have done or said the day before, God is with us in a fresh new relationship every morning.

Every night before we go to sleep, we need to confess our sins to God and receive His forgiveness. We need to do this not so that God will awaken the next morning full of love, forgiveness, and mercy toward us, but so that *we* will awaken the next morning able to receive the fullness of the love, forgiveness, and mercy He extends to us. God never drags around our unconfessed sins, but we do. The burden of guilt is something we carry. It is vital that we set down the burden of those sins so we can take up the blessings that God has prepared for us.

You can trust God to meet your needs with a provision that is fresh and good. It will be exciting and life-giving, satisfying, and sufficient.

An Extension of His Glory

I once overheard a child offer this as an excuse for his behavior: "I just couldn't help myself." To a certain extent, God meets our needs and desires to give us good gifts because it is His very nature to do so. He cannot fail to give. He cannot fail to love.

God's good gifts flow from His goodness. God's very nature of goodness motivates Him to give good gifts and to give them and give them and give them. There is no end to either God's desire to give good gifts to His children or His ability to give good gifts. And therefore, we can never fully exhaust the storehouse of good gifts that are laid up for us.

I once took an informal poll and asked people at random to tell me the first word that came to their minds to describe the nature of God. Many people responded with these words: *holy, righteous, just, absolute, eternal.* A few people said *loving* or *forgiving.* But it was only after asking dozens of people this question that someone responded with *good.*

Most people don't seem to think of God as being good to them. They tend to think of God as being demanding, exacting, and unrelenting. They see Him as prosecutor, judge, and jury. They see Him as distant, remote, and unfeeling—the Creator, the Higher Power, the Almighty. While God certainly bears all these titles and attributes, He also bears the attributes of faithful, merciful, forgiving, loving, kind, gentle, nurturing, providing, protecting, and good.

We have a lot more ability at times to imagine other people—from close family members to total strangers—doing something good for us than we have the ability to imagine that God might truly pour out an overwhelming blessing on our lives.

A provision always for good. All that God has for us is good. His supply is not only ample, but it is of the highest and finest quality. Jeremiah knew this great truth about God:

> The LORD is good to those who wait for Him,
> To the soul who seeks Him.
> It is good that one should hope and wait quietly
> For the salvation of the LORD.
>
> (LAM. 3:25–26 NKJV)

God sees the whole of our lives, beginning to ending and on into eternity. He knows what is the best for us not only now but tomorrow and next month and next year and twenty years from now. His gifts to us are always good for us.

A good parent does not give a child a gift that will make the child unhappy. Neither does he give the child everything the child thinks will make him happy. A parent gives what he believes is best for the child, in the right amounts, at the right times.

When I was a boy, there were lots of foods that I didn't particularly like. I ate them anyway. I ate them because my mother cooked them for me and she insisted that I eat them. I ate them because I was hungry and what was put before me was all that was available for me to eat. But that still didn't mean that I enjoyed the taste of all the foods that were put on my plate.

An amazing thing happened somewhere along the way to adulthood. I started liking some of the foods that I didn't like as a child. Some of the things to which I would have liked to have said "no, thank you" as a child are things I find myself ordering from menus.

That same thing happens to us as we grow in our relationship with Christ and become more conformed to His nature. Some things that we didn't like when we were in an unforgiven, sinful state become things that we dearly love. Some things that we weren't all that fond of when we were babes in Christ become things that are pleasurable to us as we mature in our faith and in our love relationship with God.

The opposite situation is also true. There were things that I craved and enjoyed as a child that I no longer like. I look back on some foods that I liked as a child and a teenager, and I think, *Why did I ever think that tasted good?* In like manner, there are things that people do when they are in sin that seem good to them at that state of their lives, but that become things they wouldn't dream of doing once they know Christ or are more mature in Christ.

Our minds are renewed when we come to Christ, and a big part of that renewal is a change in the things that we define as good, desirable, pleasurable, rewarding, and satisfying. Our definition of what is good changes as we come to Christ and grow into His likeness. However, God always sees what is absolutely good for us—things that are good for us now, good for us in every area of our lives, good for those around us, and good for us through all eternity. He gives us only the things that are truly beneficial for our growth as His children and that are beneficial for the advancement of His kingdom on this earth.

The question to ask yourself if you have an unmet need today is this: Is this thing that I need something that God defines as good for my life?

Proactive and creative in His giving. A woman once told me that one of the best Christmas presents she ever received was a stereo record player that her parents bought for her when she was eleven years old. She said, "It had never dawned on me to ask for a stereo. I'm not sure I even knew that stereo units like the one I received had been manufactured. I certainly would not have asked for such an expensive present. But my parents in their generosity gave me a stereo, and it was a gift that gave me countless hours of pleasure during my teen years. My parents continued to monitor the records that I bought. Their gift of a stereo wasn't without certain limitations about how loud or how late at night I could play it. Even so, the gift was an overwhelming one to me. It was a gift they knew I would enjoy even though I didn't know how much I would enjoy it until months had passed."

This is the way God gives to us. He gives us what He knows will bring us great pleasure and joy, even though we in our finite wisdom and understanding may not know fully what we need or desire.

God does not wait for others to initiate the provision for our innermost needs. He assumes a proactive position in meeting our needs. God may use other people in the process, but He creates, orchestrates, and engineers the solution that satisfies.

Do you believe even for a second that God is surprised by the need you are experiencing? Do you believe that your sudden lack in a certain area of your life is either a mystery or a surprise to God? To the contrary—God knows you far better than you will ever know yourself. He knew about this need in your life today long before you were ever conceived in your mother's womb. Not only did God know about that need, but He knew His provision for meeting that need. Just as your need is no surprise and no mystery to Him, neither is the provision for solving your problem or meeting your need hidden from His understanding or ability.

God will not keep anything from you that you need to know.

God will not withhold anything from you that is rightfully yours as His child.

God will not hide any aspect of His character from you.

God will not deny you any promise that He makes in His Word.

God will not shut you away from any blessing that is for your eternal benefit or that is required for the fulfillment of your purpose on this earth.

And best of all, God has already prepared for you all that you will need for every day of the rest of your life.

TWO

UNLIMITED SUPPLY

Do you believe there is a need that might be outside God's ability to meet it?

In your heart of hearts, do you believe God is going to supply only 80 percent of your needs, or perhaps 90 percent, or even 99 percent?

Not so! When Paul wrote, "My God shall supply *all* your need," he meant precisely that. All. Not a percentage of. Not a fraction of. All.

I have heard people say on a number of occasions, "Oh, yes, I have a need in my life. But God has been so good to me. . . ." What is such a person saying? In essence he is saying that he believes he has used up all of his allotted portion of blessings. His current need lies just beyond God's storeroom of supply. His current need pushes him into the category of being selfish or greedy, and therefore, he expects God to turn down his desire for yet another blessing.

Friend, God has more for you. He still has blessings that you have not received. Malachi painted a wonderful word picture about this:

> "Bring all the tithes into the storehouse,
> That there may be food in My house,
> And try Me now in this,"
> Says the LORD of hosts,
> "If I will not open for you the windows of heaven
> And pour out for you such blessing
> That there will not be room enough to receive it."
>
> (MAL. 3:10 NKJV)

We are not to think we are asking for too much from God. Malachi pointed us toward the knowledge that God has more for us than we are capable of receiving. An abundance of God's provision for us lies beyond what we have even thought to request.

Not long ago I heard about a man who said, "I cannot contain it all." This man as a child had dreamed of owning a house with a big yard so that he could buy a riding lawn mower to mow it. He loved to be outside as a boy, and he thought the idea of mowing a lawn with a riding lawn mower would be about the best thing a person could do on a Saturday afternoon.

He had been a churchgoer all his life, and even as a child, he gave his tithes and offerings to God. Over the years, he never wavered from that obedience to the Lord. He was wise in his spending and wise in all his business practices. Decade by decade, his fortune grew, and along with it, the amount of his tithes and offerings. He thanked God for all things. And by the time he was sixty years old, he lived on an estate in which he had more than an acre of lawn. Sure enough he had a riding lawn mower. And not only did he have this estate, but he also owned houses in two other areas of the country. In each place he had two automobiles, one for himself and one for his wife. And in each place, he had a riding lawn mower. Finally at age seventy-five, he said to God, "There's too much for me to contain. I don't need three riding lawn mowers, six cars, three houses, and a boat to maintain. This blessing You have poured out for me from heaven—well, Lord, I just don't have room to receive it all!"

Most of us don't have the problem that man had. But then again, most of us don't have the simple trust in God that he had all his life. He had no doubt that God would meet his needs, and that God would meet them with an over-flowing abundance. He believed that God had the ability to do or accomplish anything. And in believing that he was a beloved son of God, he had no trouble receiving the blessings that God showered upon him from above.

The man ardently sought out every bit of wisdom that God might send his way as he conducted his various business affairs. He asked God to help him in every relationship he had—not only in his relationships with his wife and children, but in his relationships with employees and even those who serviced his riding lawn mower. He asked God to help him grow in his spiritual life and in his ability to be an effective minister to others. God had given him numerous opportunities to share his business expertise with others in one-to-one counseling and in providing business wisdom to his church and various community groups. The man truly believed that God would meet *all* his needs—not some, but *all*—and that God would meet his needs in a way that was overflowing in generosity and abundance.

Do you believe about God what this man believed about God? Do you know God and trust Him as this man did? Are you truly trusting God to meet all your needs—not some, not just a high percentage, but all—even to the point that you no longer can contain all of the blessing that God pours out on you?

GOD'S STOREHOUSE OF SUPPLY

God does not meet our needs according to our resources—the talents we have, the gifts we offer, the numbers we have associated with our bank accounts or investment portfolios. No. God meets our needs according to His resources.

And what are God's resources?

My! You cannot begin to count all of God's resources. The oceans and seas are His. The continents are His. The atmosphere and all of outer space are His. All that is under the continents and all that is locked away as potential for life-giving blessing in plants and animals—*His!* We cannot begin to calculate all of God's resources that are available for His use on this earth, and we haven't even begun to count the unseen resources of heaven. His resources are immeasurable, indestructible, and inexhaustible.

God's bank account has no limitations. His storehouse of supply is beyond our imaginations in size, scope, and magnificence.

How rich is God? What does God possess? The psalmist recorded this about God's wealth:

> I am God, your God. . . .
> For every beast of the forest is Mine,
> The cattle on a thousand hills.

I know every bird of the mountains,

And everything that moves in the field is Mine.

(PSALM 50:7, 10–11)

In Haggai 2:8, the Lord declared, "The silver is Mine and the gold is Mine."

ALL THINGS ARE GOVERNED BY GOD

Everything that is in existence is owned by God, governed by God, and available to God at any given moment. He is in absolute control over anything that we might call a resource, be it animal, mineral, plant, or atmospheric in nature. He has created all and sustains all. At any given second, God could wipe out everything we know as being real, including our lives, because His power over His creation is all-encompassing.

As Christians, you and I are living in union with the Sovereign Power of the universe.

Not only is God in total and absolute authority over all *things* in the universe, but also over every *process* of the universe. The laws by which nature operates are God's laws. He made them, He can alter them, and He can change them if He so desires. All the scientific laws that we associate with healing, growth, development, and fruitfulness are His laws.

Furthermore, all things that exist but are unseen—in other words, the spiritual realm—are governed by God and are subject to His command. All of the rules or laws that pertain to good relationships, good marriages, good psychological and emotional health, a sense of well-being, effective communication, leadership, a righteous community of people, a godly attitude, development of a good character, and many other laws related to our inner being and our relationships with others are God's laws. He established them, and He continues to rule over them.

We often think of the natural world as being subject to the laws of nature, but when it comes to human nature, many people factor out God's sovereignty. God is the Author of the laws that govern human nature just as

He is the Author of the laws that govern the natural environment in which we live.

Friend, there isn't a resource or a process, seen or unseen, known or unknown, that is outside God's domain and God's governance. You are in union with Christ Jesus, God the Father, and the Holy Spirit simultaneously and continually. You are in union with God in His fullness, and that includes the fullness of His authority and power over all things.

Surely at this point Philippians 4:19 becomes really exciting! "My God shall supply all your need *according to His riches in glory*" (NKJV). We are privileged by God and given the right by God to tap into His riches in glory—riches that are far beyond anything that we can fully understand or comprehend. As Paul wrote to the Ephesians, God "is able to do exceedingly abundantly above all that we ask or think" (Eph. 3:20 NKJV). In other words, you can't begin to ask God for all that He desires to give you. You can't imagine all that He has for you. I have a pretty good imagination and a pretty good boldness in asking things of God. What an awesome statement about God's supply house to think that we can't even imagine all that is contained in God's riches and that we don't have enough time on this earth to tap into all that God has made available to us!

One of the words that most toddlers learn quickly and use to great advantage is *more*. Give a young child a sip of a milkshake or a spoonful of good-tasting pudding and that child is likely to respond, "More." Even if the child doesn't say the word, the look in his eyes is one of eager anticipation, *More!* As little children before our heavenly Father, we are like toddlers desiring more of God's goodness and more of God's riches in our lives. And just as a loving parent does not give a child just one taste of an ice-cream cone and then deny the child a second taste, neither does our loving heavenly Father give us just a taste of His goodness and then deny all future requests for His blessings.

GOD IS OUR NEED MEETER

We must recognize three significant truths about God's provision and His storehouse of unlimited supply. The first of these is that God, and God alone, is the One who provides. He is the One who holds the keys to the storehouse of unlimited supply. He is both the originator and the giver of the supply.

Paul wrote very specifically that God will supply all our need "according to His riches in glory" (Phil. 4:19). *His* supply, *His* storehouse, *His* riches, *His* possessions.

How many people in the world today believe that all of their needs can be met by a government agency or by a special program of some kind? Let me assure you, no government or special program can ever meet all of a person's needs, and certainly not the most fundamental and basic of all needs: spiritual and emotional needs. No amount of government aid can ever instill self-worth. In fact, government aid too often becomes a detriment to self-worth.

The quicker we come to the understanding that only God in Christ is the Need Meeter, the sooner we will release other people from the tremendous burden we try to place upon them to meet our needs and to provide for us all of the emotional support and love that ultimately God alone can provide. I cannot convey to you how important this is to our developing healthy and joyful relationships with other people. As long as we look to others to satisfy the deep inner longings that we sometimes cannot even fully define or describe, we will remain in a needy state. God alone is capable of meeting our deepest inner needs.

God may use certain people to meet your needs, but you must never look to those people or require them to meet your needs. To do so is to set yourself up to be devastated when those people fail you either through a willful act or through a lack of ability. No person, or persons, can be or should ever be counted upon to be your source of hope, joy, peace, contentment, creativity, or emotional security. God alone is your source for the meeting of these needs!

GOD MEETS OUR NEEDS BY CHRIST JESUS

God has a method and a means for making available to us the riches of His unlimited storehouse. His means of availability is Christ Jesus. This is the second truth we must learn.

Many people, including a good percentage of those who sit in churches every Sunday, do not know the position they have in Christ; therefore, they do not understand the privileges that are theirs in Christ. Many people live their entire lives without knowing the fullness of the provision that God has for them.

Many companies today issue identification passes to their employees. These passes give them entrance into the company and, in some cases, restrict or allow access to various departments or physical locations within the company. Our "pass" into all areas of God's storehouse is Christ Jesus. Paul wrote to the Philippians that God supplies our needs "by Christ Jesus."

Jesus brought us to the Father and mediates for us before His throne, saying, "This one believes in Me." Because of what Jesus has done for us and what Jesus declares about us, we are forgiven and cleansed of all our sin. Jesus gives us access to God the Father.

Jesus brings us again and again to the Father and says, "This is the need in Our beloved one's life. This is what We must meet."

"By Christ Jesus" we are in relationship with the Father. And thus, by Christ Jesus we are in a position to receive all that the Father has for us in the way of our inheritance as His children.

Jesus knows my name and my address. He knows precisely where to deliver God's "riches in glory."

We have the position in Christ to receive God's ample supply. Christ has an ample supply to give. And we have the privilege of receiving His supply.

THE PRIVILEGE OF INSTANT ACCESS

Furthermore, we have instant access to God's provision. There is no time in our lives when we are cut off from God, and therefore, there is no time when we are cut off from His supply.

You can be on a gurney being rolled into a surgical suite.
You can be standing at your kitchen sink washing dishes.
You can be sitting at your desk shuffling papers.

You can be out on the golf course just about to make a putt.

You can be driving in your car on a freeway.

One of the greatest privileges of your life is that you have instant access to God. You do not need to complete a certain protocol, accomplish a list of pre-requisites, or be in a certain place, holding your hands in a specific way or reciting a particular statement. You can get in touch with God instantly, directly, and personally at any time of day or night, in any situation or circumstance, either verbally or silently.

Let me paint a picture for you. Suppose that a person sees a brochure about a cruise to Alaska, and he decides he wants to go on a trip like that. He makes his reservation, saves his money, and buys his tickets. He packs his bags, and finally the day comes when he boards the ship. He goes to the first sitting of the first dinner meal and takes a look at the long, sumptuous buffet table. Then he sits down, opens a little sack, and pulls out a few crackers and a jar of peanut butter.

Someone asks him at that point what he's doing, and he replies, "I'm having dinner." This person obviously doesn't know that all his meals on the ship are covered by the price of his ticket.

When you came to Christ, *all* the provisions and abundance of Christ Jesus were made available to you. You don't have to remain in a needy state. Christ has what you need in sufficient supply, and it is available for you to access right now.

A FULL PROVISION FOR EVERY NEED

The good news for us is that these are not only needs in our lives, but because they are needs that God has created within us from birth, they are also needs for which God has created a full provision. God never sets up a situation or creates a circumstance without also building in the full provision, expression, or potential for success in that situation or circumstance. This is the third significant truth about God's provision.

God creates needs so that we might trust Him to provide for the needs, and in the process, we might grow in our relationship with Him and strengthen our ability to be and do what He has created us to be and do. Stated another way, any lack in our lives is an opportunity for us to grow in our relationship with God, and an opportunity for us to grow in our abilities and in our faith so that we can be even more effective servants of God and witnesses to God's love and grace.

For God to give His people needs and then fail to provide for the needs would be punitive and hateful. God certainly is neither! It is out of God's great love and mercy that He has built a God-shaped vacuum into our lives and then offered to freely, generously, and abundantly fill that void with His love, presence, and power. Friend, there isn't a single verse in all the Bible that describes God as uncaring, unfeeling, stingy, or tight.

YOUR SUPPLY BOX IS FULL

In Ephesians 1:3 Paul declared, "Blessed be the God and Father of our Lord Jesus Christ, who has blessed us with every spiritual blessing in the heavenly places in Christ." I want you to notice that this statement is in the past tense. Paul did not say that God is *going* to bless us with spiritual blessings once we are in heaven, or even once we fulfill certain duties, roles, or commands. Paul wrote that Jesus Christ already *has* made all these blessings available to us. They are blessings that are already laid up in God's storehouse for us to claim.

God does not have to go out and work to refill your supply box. Your supply box is already full to overflowing. Everything you are ever going to need to fulfill God's plan and purpose for your life has already been placed in your supply box, and it has been there since the moment of your conception. God has already deposited to your account all that you will ever need to withdraw.

In other words, you cannot have a need that is too great for God to meet. You cannot have a need that takes God by surprise. You cannot have a need that is beyond the supply that has already been provided by your heavenly Father and made available to you by Christ Jesus!

THREE

A WAY OUT

Have you ever confronted a problem and said, "Where's the exit sign? I want out of this situation"? It might have been a financial problem, a career-related problem, a family-related problem, or a personal problem. When anyone is in need, the first thought is usually, *How can I escape this?*

If that is the way you are feeling and thinking about a need in your life, you should be encouraged today. God *does* have a way to resolve your need!

Three questions are related to virtually all types of needs:

1. Who or what is responsible for causing the need?
2. What is necessary for the need to be met?
3. Who is responsible for meeting the need?

I believe a powerful principle related to needs ties together the answers to these questions: *Whatever created the need in your life will determine how God supplies the need and who is responsible for meeting the need.* In other words, the one responsible for causing the need is ultimately the one responsible for meeting the need, and the condition caused by the need is directly related to the solution for the need.

Financial needs require financial solutions.
Physical needs require physical solutions.
Relational needs require relational solutions.

Spiritual needs require spiritual solutions.

Needs that arise from hatred require solutions rooted in love.

In nearly all cases, the way out of a need is the same way you got into the need—only in reverse. The person primarily responsible for meeting the need is the person involved in creating the need.

NEEDS THAT GOD CREATES

God created some needs. Many Christians have not stopped to thoroughly consider that truth. They automatically assume that God solves needs, and therefore, the devil or the evil nature of man must create them. Just because God is the supreme Need Meeter does not mean that needs are not sometimes created by God in our lives so that His plan and purpose can be realized in us and through us.

Have you ever stopped to consider that God created a need in the life of Moses? Moses had been tending sheep for forty years on the back side of the desert. He was married, had children, and had a good relationship with his father-in-law, who was the priest of the people with whom Moses had settled. He had a career, a family, and a degree of status and wealth. And then God showed up.

The Lord revealed Himself to Moses in a bush that was ablaze with fire but was not consumed. God spoke to Moses and created a major problem for him: "Go back to Pharaoh. Lead My people out of Egypt and to the promised land." Moses was wanted on murder charges in Pharaoh's court. He had no status with the Hebrew people or authority to lead them anywhere. And furthermore, he had no public-speaking ability. Problems? Yes, huge problems.

As is true for all problems that God creates, we have only one choice: obey or disobey God's demand on our lives. To obey is to put ourselves into a position for God to provide for our need. To disobey is to put ourselves outside the boundaries of God's provision. Moses obeyed.

Consider the situation of a thirty-six-year-old man who is married, has a family, has a good job, and has bought a house in a nice neighborhood. And then, consider what happens if God calls that man to preach the gospel. God creates a whole host of needs for that man—where to go to seminary, how to pay for seminary, where to live, how to help his children and wife make the move, and on and on. To obey is to see God's provision. To disobey is to be miserable.

Many people respond to God's demand on their lives by blaming God, blaming others, or sulking in their pain. The better approach is to ask, "God, what is Your goal for me? What do You want me to do? Help me to trust You to fulfill what You are calling me to do and be."

When God creates a need, He determines what is necessary for meeting the need, and He is responsible for meeting the need.

NEEDS THAT WE CREATE FOR OURSELVES

We create other needs for ourselves. Needs in this area are very often material, physical, financial, or relational.

Many of our self-created needs arise because of unwise decisions. The need will be met, in part, by our making wise decisions and having the courage, skill, and determination to follow through on them. Let me give you an example. Suppose you have engaged in a bad health habit, which over time has caused an unhealthy situation in your body. Perhaps you have eaten foods that are too high in cholesterol and fat content, and you are now facing a higher risk for heart attack and stroke. What will solve this need? Well, the solution in part will involve your making a wise decision to cut down your fat and cholesterol intake, to engage in more active exercise, and to have periodic physical checks on this condition.

What is the way out of a need created by an unwise decision? A wise decision. And who is primarily responsible for meeting the need? The person who has made the unwise decision.

What is God's role in this? I believe that God will give any person wisdom if he asks for it. James 1:5–6 tells us, "If any of you lacks wisdom, let him ask of God, who gives to all liberally and without reproach, and it will be given to him. But let him ask in faith" (NKJV). I believe that God will give daily guidance to any person who requests it, and that He will give courage, fortitude, and willpower to any person who requests these qualities.

In some cases, people create needs in their relationships, perhaps through ignorance and carelessness, but often through rebellion and self-centeredness. Hurtful words may be spoken; estrangement may arise; divisiveness may take root. The relationship is in need.

What is the way out of this type of need? Generally speaking, it will be the opposite of what created the need. Consider the man who is neglectful of his wife. Perhaps he spends fifteen hours a day at the office and gives his wife no priority when it comes to scheduling his weekend hours. What is the solution for the need? A big part of it is likely to be a reprioritizing of plans and schedules so that the man can spend more time with his wife. Who is responsible for meeting the need? The man. What is God's role? I believe God will give the man wisdom about *how* to reprioritize his time and efforts, and will help heal the heart of the wife and make her more open to a full reconciliation with her husband.

If unkind words have been spoken, kind words need to be spoken.
If dishonesty has become a pattern, honesty needs to prevail.
If lies have been told, the truth needs to be told.
If hateful actions have been taken, loving actions need to be pursued.

Jesus told a parable about a man who created needs for himself. We know it as the parable of the prodigal son (Luke 15:11–24). Through a series of wrong conclusions and bad decisions, the young man created needs in his life. He learned what we all learn: bad decisions produce bad consequences.

Some of the needs in the young man's life were no doubt legitimate. He had a need to prove himself and fulfill his personal destiny, as well as a need to establish his own identity. Other needs might *not* have been of his own choosing. He might have experienced feelings of rejection. The problem, however, arose because the young man did not know *how* to resolve his needs. He *left* home rather than confront his neediness *at* home. We can never outrun or escape our neediness.

The prodigal son ended up homeless, hopeless, rejected, criticized, left out, and with a deep longing for love. The good news of this story is that no matter how needy we become—and regardless of the fact that we might have brought some needs on ourselves—God loves us, accepts us, forgives us, and *helps us to resolve our needs.* He will not do our part, but He will assist us so that our efforts will succeed and we will have both the courage and the endurance necessary to see a problem resolved fully or a need met fully.

NEEDS THAT ARE CREATED BY OTHERS

There are some needs that we don't ask for and we don't create, but that others create for us. Joseph was certainly a person who experienced this type of need. He was sold into slavery by his brothers through no fault of his own, other than telling his brothers two of his dreams. While in Egypt and in slavery, Joseph was falsely accused by Potiphar's wife, and as a result of the false charge, he found himself in prison even though he had acted righteously before God. Yes, Joseph had problems created by others!

One time after an In Touch rally, a woman greeted me. She put a note in my hand and said with great insistence, "Please read this." When I opened her note later, I found that it said:

> I feel hopeless. I have no purpose in life. I am angry with God. But I believe what you said tonight and I am accepting Jesus Christ as my Savior. Suicide and hell would be worse.

At the bottom of the note she had written: "Adult 24. Child of alcoholic father. Mother in mental hospitals most of my life. Sexually and physically abused as a child."

This young woman, like Joseph, had not asked for the troubles of her life. But also like Joseph, she had made a decision to trust God with her life.

In cases where others create problems for us, God's role is one of deliverance from evil. Total and abiding trust in God is our only hope.

NEEDS THAT WE INHERIT FROM OTHERS

Some people have had some needs so long that they can't remember how they acquired the needs or from whom. Needs in this category are very often emotional in nature, and a good number of them relate to needs that begin early in life.

Some of these emotional needs are rooted in parental rejection, abuse, separation, hateful criticism, cutting remarks, or neglect. Others arise out of repeated failures. What can be done in these cases?

Well, first we must recognize that these needs are usually deep-seated and that they will take time to reverse. There are no quick cures for the feelings, hurts, and emotional needs that arise from bad parenting early in a child's life. Long-term and loving commitments are required. What brings about the healing, however, is often the opposite of what caused the pain—being accepted, loved, nurtured, praised, valued, included, honored, treated with dignity and respect. In cases of repeated failures, the need may be best met through information, wise counsel, acquired skills, and opportunities for incremental and consistent successes.

The person primarily responsible for meeting needs arising from repeated failure is the "bad teacher" or the "inattentive student." The failures may be self-created through rebellion that caused the person to reject sound teaching or through lack of discipline that resulted in a failure to practice or maintain good skills and habits. The failure may result from bad information or bad role modeling. The need will be met through good teaching, good role modeling, diligent practice, a submissive attitude, and an eagerness to be instructed and to learn. The errant student is responsible for finding a good teacher since in all likelihood, the bad teacher will be incapable of providing good teaching.

In both the case of an emotional need arising from bad parenting and the case of a failure-related need arising from bad past performance, the person must be able to recognize his own need if he is going to be able to participate in meeting his need. One difficulty in solving these types of needs is that the needy person often admits only to having rather nebulous, undefined, foggy or fuzzy types of inner feelings. There is restlessness, but there is little understanding of what originally caused such vague, yet persistent, feelings. The person tends to know that something is wrong or missing, but he is unsure about what.

In my experience, a critical step is taken when the person will ultimately admit to having one or more of these needs:

- I need acceptance.
- I need successes in what I attempt to do.
- I need approval.
- I need to be loved genuinely and unconditionally.
- I need attention.
- I need friendship or companionship.
- I need to feel that my life is worthwhile and valued.
- I need to be needed by someone.
- I need a vacation (or a break).
- I need a rest.
- I need a challenge.

Identifying the type of need is the first step toward recognizing what the solution for the need might be. If a vacation or a prolonged break is needed, the need will be met through planning and then taking a vacation or prolonged break. If the need is friendship or companionship, the need will be met through engaging in activities that give an opportunity for friendships to develop.

And ultimately when it comes to meeting the emotional or deep inner needs of another person—the needs that may have no known source or specific cause—the responsibility for need meeting is going to fall upon three sources, each of which may have a different level of responsibility: (1) the person with the emotional need; (2) loving Christian friends; and (3) God Himself.

It is very difficult to help a person with a deep-seated or long-standing emotional need unless he is willing to receive help and in some way engage actively in meeting the need. The person who turns his back on all help, wise counsel, or prayer will probably continue to experience need regardless of what others do.

In some cases, people will say to themselves and others, "Well, if this is a problem, God will fix it." In saying this, they expect God to completely override their will, emotions, and thought processes—something God does not do except in the most extreme cases where His eternal plan and purpose are involved. A do-nothing attitude toward a need results in a nothing-done state. We are never to expect God to do everything while we sit back and do nothing. In the Gospel of John, Jesus described the Holy Spirit as our Helper, our Counselor, our Advocate. He is not described as the One who will do everything for us and require nothing of us.

An older farmer gave this advice to a younger farmer: "Ask God to show you what to plant and when to plant. Then plant the best seed you can buy. Ask God to grow the seeds. Then cultivate the ground, pull the weeds, and fertilize the plants as they grow. Ask God to produce a great harvest. Then go out and gather the harvest when it is ripe. Ask God to show you how to market your produce. Then take your produce to market. Don't try to do God's part. And don't expect God to do yours."

INVOLVEMENT WITH OTHERS

No one person's needs can be met fully by just one other person. The reason lies in the question, How much is enough? You can ask that question of virtually anything in life. In human terms, there is never enough that any human being can do, have, or be in order to meet a need completely, especially an emotional or spiritual inner need.

A human being who is starving for affection can never get enough affection from one other human being. A person who is frightened and lonely deep down inside can never get a feeling of security or companionship from a single relationship. He or she can never get close enough to another human being. I have watched with sadness as marriages have become estranged over this very issue. One person in the relationship is needy and so desperate to have a deep inner need met that he or she will cling to the spouse until the spouse is drained dry and is left feeling bewildered, exhausted, sad, angry, and frustrated—often all at the same time. A person with deep inner needs seems to draw upon others with a relentless, insatiable emotional hunger, and virtually nothing that any other person does is enough to satisfy the inner need.

Friends, contributors, employers, employees, volunteers, family members, skilled consultants and experts, hired specialists, and numerous other categories of people are required in some way for nearly all types of material, physical, financial, and relational needs to be met.

In the realm of emotional healing, the person with a need will need a body of believers to bring about a total meeting of the need. If the person needs approval for the talents and gifts that God has given him, he will need approval from several people, not just one, for him to feel that the approval is valid. The body of Christ should provide such approval. If the person needs friendship, he will need the friendship of several people, not just one person. The body of Christ should provide such friendship.

If the person needs sound teaching or new skills, the person will need several teachers to provide that instruction, not just one teacher. The body of Christ should provide such instruction in the form of pastors and teachers who are good role models and who provide consistently wise instruction from the pulpit, in Sunday school classes, in small group meetings, at retreats and seminars, over the airwaves, in the form of books and recordings, and through one-on-one conversations and counseling sessions.

Again, an inner need cannot be met by an external solution, including the external solutions manifested in another human being. No one person can totally satisfy all of the inner need in another person. We are called to be part of and to participate fully in the body of Christ.

FALSE SOLUTIONS TO NEED MEETING

In many cases, the behavior of a person is rooted in his perception that what he is doing *externally* will bring about the solution to his deep needs *internally*. But external solutions don't work for deep emotional or spiritual needs.

Let me give you a couple of examples.

Let's consider a man who works sixty hours a week at his job. All his energies, seven days a week, are aimed at getting ahead in his career. Outwardly this man claims that he must work long hours either to keep his job or to advance in his job. Or he may claim that he is expending all the time and effort for the good of his family. At the core of his being, however, is a deep need to be accepted, recognized, and rewarded for who he is as a person. He has a deep need to achieve in order to have a place in the social world that he doesn't have. All his energies are channeled into the workplace in hopes that somebody will value him enough, recognize him enough, reward him enough, or accept him as being worthy. He is trying to meet internal needs through external means.

If you were to ask such a person whether he had needs, he would likely say, "No, I don't have any needs. I'm just a hard worker." The reality is, such a man often does not know within himself the true nature of his inner needs, and he has been deceived into thinking that he can increase his value to others, and ultimately to God, through hard work. Such a person is driven by inner needs, but he will not solve the needs through the work he does.

Let's consider a woman who gets involved in every volunteer effort and every church committee available. From dawn to dusk she does good works for her church and her community. She says she is just trying to be a good Christian. In reality, however, she is struggling with a sense of failure before God. She feels unworthy of God's love and acceptance. She is haunted by incidents long in her past in which she felt rejection, pain, and sorrow. She might have been involved in some type of sin, either her own or that of another person, and she feels unclean and of little value before God. Her efforts are an external attempt to compensate for an internal need.

Such a woman likely does not know that she is attempting to meet inner needs through her relentless work on behalf of others. In truth, she feels driven to give of herself to make herself worthy of God's love and forgiveness. She is striving to earn what Jesus has already offered to her freely.

I have talked to a number of men and women who fit the profiles I have given here, and in every case, if I am able to talk to the persons long enough and they are willing to be honest with themselves and with me, we get to the point where we come face-to-face with a deep emotional or spiritual need in their lives, one that often goes all the way back to their early years.

The same emotional need that drives a person to work himself to the point of exhaustion or illness or perhaps even stroke, heart attack, or death, is the same need that often drives a person to promiscuity, alcoholism, or substance abuse. It is the deep inner need for acceptance, love, value, worthiness, and forgiveness from God.

Until that inner need is faced, and then met through receiving the love and forgiveness of God made possible through the cross of Jesus Christ, the person is likely to continue to pursue external solutions, which are ultimately false solutions.

WHEN ARE EXTERNAL SOLUTIONS VALID?

Things can never take the place of relationships. Neither things nor relationships resolve inner needs. This is not to say, however, that all external solutions are invalid. External solutions work for meeting external needs.

Consider the situation in which a person has a home literally washed off its foundation by a hundred-year flood. That is an external need. It is not at all rooted in the inner lives of the family members who lived in the home.

What is likely to meet the need that this flood-ravaged family has experienced? The caring generosity of neighbors and community members, hard work to earn enough money to rebuild the home, wise decisions about where to rebuild, continued love and encouragement to one another in the face of such a challenge. External solutions will work because the need is external.

Consider the situation in which a child falls ill to a fever that was transmitted by a tick while he was out hiking with a group of Scouts. What will bring about a solution to that problem? Good medicine, good support of prayer and love and encouragement from family members and friends, and ongoing precautions. External solutions will work because the need is external.

External solutions work for external needs.

Internal solutions are required to meet internal needs.

WHAT IS GOD'S ROLE?

God's role varies according to the nature of the need. Sometimes God's role is to instruct us in the way we should go. It is then our responsibility to do what He has told us to do.

At other times God's role in meeting our needs is to supply Himself. God the Holy Spirit has been given to those who believe in Jesus Christ to be our Comforter, Counselor, Spirit of truth, and Helper. Jesus used these words to describe the work of the Holy Spirit in us. Guidance, comfort, courage, insight, truth, discernment, wisdom, understanding, peacefulness, strength—all of these are imparted to us by the Holy Spirit to help us see clearly and then walk boldly in the path God puts before us.

What is vital for us to recognize is this: at all times God has a role. Furthermore, we must always acknowledge His role as the most important role.

When we talk about having our needs met, we human beings often look to everyone except to God. We seek answers from relatives, friends, and a host of other sources—some helpful, others harmful to our spirits—rather than look to God.

The ultimate source for meeting all need is God. He uses a variety of methods and instruments to meet our needs, but He is the Author and Originator of all that we need, both in the outer material, natural, and physical realm, and in the inner emotional, mental, and spiritual realm.

Many of the ways in which He helps us can be found in His Word. The Bible not only defines human need but also presents God's methods for resolving human need.

Furthermore, God's Word presents both a right and a wrong way for meeting our needs. Example after example is provided to show how God works and to show the futility of man's methods.

And finally, the good news about God's methods for meeting needs is this: there is no negative side effect. When we follow God's method for meeting needs, we are not left with a residual feeling of anxiety, guilt, frustration, or embarrassment. When God meets our needs, He does so in a way that leaves us feeling a deep inner peace, satisfaction, and sense of fulfillment.

Many times God will reveal a plan for meeting your need, and that plan very often includes something specific that you must do.

A young man was discussing his love life—or rather, his lack of a love life—with his grandfather. He mentioned to his grandfather that he hadn't been out on a date in several months. He finally gave a big sigh and said to his grandfather, "Gramps, I guess I'm just going to have to trust God to send me a wife."

His grandfather replied with a twinkle in his eye, "I suspect that God would be a lot more eager to help you if He knew you had the nerve to ask the girl He sends you out on a date."

The point is, we usually have to do something to bring God's answer to bear on our need. Certainly we can trust God to help us, lead us, guide us, bring relationships our way, and give us the courage to act. We also must be willing to do our part: ask, seek, knock, work, plan, prepare, initiate contacts, be open to opportunities.

Are you willing to do things God's way?

Are you willing to read God's Word and communicate with God until you have certainty about His plan and His timing?

Are you willing to do what God reveals to you to do?

These are key questions you must ask yourself.

GOD'S PLAN INCLUDES GOD'S PERFECT TIMING

Jesus has a method and a procedure to bring you through the storm you are experiencing, and He also has a specific timetable for His method and procedure. God's timing is perfect, even though His timing may not be your timing.

Notice what happened when Jesus sent the disciples away after He miraculously had fed five thousand families from a few loaves and fish. The Bible says that Jesus "made His disciples get into the boat and go before Him to the other side" (Matt. 14:22 NKJV). The implication is that they didn't want to go.

Jesus insisted. He wanted personally to send the multitudes away, and He also wanted time alone with the Father. His reasons were *His* reasons.

God never has to explain Himself to us or give us a reason for what He does. He never needs to reveal to us the reason for a storm in our lives unless He desires to do so and chooses to do so. There are some reasons that we simply never need to know.

What we do need to know is that Jesus is with us in the storm, regardless of its nature or origin, and that God has a divine plan and purpose in place for our lives.

The storm on the sea, the passage of the disciples from one point to the next, and Jesus' prayer time were all in a perfect concert of time from the Father's perspective.

There is no sense of hurry about this scene, from the divine perspective. Jesus knew the storm was raging, but there is no indication whatsoever that Jesus hurried His prayer time. Jesus knew that the disciples were going to end up exactly where He intended for them to be. He had no fear whatsoever that the storm was going to blow the disciples off course. They might have thought they were going to be off course or late in their arrival, but Jesus knew they were going to arrive exactly where they were supposed to be, when they were supposed to be there. There is no indication that Jesus was running to them across the sea, as if He had to get there in the nick of time. No! Jesus was walking to them as if everything was happening and unfolding precisely as God had ordained—and indeed, it was.

Jesus was not only the Sovereign of the sea, but also the sovereign Lord of the disciples' lives. That being the case, Jesus was totally in charge of every aspect of the experience.

What a wonderful assurance we should draw from this story for our lives. Is Jesus the Lord of all things or only some things? Is He Lord over time, situations, all the material universe, and all circumstances? Indeed, He is! Is He Lord over your life? That is a question only you can answer. The truth, however, is that if you have made Jesus the Lord of your life, and He is the rightful King of all kings and Lord of all lords, then there isn't a situation, circumstance, or period of time over which Jesus does not have absolute control and sovereignty. He will make certain that all things come together for your good, in His timing and according to His chosen methods, if you will only trust Him completely to be the Lord of your life.

Have you ever thought about the fact that the Lord can cause any storm in your life to carry you to the place where He intends for you to arrive? Many of us think that it is up to us to decide where we are going to be five years from now, or even that it is up to us to decide exactly what we are going to do tomorrow, next week, or next year. If we claim Jesus as our Lord, then those decisions are up to Him, not us. We can make plans, and we are wise to do so, but our plans must always be the result of prayer and made with total flexibility that if this is not what God desires for us to do, we will be quick to alter our course.

James addressed this very issue:

Come now, you who say, "Today or tomorrow we will go to such and such a city, spend a year there, buy and sell, and make a profit"; whereas you do not know what will happen tomorrow. For what is your life? It is even a vapor that appears for a little time and then vanishes away. Instead you ought to say, "If the Lord wills, we shall live and do this or that." But now you boast in your arrogance. All such boasting is evil.

(JAMES 4:13–16 NKJV)

The disciples should never have experienced a single moment of doubt that they were precisely where God wanted them to be and that He was in control of their lives and would bring them through the storm. Why is that so? Because Jesus had insisted that they get into the boat and go before Him to the other side. Jesus will not tell you to do something and then change His mind about it and not tell you. Jesus will not tell you to get into a boat and go before Him to the other side if He does not intend to meet you on the other shore. Jesus had made it very plain to His disciples where they were to go, how they were to get there, and that He would meet them there.

Note what Jesus did *not* tell His disciples. He did not tell them their time of arrival. Neither did He tell them how He was getting to the other side of the sea. He said, "Get in the boat, row to the other side, and I'll meet you over there."

The Lord may not tell you every detail of His plan. Your position is not to require every detail or to know all things, but to obey what the Lord tells you to do. How the Lord does His part, and what the Lord's timing may be, is the Lord's business, not yours.

This is critically important to the way you face needs and storms. The Lord knows precisely how He is going to meet your need or calm your storm. He knows all the methods He is going to use, and for which purposes He will use them. He knows exactly when He is going to exact His purposes to meet your need or calm your storm. Your position is to trust God and, in your obedience and trust, to do what you know to do and leave all other matters to God's sovereignty.

GOD'S METHODS ARE NOT WITHOUT PAIN

We can and must trust God explicitly when it comes to both method and timing for our needs to be met. That does not ensure, however, that the process will be painless. What we can count on is that God's method will always be effective and eternally beneficial.

It was not until I was into my forties that I began to deal with some of the inner wounds from my past. I became increasingly restless in my spirit and found myself asking God more frequently, "What's going on here? Something isn't right." I couldn't recognize the cause of my frustration and uneasiness. I asked the Lord to reveal to me the cause of the inner tension I felt. And He began to do His surgery in my life.

The process was not quick and it was not without pain. I had layers and layers of emotional wounds that needed to be revealed and healed: feelings of loneliness, rejection, abusive criticism, unworthiness, and guilt that began early in my childhood. My healing of emotional wounds was not a matter of saying a quick prayer, "Jesus, please heal me. Amen." No, it was a process that required years of introspection, yielding to the healing power of God, and wise counsel from godly men who knew how to listen with an open mind and how to listen to the Holy Spirit and follow His leading in the advice they gave me.

Did I enjoy the process? No, not really. I'm not sure that divine surgery is something that any person enjoys, or even that it is a process that God intends for us to enjoy.

Did I benefit from the process? More than words can convey. I am not the same person I once was in the innermost parts of my being. Through this process of subjecting myself to God's healing power, I learned a great deal more about myself and vastly more about God and His love. I came to experience the feeling of God's love for me in a way that I had never known before. I developed a more intimate relationship with God than I had ever had in the past. My trust in God became complete; my faith grew stronger; my spiritual sensitivity increased; my awareness of God at work became sharper. I developed spiritually in ways I can't even describe other than to say my relationship with God became richer, more intense, more satisfying, and more all-encompassing, and it continues to become increasingly richer, more intense, more satisfying, and more all-encompassing as time passes.

Am I certain without a shadow of a doubt that God heals emotional wounds? Absolutely. Am I certain that He will do in you what He has done in me if you will yield yourself to His healing presence and power as I yielded myself to Him? Absolutely.

PATIENCE IN THE MIDST OF GOD'S PROCESS

Financial problems often develop over months and years. Paying off one's debts can take equally long.

Family and marital problems usually build slowly over years and sometimes decades. Solutions can be slow in coming and may take years of family and personal counseling.

Emotional wounds can occur quickly. It may take only a few minutes for a person to be hurt deeply. But emotional bitterness, resentment, and hatred often seethe for years before a person seeks healing. Emotional healing takes time.

God can heal or resolve both external and internal needs instantly, but in the vast majority of cases, individuals who are truly going to be healed are going to have to walk through a process that takes time.

A woman recently asked a friend of mine, "How long is it going to take for God to heal me of the pain I feel over the incest in my childhood?" The woman had been in therapy for years and was still receiving counseling for problems rooted in that terrible abuse of thirty years ago. My friend replied, "I don't know. Only God has the timetable."

That answer may not be satisfying to the person experiencing pain, but it is an honest answer. An accident can do serious damage to the physical body in a matter of seconds. Healing from those injuries can take months, even years. A disease can be quite advanced before its symptoms drive a person to seek help. Healing from such a disease can require months or years of treatment. So, too, our emotional wounds. A single act of sexual abuse, a particularly embarrassing situation, or one act of rejection can cause emotional pain that may take years to undo or overcome. Only God knows all the pieces to the puzzle and what it will take for a person to regain full health and wholeness.

If you or someone you love is in the process of being healed, have patience. God calls us to be steadfast and to be faithful in our obedience to Him as He renews us, regenerates us, and creates in us the likeness of Jesus Christ.

Even the person who experiences a miraculous physical cure often requires weeks or months of therapy to regain full strength and function. So, too, with emotional healing. The healing process is one of healing and then strengthening for the future. A major part of the process is not only dealing with the past, but also acquiring skills, strategies, and a new perspective for facing the future successfully. Emotional healing requires that we develop new ways of thinking, responding, feeling, and relating. It requires that we approach life with a new outlook and a new level of trust in God.

Don't allow yourself to become discouraged by the pain that you may experience at the outset of an emotional healing process or by the fact that your emotional healing is not instantaneous. Be encouraged that God is at work and He is remaking you into the person He truly created you to be.

Consider the experience of Jeremiah the prophet, who heard the Lord say to him,

"Arise and go down to the potter's house, and there I will cause you to hear My words." Then I went down to the potter's house, and there he was, making something at the wheel. And the vessel that he made of clay was marred in the hand of the potter; so he made it again into another vessel, as it seemed good to the potter to make. Then the word of the LORD came to me, saying: . . . "Look, as the clay is in the potter's hand, so are you in My hand."

(JER. 18:2–6 NKJV)

When we undergo an experience of emotional healing, it is often as if we are broken so that the Lord can completely remake us. Emotional healing is a re-fashioning process. The clay is still the same, the end design is still the same, but the process requires a breaking and a rebuilding so that the flaws can be removed.

Not only are we to remain steadfast, but we are to be joyful that God is at work in our lives. We are to thank Him daily that He is healing us, restoring us, and making us whole. We are who we are, each one of us, because the Lord is making us who we are. We are His workmanship. Praise God that He is providing you with a way out. He is with you every step of the way as you follow His leading, and He will bring you to a complete resolution of your need.

Paul encouraged the Philippians by writing at the beginning of his letter to them, "He who has begun a good work in you will complete it until the day of Jesus Christ" (Phil. 1:6 NKJV).

Paul wrote to the Thessalonians a similar word of encouragement: "He who calls you is faithful, who also will do it" (1 Thess. 5:24 NKJV).

Rejoice over the fact that God provides the way out, and His presence will enable you to pursue that way out until *all* your need has been met!

FOUR

HIS PRESENCE

Are you aware that God is with you always?

Many Christians readily proclaim, "God is always there," but if they are pressed for an honest response, they will also admit, "I don't always feel God. I'm not always aware of His presence with me." Too often this is true when we experience periods of intense neediness or when we truly confront our inner state of neediness for the first time.

In the previous chapter we discussed primarily *how* God provides a way out for us when we have need, and we briefly touched upon the nature of God as He walks with us through our need all the way to His full provision and blessing. In this chapter, I want to focus on the nature of God's relationship with us and how we can fully experience the provision of His presence.

DELIGHTING IN THE LORD

Psalm 37:4 gives us one of the most precious and sweet promises of God related to our desires:

> Delight yourself in the LORD;
> And He will give you the desires of your heart.

How many people do you know who have that verse underlined or highlighted in their Bibles?

But look at the first line of that verse: "Delight yourself also in the Lord." When you delight yourself in another person, you spend as much time as possible with that person, and you get to know that person as well as possible. When you are delighted in your relationship with another person, you are fulfilled, complete, satisfied, content, and joyful in your relationship. If you experience such a relationship, many material and physical things usually become less important.

Think back to a time when you were very much in love with another person. You could spend hours and hours with that person doing virtually nothing, with nothing, and at very little expense. Just taking a long walk with that person or sitting on a porch swing by the hour with that person was sheer delight. Driving to get an ice-cream cone and sitting in the car watching the people go by— those were satisfying and enjoyable moments. You weren't concerned about the designer label on the clothes you were wearing, the make of the watch on your wrist, or even the model of the car you were sitting in. You weren't concerned about having a lot of other people around you. You were fully content just to be in the presence of the one you loved. The most important thing to you in the moments you spent together was the relationship you were building.

And so it is when we come to delight in our relationship with God. Nothing else really matters when we experience an intimate time with the Lord. Everything else pales in comparison to Him. As the old Gospel song "Turn Your Eyes Upon Jesus" says, in the light of Jesus' glory and grace, "the things of earth will grow strangely dim."

Are you content when you are with the Lord? Do you truly delight in Him? Are you spending enough time with the Lord to become delighted in Him?

I have discovered over the years that most people I meet haven't taken the time or made the effort to get to know the Lord. Not really. Not deeply. Not in an intimate way that allows them to feel God's heartbeat and to know God's vast and eternal love.

The reasons for their failure to know the Lord in a deep and satisfying way are many—fear of God's judgment, fear of what others might say, lack of information, poor teaching in the past, a failure of perception or understanding, a lack of making the Lord a priority.

Once a person truly gets to know the Lord, however, that person is going to discover that it is a delight to know the Lord. No times are sweeter than the times spent with Him. No times are more fulfilling, satisfying, or joyful than the times spent basking in His presence.

When our relationship is one of delight in the Lord, we are not going to want to do things, possess or use things, or enter into any relationship that will damage in any way our relationship with the Lord. Again, think back to the way you felt when you were deeply in love. To the best of your ability, you didn't let anything come between you and your loved one. Nothing mattered as much as keeping your relationship as wonderful as it was on the first day you fell in love.

So it is with the person who delights himself in the Lord. Such a person will not want anything that might inhibit, hinder, stall, or interfere with his relationship with the Lord. In terms we have discussed previously, the person will want only what is good for the relationship.

When we seek the Lord and delight ourselves in Him, we want only what is pleasing to Him and only what He wants us to have. Furthermore, we will be satisfied completely with what the Lord gives us.

As 1 John 1:3 tells us, "Truly our fellowship is with the Father and with His Son Jesus Christ" (NKJV). That's the ultimate fellowship! Knowing God. Communicating with Him—pouring out our hearts to Him and hearing His desires, His plan for us, His purposes. Loving Him with all our hearts and receiving an awareness of His vast love. Being at peace with God and knowing God's peace in our hearts. Praising God and being filled with God's joy. Being in a position to say, *"My* God." That is truly what it means to have fellowship with God.

GOD'S PROMISE TO MEET OUR NEEDS

When God meets our inner needs with the provision of His presence, we can be assured always that part of His provision will be to give us these things:

- Contentment—deep and abiding inner peace and calm
- Strength—great courage and fortitude to endure all things

- Fulfillment—a full and satisfying feeling of supply related to our purpose on this earth

Throughout this part of the book, we have been focusing on God's need-meeting promise in Philippians 4:19: "My God shall supply all your need according to His riches in glory by Christ Jesus" (NKJV). To fully understand this verse, we must understand its context.

Paul's entire letter to the Philippians is related to needs and need meeting. The Philippians were tremendously helpful in meeting Paul's material and financial needs. Paul began his letter to them by saying, "I thank my God upon every remembrance of you, always in every prayer of mine making request for you all with joy, for your fellowship in the gospel from the first day until now" (Phil. 1:3–5). Their *fellowship* in the gospel is translated in one version as their *participation* in the gospel—in other words, the things that the Philippians did to help Paul spread the gospel and teach the new believers.

In the fourth chapter of Philippians, Paul again thanked them for their support:

But I rejoiced in the Lord greatly that now at last your care for me has flourished again; though you surely did care, but you lacked opportunity. Not that I speak in regard to need, for I have learned in whatever state I am, to be content: I know how to be abased, and I know how to abound. Everywhere and in all things I have learned both to be full and to be hungry, both to abound and to suffer need. I can do all things through Christ who strengthens me. Nevertheless you have done well that you shared in my distress. Now you Philippians know also that in the beginning of the gospel, when I departed from Macedonia, no church shared with me concerning giving and receiving but you only. For even in Thessalonica you sent aid once and again for my necessities. Not that I seek the gift, but I seek the fruit that abounds to your account. Indeed I have all and abound. I am full, having received from Epaphroditus the things sent from you, a sweet-smelling aroma, an acceptable sacrifice, well pleasing to God. And my God shall supply all your need according to His riches in glory by Christ Jesus.

(PHIL. 4:10–19 NKJV)

I want you to notice two things in this passage. First, Paul was a man who knew about need. He was writing the letter to the Philippians from a prison cell in Rome, so he certainly had a keen awareness of his external needs even as he wrote. Paul never made a claim that the Christian life is a need-free life, or that as Christians, we can mature to the point that we never face need. Paul knew that needs exist for us every day of our lives. We never outgrow our neediness or mature to the point that we don't have needs.

Second, Paul was willing to admit his neediness and to share what he learned about needs and how to deal with them. Paul encouraged the Philippians in the truths he learned from having experienced needs. Never be ashamed of your past needs or your current neediness. Be quick to encourage others by telling them how God has met your needs in the past and how you believe He will meet their needs.

CONTENT IN ALL STATES

Paul said that he learned to be content regardless of his circumstances—in whatever state he was in. Paul was not content *with* troubles, trials, suffering, pain, or need. He felt pain and need just as much as any other person. But he learned to be content *in* times of difficulty. His internal state was one of contentment even when his outward state was one of turmoil, trial, or trouble.

No stranger to outer pain and suffering, Paul was stoned and left for dead in Lystra, beaten and imprisoned in Philippi, and persecuted and defamed publicly nearly everywhere he went. To those in the Corinthian church who compared him to other preachers, Paul wrote that he was "in labors more abundant, in stripes above measure, in prisons more frequently, in deaths often" (2 Cor. 11:23 NKJV). He then went on to detail for the Corinthians some of the needs and troubles he had experienced in his ministry:

> From the Jews five times I received forty stripes minus one. Three times I was
> beaten with rods; once I was stoned; three times I was shipwrecked; a night
> and a day I have been in the deep; in journeys often, in perils of waters, in

perils of robbers, in perils of my own countrymen, in perils of the Gentiles, in perils in the city, in perils in the wilderness, in perils in the sea, in perils among false brethren; in weariness and toil, in sleeplessness often, in hunger and thirst, in fastings often, in cold and nakedness—besides the other things, what comes upon me daily: my deep concern for all the churches.

(2 COR. 11:24–28 NKJV)

Few people can match Paul in severity and frequency of need and suffering externally. Yet Paul wrote that in the midst of such outer troubles, he learned to be content internally.

How many truly contented people do you know?

I suspect that the number is very few. And yet if you look closely at the lives of those who truly and genuinely are contented, you are going to find that their contentment has nothing whatsoever to do with material things, relationships, or achievements. I've met truly contented people who were single, and I've met some who were married. I have met genuinely contented people who were poor, and a few who had been given great wealth. I have met contented people who were totally without fame and recognition, and in many ways, without fantastic jobs or great successes, and I've met a few who were content regardless of their fame and success.

In many cases, the very thing that people think will bring them contentment turns out to be the very thing that creates more problems and turmoil for them. In the end, only the Lord Jesus Christ Himself can bring about contentment in a person's life. Paul was able to say, "I have learned in whatever state I am, to be content: I know how to be abased, and I know how to abound. Everywhere and in all things I have learned both to be full and to be hungry, both to abound and to suffer need. I can do all things through Christ who strengthens me" (Phil. 4:11–13).

Be careful that you don't misread these verses. Paul did not say that Christ strengthened him only when he was struggling, suffering, hungry, or abased. Christ strengthened Paul in all states in which he found himself. He strengthened Paul when he was full, abounding, safe, and without pain or struggle. We often don't think about this. Paul had no less need for Christ's strength when things were good. In times of abounding, Paul needed Christ's strength to keep him humble, keenly aware of others and generous toward them, thankful, energized, and an active witness of God's power. When things are going well for us, we need Christ's strength to keep us from pride, laziness, and self-sufficiency.

Paul said that he learned to be content "in whatever state I am." His contentment was in Christ—not in things or in circumstances. His contentment lay in his relationship with the Need Meeter, not in the fact that his needs were met momentarily.

I heard about a man who experienced great contentment and love in the presence of his wife just by holding her hand. The man's wife suffered with a terminal disease for three years before she died, and as she became weaker and weaker in the final months, the man pulled his chair close to hers, and they held hands and stared into each other's eyes. No words needed to be spoken. No physical embrace needed to be shared. The love was just as rich and freely flowing between them through the looks in their eyes and the touch of their fingertips. No grasping. No desperate clinging. No clamoring for attention. No pleas for acts of affection.

True contentment is always marked by a lack of striving—a lack of grasping, a lack of demanding, a lack of insistence.

True contentment lies not in having, but in knowing—of knowing that you are accepted, loved, forgiven, valued in spite of what you may or may not have in your hands or surrounding you.

True contentment is not rooted in environment or in any aspect of the natural and spiritual world. Ultimate contentment is rooted in relationship with Jesus Christ and in Him alone.

STRENGTH TO FACE ALL CIRCUMSTANCES

Paul also taught that he had learned to experience strength in all things. He might have had times when he felt weak in his flesh, but he knew that even in those times of natural and physical weakness, he could experience the strength of Christ internally. Paul wrote to the Corinthians about his ability to feel strong spiritually in the face of physical weakness:

A thorn in the flesh was given to me, a messenger of Satan to buffet me, lest I be exalted above measure. Concerning this thing I pleaded with the Lord three times that it might depart from me. And He said to me, "My grace is sufficient for you, for My strength is made perfect in weakness." Therefore most gladly I will rather boast in my infirmities, that the power of Christ may rest upon me. Therefore I take pleasure in infirmities, in reproaches, in needs, in persecutions, in distresses, for Christ's sake. For when I am weak, then I am strong.

(2 COR. 12:7–10 NKJV)

Paul's thorn-in-the-flesh experience brought him to the position where he could fully allow the strength of Christ to be his strength. Paul was not saying that he delighted in the pain and suffering; rather, he had learned those were opportunities when he could and would feel an even greater flow of Christ's strength in his inner being. Paul's reliance upon Christ's strength became a vivid witness to others who saw his physical suffering, and for that, Paul was grateful.

Some people today will claim, "Troubles make you strong." They are wrong. Troubles destroy some people. Troubles weaken others. There is nothing inherent about troubles that results in making us strong emotionally and spiritually. The truth, as Paul stated it so well, is that when we rely upon Christ Jesus in our times of trouble, *He* makes us strong. He imparts His strength to us and as we receive His strength, we are made strong.

A FULL SUPPLY FOR ALL THAT IS LACKING

Paul said that he learned to experience "supply" for all his needs. We do not know what gifts Epaphroditus brought from the Philippians to Paul. We do know that Paul regarded their gift as pleasing to God and more than sufficient. To be supplied to the point that you can say, "I have all and abound," is to be fully satisfied (Phil. 4:18). Paul saw all his needs as being met, and out of that inner feeling of satisfaction, he boldly declared to the Philippians his assurance that they, too, would have all their need supplied by God according to His riches in glory by Christ Jesus (v. 19).

Most people tend to think that the gifts Epaphroditus brought to Paul were only material. The gift no doubt was at least partly material since the family and friends of Roman prisoners were expected to provide material provision for those detained by Roman officials, especially those under house arrest as Paul appeared to be. But prisoners' needs then and now are not merely material. They are also social, emotional, and spiritual.

Paul was undoubtedly encouraged by the friendship of Epaphroditus. Paul could communicate fully with him about matters pertaining to his faith and to the work of the Lord. Paul no doubt could both laugh and cry with him. Such Christ-centered friendship is priceless!

Furthermore, Epaphroditus no doubt brought a good word about Paul's friends in Philippi and elsewhere in the regions where Paul had traveled and ministered. How encouraging that must have been to Paul—to know that his work had not been in vain, that his efforts were bearing fruit, that the work of the Lord was going forward, that the church in Philippi was strong. We all need others to affirm that our efforts have been valuable and beneficial to them. We need their gifts, their friendship, and their encouragement that our lives have had purpose and meaning. Through such affirmation, we experience a full feeling in our hearts that we call fulfillment. A deep satisfaction comes when we know we truly have helped others in an eternally beneficial way.

Paul received a full blessing from Epaphroditus—material provision for his external needs but also emotional and spiritual encouragement that was a provision for Paul's inner needs.

Wouldn't we all like to be able to say with Paul that regardless of what happens to us, we are content, strong, and fully satisfied? In truth, we can have that inner state of being.

A LEARNING PROCESS

We should also note that it was a learning process for Paul. He said very plainly, "I have learned . . ." (vv. 11–12). Paul didn't instantly reach a state of inner contentment, strength, and satisfaction. He grew into that state of being as he "learned Christ."

What Paul had learned, we can learn. Paul made that very clear. Even if you have never felt much peace in your life, you can learn to be content. If you have always thought of yourself as weak and needy, you can learn to be strong, and if you have thought of yourself as strong, you can learn to be stronger. If you have felt uncertain about your purpose in life and whether you are fulfilling it before God, you can learn to experience inner fulfillment as well as learn what it means to receive an abundance of external blessing.

This learning process is part of a growing relationship with the Lord. It ultimately is "learning God." It is knowing the Lord and delighting in Him with increasing delight.

EXPERIENCING GOD'S PROVISION IN CRISIS TIMES

God desires that we experience Him always and that we draw contentment, strength, and total satisfaction from our relationship with Him at all times. It is especially important, however, that we experience the provision of God's presence in the stormy times of our lives, the times when we are keenly aware of our needs or neediness. Such times come for us all.

Every person's life is marked by storms of one kind or another. The reality for each of us is that we are in a storm, have just emerged from a storm, or are about to enter a storm. No geographic area of the earth is immune from natural atmospheric storms, and no person or relationship is immune from inner storms. Since we cannot avoid storms, we must learn to deal with them.

All kinds of atmospheric storms impact us on this earth—windstorms, sandstorms, rainstorms, thunderstorms, snowstorms. At times these storms are driving, blinding, destructive, and costly, even at the cost of life itself. Such storms often make the headlines—they evoke a ripple effect of devastation in the general public and, in many cases, bring about a response of public compassion and concern.

We also face a number of emotional storms in our lives, no less blinding, destructive, and devastating. If these storms are known by the public, even a small group of friends, they also have a ripple effect. No emotional storm impacts only one person.

The response to emotional storms is somewhat different from the response to atmospheric storms. Some respond to the victims of emotional storms with compassion and concern, others shun the persons at the center of the storms, and still others tend to be critical of those who experience emotional storms, usually blaming them in some way for what has happened. In dealing with a storm, we are called to examine the way in which we confront a storm and the manner in which we respond to both the instigators and the victims of that storm.

What happens if the emotional storm a person experiences is not readily known by others? Does the storm impact others any less? Not really. An emotional storm within a person or family will spill over to impact others in ways that may not be readily understood or even identified as relating to the storm. For example, anger that brews within a person is likely to erupt suddenly and sometimes violently, and often it is aimed at someone who was not the initial reason for the anger. The innocent victims of such anger are left wondering, *Where did that come from? What brought that on?* They have no understanding of the inner emotional storm that had been raging and very likely is continuing to rage in silence within the person.

The conclusion we must draw is this: storms occur, and storms cause damage—sooner or later, to greater or lesser degrees—unless they are dealt with by the only One capable of truly calming a natural or emotional storm, Jesus Christ.

In learning to deal with life's storms, we must turn to Jesus and discover the provision that He makes for us when storms strike.

OUR RESPONSE TO THE STORM

Let us keep in mind as we study Christ's provision that the *nature* of the storm is not at issue. The storm may be in a marriage, in health, in finances, in work, in a relationship with children. What we do in the aftermath of a storm, and especially to keep another storm from arising, is very important, and it relates to the nature of the storm. But while we are in a storm, its nature is not an important issue.

A storm hits the whole of one's life. If you are having financial difficulties, such a storm will have a profound effect on your marriage and family life, your performance at work and in other areas, and ultimately, if the financial difficulty is not resolved, it may even impact your health. A storm in your marriage will impact your children, your finances, your work, and your health.

Neither is the *cause* of the storm at issue. When you are in the midst of a storm, your primary concern is with survival. Pointing a finger at the person or circumstance that caused the storm is not a productive response. After the storm has passed, you may be wise to take a good, long, objective look at what caused the storm so that if at all possible, you can avoid or avert such a storm in the future. You may be wise to alter your relationship with a storm-causing person in some way, preferably to seek loving reconciliation and greater communication and understanding with that person. But during the storm itself, your concern is not going to be primarily with the cause of the storm.

What is your concern in the midst of a storm? How can you survive the storm? How can you live through the situation or circumstance? How can you emerge from the storm?

God's Word assures us that Jesus provides answers to these critical questions. One example of the way Jesus deals with those who are experiencing a storm is found in Matthew 14:22–34. Let's focus on several different aspects of the story.

Jesus had just finished a full day of tremendous ministry—preaching, teaching, and healing a great multitude of people who followed Him out into a desolate area. Before sending the people away, Jesus had multiplied five loaves and two fish to feed the hungry crowd of five thousand men and their families. Then, no doubt in exhaustion, Jesus

> made His disciples get into the boat and go before Him to the other side, while He sent the multitudes away. And when He had sent the multitudes away, He went up on the mountain by Himself to pray. Now when evening

came, He was alone there. But the boat was now in the middle of the sea, tossed by the waves, for the wind was contrary.

(MATT. 14:22–24 NKJV)

In the fourth watch of the night, sometime between three and six o'clock in the early morning, Jesus went to His disciples who were struggling in the storm; He walked on the sea to them. When the disciples saw Him walking on the sea, they cried out in their fear, "It is a ghost!" Here is how Matthew told the rest of this story:

> Immediately Jesus spoke to them, saying, "Be of good cheer! It is I; do not be afraid." And Peter answered Him and said, "Lord, if it is You, command me to come to You on the water." So He said, "Come." And when Peter had come down out of the boat, he walked on the water to go to Jesus. But when he saw that the wind was boisterous, he was afraid; and beginning to sink he cried out, saying, "Lord, save me!" And immediately Jesus stretched out His hand and caught him, and said to him, "O you of little faith, why did you doubt?" And when they got into the boat, the wind ceased. Then those who were in the boat came and worshiped Him, saying, "Truly You are the Son of God." When they had crossed over, they came to the land of Gennesaret.
>
> (MATT. 14:27–34 NKJV)

The first thing that we are wise to recognize when a storm strikes is that Jesus is present with us in the storm, just as He was present for His disciples in this story. Jesus is present. He is with us at all times, in all circumstances. There is never a single moment of your life in which Jesus is not there for you and with you.

AWARENESS OF HIS PRESENCE

Nothing can match the power of an awareness that Jesus is present. The presence of friends, advisers, and colleagues can never match the presence of Jesus.

The disciples had been struggling all night without making any progress. Storms arose suddenly in the Galilee area. The winds came across the land from the Mediterranean Sea and then rushed down the steep valleys into the Sea of Galilee, beating the sea almost as if a giant hand mixer were lowered into the waters. The disciples had struggled against such a wind for at least nine hours and had gone a distance of only about five miles, no doubt fighting for every inch of progress they made to keep the boat from capsizing.

Storms strike us quickly at times and often fiercely. We may feel as if there is no way out—everything becomes an intense struggle that seems overwhelming.

A woman once said to me about the day that her husband told her he was filing for a divorce, "Everything began to spin. I felt as if I was hanging on to the edge of a world that had gone out of control. For the next few weeks, it was all I could do to hang on. It was a tremendous effort just to get up and get my children off to school and go through the basic routines of what needed to be done in my life. Nothing else mattered—just getting through the day took all of my energy and strength." Emotional storms are often that violent and all-consuming.

Jesus knows about storms. You can be assured that He knows every detail about the storm you are experiencing. He knows far more about the storm than you know or will ever know. Furthermore, He knew that His disciples were struggling and battling the storm with all their strength. He knew they were in one of those periods that no doubt seemed to them to be the fight of their lives. He knows how you struggle when you are in a storm. And Jesus' response was this: *He came to them.*

Notice that He did not calm the storm from afar, although He could have done that. He had calmed a natural, physical storm on the Sea of Galilee at a previous time. This time, Jesus chose *not* to calm the storm as He had done before.

Neither did Jesus ignore the storm, knowing in His sovereignty that the storm would eventually blow over without loss of life or property.

Rather, Jesus knew that in this particular storm, the most important thing that His disciples could experience was *an awareness of His presence.* Note that I did not say Jesus' *presence*, but *an awareness of His presence.*

Jesus was just as present with His disciples while He was up on the mountain in prayer as He was when He walked on the sea to them. They were never out of His sight or His concern.

But the disciples were not aware that Jesus knew or cared about them. Their thoughts were not on Jesus, even though His focus was on them. Their thoughts were so much on things other than Jesus that when Jesus appeared to them walking on the sea, they thought He was a ghost! They were frightened at the sight of Him.

We are so like these disciples! We often fail to look for Jesus in the midst of our storms, and we fail to recognize Him when He comes.

The likelihood is that Jesus may not come to you in precisely the way you expect Him to come. He may not come to you in a form that you quickly recognize. Probably the last thing on the earth that the disciples expected that night was to see Jesus walking on the water to them, yet that is the way Jesus chose to reveal Himself to them. Jesus may come to you in a totally unexpected fashion. And if you are not aware that He is present with you or that He cares enough to come to you in your storm, your response to the Lord may be the same as that of the disciples: fear and lack of recognition.

Let me give you a very practical example. A woman once told me of her reaction when her family physician said to her, "You have cancer." She said to me, "Dr. Stanley, it was as if my doctor had just thrown a black blanket of fear over me. I could hardly think. My eyes wouldn't focus. My ears seemed to ring. I was so stunned I felt paralyzed, incapable of moving. I didn't even hear the rest of what the doctor had to say, which was to tell me that he thought this cancer could be stopped with radiation treatments since it was in very early stages. If my daughter hadn't been with me during that appointment, I'm not sure I could have made it out of his office and to the car—I was that much in a fog.

"The next week, I made my first visit to the radiologist that my physician had recommended. I walked into his office and then into the radiology room filled with fear. What I hadn't expected at all was that this man might be a Christian, or that he might be aware of how I was feeling inside. I was completely surprised when he asked me, 'Are you afraid?' I admitted to him that I was fearful, not only of the cancer but also of the radiation. Then he said to me, 'I am a Christian, and I believe that prayer can help a person in times like these. Would it be all right with you if I said a prayer for you?' I said, 'Most certainly.' He prayed a sweet but very powerful prayer and as he prayed, I could feel my body relaxing. He took time to talk to me about both the cancer and the radiation treatments. I sensed that he truly cared about me, and I became more confident about what I was facing.

"The next time I went to see him I was less afraid. I told him how much his prayer had meant to me, and he asked if we might pray together again before my second treatment. Of course I agreed! This happened each time I went for treatments—thirty-two in all. I tell people now that I had thirty-two radiation treatments and thirty-two prayer treatments!

"By the time I had my last treatment, I was almost sorry it was my last visit to see him—not that I wanted more radiation, mind you, but I had come to appreciate this man's prayers and his calm and reassuring faith. It was a few weeks later that the thought struck me, *Why, that was Jesus coming to me through the form and skills of that radiologist! The love and power of Jesus in him gave me hope and eased my fears. The presence of Jesus in him had become a part of my healing process!*"

I don't know the way in which Jesus will come to you in your storm, but I can say to you in full confidence: Jesus will come to you in the precise way and form that you need Him the most. Trust Him to reveal Himself to you. He wants you to know that He is with you in the midst of the storm.

FEELINGS OF TOTAL ASSURANCE

Why is an awareness of Jesus' presence so important?

When we become aware of Jesus with us, several things happen to us. Taken together, these things add up to total assurance.

Comforted

When we are aware that Jesus is with us, we immediately become comforted. Each of us knows that when we are alone, it is much easier to feel fearful, but if we have even one friend with us in a time of trouble, we take comfort in his presence. Jesus is the Friend of friends. One of the terms given to the Holy Spirit is that of *Comforter*. When you are aware that Jesus is with you in your storm, you can't help being comforted by His presence.

More Courageous

We take courage that we can face what lies before us. Who comes to us in our storm? The King of kings, the Lord of lords, the almighty, all-sufficient, all-powerful, all-wise, all-loving Savior and Deliverer! With Jesus beside us, who can stand against us? We cannot help feeling more courageous when we are aware that Jesus is by our side.

More Confident

We become confident that God will see us through. Confidence is directly related to our knowing that a current trial or time of trouble will come to an end. When Jesus appears—throughout the Gospel books of the New Testament and in every instance we can cite in our lives today—He comes as Victor. The devil cannot remain where Jesus dwells. The enemy cannot succeed when Jesus arrives on the scene. Our confidence is no longer in ourselves to be able to survive, to endure, or to conquer; our confidence is in Jesus. Our confidence is based upon who Jesus is and what He will do for us, which always will be for our ultimate and eternal good (Rom. 8:28).

NO STORM CAN DRIVE JESUS AWAY

An awareness of Jesus' presence also reminds us that *no* storm can separate us from the Lord. No matter how fierce the storm rages or how powerful it seems to be against us, the storm cannot separate us from God's love, forgiveness, help, or promises. Paul wrote to the Romans,

> Who shall separate us from the love of Christ? Shall tribulation, or distress, or persecution, or famine, or nakedness, or peril, or sword ? . . . Yet in all these things we are more than conquerors through Him who loved us. For

CAN YOU STILL TRUST GOD?

I am persuaded that neither death nor life, nor angels nor principalities nor powers, nor things present nor things to come, nor height nor depth, nor any other created thing, shall be able to separate us from the love of God which is in Christ Jesus our Lord.

(ROM. 8:35, 37–39 NKJV)

The truth of the Lord's ever-presence (omnipresence) comes to us each time we become aware that He is with us in a storm. Just before His arrest and crucifixion, Jesus spoke to His disciples about His abiding presence with them. He said, "I will not leave you orphans; I will come to you" (John 14:18 NKJV). He promised them that He would send the Holy Spirit to them as their Helper.

As Jesus spoke to His disciples after His resurrection, preparing them for His ascension to heaven, He said, "Lo, I am with you always, even to the end of the age" (Matt. 28:20). In the form of the Holy Spirit, Jesus is with us at all times. He is *always* present in our lives, every minute of every hour of every day.

How blessed we are to live in the time of the Holy Spirit! When Jesus was alive on the earth, He could not be in two places at one time. But now, Jesus is free of all constraints of time and space. By the power of the Holy Spirit, He is with each of those who believe in Him at all times. We never need to call for Jesus to show up. He is already present. We may have a sudden awareness of His presence, so much so that it feels as if He just showed up, but it is not a sudden coming of Jesus—rather, a sudden awareness on our part.

ASK THE LORD TO REVEAL HIMSELF

How might we become aware of Jesus' presence? By asking Him to reveal Himself to us.

So often, we ask the wrong questions of the Lord. We say, "Where are You, God? Why don't You show up? Can't You see what's happening to me? Can't You see how I am struggling? Can't You see the pain I'm in?" The answer of the Lord, of course, is, "I'm right here with you. I know exactly what's going on!"

Our question of the Lord should be, "What is keeping me from seeing You? Help me to see You and to experience Your presence!"

One of the most intense emotional storms described in the New Testament is that experienced by Mary and Martha in the aftermath of their brother's death. Lazarus became sick, and Mary and Martha sent word to Jesus, saying, "Lord, behold, he whom You love is sick" (John 11:3). Jesus responded by saying, "This sickness is not unto death, but for the glory of God, that the Son of God may be glorified through it" (v. 4 NKJV).

Jesus stayed where He was for two more days, and then He said to His disciples, "Let us go to Judea again . . . Our friend Lazarus sleeps, but I go that I may wake him up" (vv. 7, 11 NKJV). The disciples couldn't understand Jesus' reasoning since they knew it was dangerous for them to return to Judea, and they also figured that if Lazarus was sleeping, he was getting better. Jesus finally said to them plainly, "Lazarus is dead. And I am glad for your sakes that I was not there, that you may believe. Nevertheless, let us go to him" (vv. 14–15).

Now on the surface it may appear that Jesus was not present or aware of Lazarus in that terrible storm of sickness. In truth, Jesus was very aware of all that was happening to His friend as well as what was happening to Mary and Martha. He knew exactly the full plan and purpose of God in the storm they were experiencing. He knew the moment that Lazarus died.

By the time Jesus arrived in Bethany, Lazarus had been in the tomb four days. Mourners who had filled the house of Martha and Mary were attempting to comfort them. As soon as Martha heard that Jesus had arrived on the scene, she ran out to meet Him, saying, "Lord, if You had been here, my brother would not have died" (v. 21 NKJV). Even Martha, who knew Jesus so well, assumed that Jesus had not been present in their lives. She went on to make a great statement of faith, however, saying, "But even now I know that whatever You ask of God, God will give You" (v. 22 NKJV). She didn't expect that Jesus would be able to ask or receive anything related to Lazarus, but her faith remained in Jesus that He was no less the Healer, Deliverer, and Savior.

Martha and Mary might very well have talked to each other prior to Jesus' arrival and said, "Why hasn't Jesus come? Surely He loves us. He has been in our home. We have shared meals with Him, laughed with Him, heard Him teach. He knows how much we love Him, and we know He loves us. So where is He?" Those are the kinds of questions we ask today when we, as Christian believers, experience storms.

The real question, however, should be, "What is Your purpose in this, Lord? Why am I slow to see Your presence and to catch a glimpse of Your plan?"

Jesus did not respond directly to Martha's statements, but He spoke God's plan to her: "Your brother will rise again" (v. 23 NKJV). Martha did not understand what He meant. She said, "I know that he will rise again in the resurrection at the last day" (v. 24). Jesus then said to her, "I am the resurrection and the life. He who believes in Me, though he may die, he shall live. And whoever lives and believes in Me shall never die. Do you believe this?" (vv. 25–26 NKJV).

Jesus went on to Lazarus's tomb and insisted that the stone be rolled away. He then prayed, "Father, I thank You that You have heard Me. And I know that You always hear Me, but because of the people who are standing by I said this, that they may believe that You sent Me" (vv. 41–42 NKJV). He then cried with a loud voice, "Lazarus, come forth!" (v. 43). And Lazarus came walking out of that tomb, restored to life four days after his death.

What was Jesus' message to Martha and Mary and to all who experienced the evidence of that miracle? It is the simple message that *Jesus is*. Wherever *Jesus is*, there one finds the full operation of the fullness of Jesus.

We say, "Where *were* You, Jesus?" or we say, "When Jesus comes . . ." The fact is, *Jesus is*. God revealed Himself to Moses in precisely this way, saying, "I AM" (Ex. 3:14). *Jesus is*.

He is never going to be more your Savior, your Healer, your Deliverer, or your Lord than He is right now. He is the same yesterday, today, and forever. The fullness of who He is, *is* with you right now. There is no more of Jesus left to show up. All of Him is present with you. All of Him has been with you. And all of Him *will* continue to be with you.

Jesus declared to Mary and Martha the truth that rings down through the generations to us, "I *am* the resurrection and the life." When we become aware of the presence of Jesus with us in a storm, we must become aware that

Jesus is with us in the fullness of His power to be the resurrection and the life. No matter how battered, bruised, or even dead we may feel inside as the result of our struggle, Jesus is with us to raise us up into newness of life. No matter how exhausted, broken, or devastated we may feel, Jesus is present with us to restore us, heal us, and energize us. He always comes to give us life and to give us life more abundantly (John 10:10). His very presence with us infuses life into our being.

WHY NOT AN AWARENESS OF CHRIST JESUS SOONER?

Why doesn't Jesus reveal Himself to us sooner than later? Why wait until the disciples were weary from rowing all night against a contrary wind? Why wait until Lazarus had been in the tomb four days? Because then the disciples were ready to become aware of Jesus. Then Mary and Martha, as well as the disciples, were ready to experience the great miracle that confirmed Jesus as Messiah and gave evidence that Jesus would rise from His own death and be the resurrection for all who believe in Him.

The "late" appearing of Jesus was not a lack of His presence but Christ's appearance in such a way and in the fullness of time so that those in need—the disciples, and Mary and Martha—might truly *become* aware of His presence.

If you are not experiencing the full presence of Jesus in your storm or time of trouble, ask the Lord to show you what is keeping you from experiencing His full and immediate presence. Ask Him to show you what He desires for you to recognize, learn, or experience as part of your having an awareness of His presence.

THE SAMARITAN SENT TO YOU

It is also important that you ask the Lord to help you recognize every person He sends to help you. Just as the Lord sent a Christian radiologist to help the woman whose story is told earlier in this chapter, so Jesus may send you very precise help in the form of a specific person. Don't miss that messenger of God's love and mercy!

Jesus told a story about a person who experienced a severe storm in his life. While on the road that led down to Jericho from Jerusalem, the man was beaten, robbed, and left for dead. Two men passed by without offering assistance to the injured man, and then, Jesus said, a man from Samaria spotted him, stopped, assisted him, and took him to a safe shelter in Jericho where he paid for the injured man's lodging and further medical help. Jesus asked those who heard this story, "Which of these three do you think was neighbor to him who fell among the thieves?" The people quickly replied, "He who showed mercy on him." Jesus then said, "Go and do likewise" (Luke 10:30–37 NKJV).

How many times has Jesus come to you in the form of a good Samaritan—someone who rescued you, ministered to you, cared for you, gave practical assistance to you, and looked out for your best interests? How many times have you been the recipient of someone's unrequested kindness? Have you seen Jesus at work in that experience or incident? Have you been aware that Jesus is the One who was behind the scenes all the time, ministering to you through that person, very much present in your time of need?

One reason you are not aware of Jesus' presence is that you have not asked Jesus just who He is using to bring about God's perfect plan and purpose in your life. It may be a person you never would have suspected.

A DIRECT REVELATION OF HIS PRESENCE

Many times, Jesus may not even use a person to make you aware of His presence. He may speak to you directly through a vision, through a message that someone preaches to you, or through the Word of God as you read it.

I once heard about a minister who was pastoring two small churches, preaching in each church every other Sunday. He was weary from the constant travel and the many needs that he saw in each of his small, rural congregations. He was struggling to do his best and remain encouraged in the Lord. He began to doubt his ability to minister adequately to the people.

He walked into his pastor's study on Monday morning and noticed that a Bible lay open on his desk. Thinking that perhaps he had left it open there on Saturday afternoon, he closed it and shelved it. The following Monday, the Bible was again open on his desk. He stopped to read the two pages that were open. Part of what he read was Luke 9:62. The words just seemed to leap off the page to him: "No one, having put his hand to the plow, and looking back, is fit for the kingdom of God."

He immediately fell to his knees, asking the Lord to forgive him for doubting the Lord's call on his life and for failing to rely completely on the Lord for the ability to minister to the people.

The next Monday morning, the Bible again lay open. The minister had no secretary, and as far as he knew, nobody in the church had a key to his private office. Yet Monday morning after Monday morning, his Bible was open on his desk when he walked into his office. Each Monday, words seemed to leap off the pages to him, encouraging him in his ministry and building him up in his faith.

Finally the preacher asked the Lord to reveal to him who was ministering to him in such a profound way so that he might thank the person. The Lord brought to mind the janitor who cleaned up the church after the Sunday morning service. Sure enough, the man had a key that gave him entrance to all areas of the church, including the pastor's study. The preacher went to call upon the man.

He said, "Thank you for leaving the open Bible for me to read each Monday. You'll never know how much the Lord has used these passages of Scripture to help me and to build me up so that I can do the job He has called me to do."

The man seemed a little puzzled. "Aren't you the one who has been giving me these verses to read?" the pastor asked.

The man replied, "No, sir. Wish I was. But you see, Preacher, I can't read. It seems every time I go into your study, though, there's your Bible lying facedown on the floor. I thought you were dropping it on purpose for me to read. So I picked it up real careful like and laid it on your desk to the open part, thinking maybe you'd make a sermon of what was there so I could get the message from the pulpit, seeing as I couldn't read the pages for myself. And sure enough, it seems like you've been preaching right to me these past couple of months."

The preacher never discovered who or what had caused his study Bible to tumble to the floor each week. The cause didn't really matter. What mattered was that the preacher chose to see Jesus in the pages of the Bible that lay open before him, and then to share the Jesus of the Bible with others. He could have dismissed what was happening as coincidence or something very mysterious— not unlike the disciples thinking they were seeing a ghost. Rather, the preacher chose to see Jesus at work. He saw Jesus using an unusual situation in which to reveal Himself and to make the preacher aware of His presence.

As you read the Bible, look for Jesus to speak to you directly and intimately with a message that you know is just for you in the midst of your storm. What is Jesus doing in the passage that He brings to your mind or seems to highlight on the pages you are reading in your Bible? Jesus desires to do that same work or to teach you that same lesson in your life, even in the midst of the storm. He is there with you. Receive His comforting presence!

Jesus *will* show Himself to you. If you are eager to experience His presence, He will enable you to experience Him. He is already present. Ask Him for spiritual eyes to see Him at work, and spiritual ears to hear His words to you.

PART TWO

GOD COMMUNICATES
WITH YOU

FIVE

ASK, SEEK, AND KNOCK

If I asked whether or not you knew how to pray, you would probably answer, "Sure I do! All Christians know how to pray!" However, if you seriously examined the track record of your answered prayers, you might not be so sure.

In Matthew 7:7–11, Jesus emphasized an important principle about prayer. Dispelling the assumption that prayer simply "comes naturally" for Christians, He asserted that prayer is an intentional, learned activity for God's children. In this passage, the Lord was quite simply showing the disciples the three basic steps for an effective prayer life: ask, seek, and knock.

Unfortunately, well-meaning Christians can miss fantastic opportunities and blessings because they have taken a completely passive role in their prayer lives. Too often, seeking and knocking are overlooked as the believer merely asks God for something once or twice and then sits back and forgets all about the matter.

For example, when a high school student begins to make college plans, what would happen if he simply sat on the couch and said, "Lord, please show me exactly where You want me to go to college"? Now, on the surface, this seems to be the best way to start the process. But what if the young man never gets off the couch? Instead of talking with other students, visiting campuses, ordering catalogs, reviewing school websites, and meeting with counselors, the boy simply sits and waits for an answer from the Lord. Most likely he would still be sitting there when classes started the next fall!

Or think about someone who honestly desires a deeper understanding of Scripture, sets his Bible down on the table, and prays, "Lord, please open up the truths of the Scriptures to me. I desperately want to understand Your Word." That person can pray continuously, but the only way for him to get a deeper understanding of the Bible would be not simply to ask, but also to seek by digging into the Word of God. Even that is not enough! He would have to knock on the doors of some Scriptures, dealing with difficult passages in order to see them open up in their fullness.

What about matters of spiritual warfare? How should a Christian pray when he is under attack? Do two-sentence platitudes work then? If you ever hope to defeat your spiritual enemy—and you have a very real enemy—you must begin with prayer.

LEARNING TO PRAY THE BIBLE WAY

When you pray, do you have confidence that God will answer, or do you feel unworthy of His attention? Are your prayers specific or general? Is your prayer life a haphazard response to needs and desires, or nourishment for the life of the Lord Jesus Christ within you? One of the simplest but most profound passages on prayer in all the Bible is found in the Sermon on the Mount:

> Ask, and it will be given to you; seek, and you will find; knock, and it will
> be opened to you. For everyone who asks receives, and he who seeks finds,
> and to him who knocks it will be opened. Or what man is there among you
> who, when his son asks for a loaf, will give him a stone? Or if he asks for a
> fish, he will not give him a snake, will he? If you then, being evil, know how
> to give good gifts to your children, how much more will your Father who is
> in heaven give what is good to those who ask Him!
>
> (MATT. 7:7–11)

Prayer is not only asking and receiving, but also giving thanks to, adoring, and praising the Lord God. There are two responsibilities in prayer—God's responsibility and our responsibility. You cannot have one without the other;

prayer is both divine and human. Notice the Lord's intensity in the progression in this passage: "ask . . . seek . . . knock." Clearly Jesus had in mind that we are to become actively involved in the prayer process. Prayer is not a spectator sport!

Every request, every desire of our hearts, and every need should begin with prayer—asking God for permission, seeking to know His will. Because Jesus Christ has come into our lives and because He has now *become* our Life, we have the privilege and the authority to approach Him and make a request (Eph. 3:11–12; Heb. 4:16).

God is always in the process of answering prayer. This message is the primary purpose of Matthew 7:7–11. Somebody may ask, "Does that mean anybody and everybody can ask, seek, knock, and find?" No, because the Sermon on the Mount is addressed to the followers of Christ. He is talking about His own children.

There is a vital element in prayer that most people overlook, which is steadfastness in prayer. We may not see anything happening, but a delay between our asking and our receiving doesn't mean that God refuses to answer our prayers. In Luke 18:1–8, Jesus told a parable of a persistent widow who bothered a judge so much that he finally gave her what she wanted. Christ used this example to teach His followers how they ought to pray, not losing heart. Why did Jesus place this emphasis on perseverance? Because He very often delays answering prayer requests, even if your request is, in fact, the will of God. Why does God delay? If He sees within us attitudes of rebellion, bitterness, or unforgiveness, or if He notices certain unhealthy habits in our lifestyles, God postpones the answer for His children. He may already have it packaged and ready to send your way, but He cannot and will not do so until you are in a spiritual position to receive it.

A second reason for God's delay is that He is in the process of testing our sincerity in order to build into us a persistent spirit. If we are really earnest, we will not make our request known just once and then give up if it goes unanswered for a time. That is why God says to pray, and to keep on praying, asking, seeking, and knocking. Persevere. Don't give up. Endure. Hang in there—even when you do not see any evidence that God will answer your prayer in the way you hope He will.

Third, God often delays answering prayer in order to build our faith. He strengthens our trust by testing us. How does God test us? Sometimes by withdrawing. As you and I begin to ask, seek, and knock, something happens in our walk with God. When we talk to Him, we are building and nourishing our relationship with Him. We are getting to know Him—who He is and how He operates. Do you realize that once you have become one of His children, what God wants to give you above everything else is Himself? He wants you to know Him.

A fourth reason for God's delays is to develop patience within us as we endure in prayer until His timing is right. God's timing does not always match our own. He is far more interested in our knowing Him than our getting from Him everything our hearts desire.

Would you say that prayer is a vital part of your daily schedule? There is no way for Jesus Christ to be a part of my life unless I am a praying man. I talk, share, and relate with Him all day long. He is my Life! I can tell you every moment I spend with Him is a blessing.

I know countless Christians who become involved in so many activities that prayer begins to shift aside as they diligently go about serving the Lord in their own strength and wisdom. One of the primary reasons we do not pray is that we have busied ourselves with so many distractions that we don't have time for the truly important things. Why do we do this? I'm convinced it's a matter of denial and avoidance. We're not willing for God to take His scalpel, open us up all the way down to our innermost beings, and deal with things that we have never overcome.

Do you realize that one of the largest veins of gold ever discovered in America was found only three feet from where previous miners had stopped digging? Christians often experience the same problem; just beyond where we quit, just out of reach from where we are willing to go, is God's greatest blessing.

If you petition God and He shows you clearly that it is not His will, then naturally you should stop praying about it. However, if there is something that you believe God is working out in your life, or if there is a serious, deep-felt need, do not stop praying. God wants to answer that prayer. I can think of times when everything in me wanted to stop, and I would just keep on praying and crying out to God. Sure enough, suddenly, with no warning, the veil would lift—and there would be the answer, staring me right in the face. If I had quit the day before, I would have made some foolish decision on my own and missed what God wanted to provide.

Nowhere does the Bible say that prayer is easy. It involves a struggle—there will be times when Satan will attack you as you are on your knees, harassing you with doubt and sending distracting thoughts into your mind. One of Satan's most effective weapons is to cause you to have feelings of worthlessness before God. I am speaking not of proper humility, but of an unhealthy sense of unworthiness. Scripture shatters this fear by boldly proclaiming that you and I have freedom in Christ to approach the very throne of God in prayer. When you go to the Lord, do not be meek and embarrassed; instead, bow before Him and rejoice! Exclaim, "Lord Jesus, I praise Your name that You are my Life. I thank You that I can come to You in confidence because You have told me to ask, seek, and knock. Lord, I'm coming as Your child, confident that You are listening to what I am saying. Certain that You will give me direction for my life. Confident that You are going to answer my prayer. I praise You and I accept ahead of time the answers for my prayer. Praise God. Amen!"

We do not always like the answers that God gives. He did not promise to give us anything we request; instead, He promises in Matthew 7:11 that everything He gives is good for us. Surely you would not want God to give you something that would harm you or ultimately destroy your life, would you? For that reason, Jesus sets the limitation up front; He says that He will give us only what is good.

Do not worry about asking God for something too big. You cannot ask God for anything so monumental that He cannot do it if He deems it to be good. God is honored by large, difficult, and impossible requests when we ask, seek, knock, and trust our loving Father always to answer for our good.

If you will actively apply this simple truth, God will transform your prayer life, which will in turn transform your relationships, effectiveness, family, business, and all other aspects of your life. The privilege of prayer is a heritage that belongs to every child of God, a potential that is beyond human understanding. It is a work of God's grace that He has given to each one of us. It is my prayer that you will not let that heritage be wasted in your life. Allow God to make you the man, woman, or young person that He desires you to be. Learn to relate to Him. Nourish that inner being of Christ in your prayer life. Make your daily prayer life an ongoing, intimate relationship of conversation with the Lord Jesus Christ.

Once you establish a prayer life with God, you will begin to harness His strength to fight your spiritual battles. When you fight your battles on your knees, you'll win every time!

A REAL ENEMY

We hear about conflicts and attacks taking place all over the world, but they often seem very distant. The truth is that every single one of us faces a war each day—we battle the devil. Yet many people do not recognize the work of Satan; they mistake his assault for the struggles of everyday life.

An enemy always wants to be camouflaged and covered so he can walk in the shadows undetected. Satan loves for people to doubt his existence, but do not be deceived—he is very real. Jesus clearly recognized the reality of the devil, who tempted Him in the wilderness (Matt. 4:1). And we know Paul believed the scriptural account of Satan's temptation in the Garden (Gen. 3) because in 2 Corinthians 11:3, he referred to the serpent that deceived Eve.

Satan is a liar. He tries to convince us that he does not exist. He wants us to believe that all religions are the same and everybody will get to heaven by one way or another. That is the way he operates: it all sounds good, but it is a lie.

Our enemy is very deliberate in the way he approaches us. He appeals to our minds first. We do not immediately act according to our temptations. The downward spiral begins with our thoughts. Our bodies simply turn in the direction our minds are facing.

We read in 2 Corinthians 10:5: "We are destroying speculations and every lofty thing raised up against the knowledge of God, and we are taking every thought captive to the obedience of Christ." We must deliberately take control of our thinking because the mind is the battleground where Satan confronts us. If we are to win the battle against Satan, we must bring our thoughts under the control of the Lord Jesus Christ.

Satan is a formidable foe. We may be able to control some of our thoughts, but we cannot resist him on our own. Left to our natural devices, we will sin by saying, "It's okay. Everybody does it. That does not apply to our culture—the Bible is outdated." Such thinking stems from allowing the devil entrance into our minds. We must actively guard our thinking against his deceitfulness.

The battle for our salvation was won at the cross. The devil knows he is a defeated foe, destined for eternity in hell. Since he cannot take a single child of God with him, he tries to destroy our witness instead. However, when we recognize Satan's deception and depend upon the strength of Jesus Christ to resist him, we can be confident of victory.

THE STRENGTH TO STAND

Have you ever faced circumstances so overwhelming that you wondered how you would stand up under them? At times, we all have feelings of weakness. Though none of us enjoy those experiences, periods of powerlessness and vulnerability are not necessarily negative. If our weakness results in self-pity, despair, or sin, then it is harmful, but if it drives us to dependency upon God, it is beneficial. Oftentimes fear and discouragement are caused by satanic attack—a willful, determined assault by the devil for the purpose of harming your spirit, soul, or body.

Satan is not omnipotent, but he is nonetheless a very powerful adversary. God does not leave us to fend for ourselves, however, and He wants us to understand the fullness and certainty of His supernatural capacity to help us. That is why Ephesians 6:10 tells us to be strong in the Lord and the power of His might. When you trust Jesus as your Savior, the Holy Spirit comes to indwell you. Living inside you is a member of the Trinity who has supernatural power—power greater than Satan's—to enable you to stand firm. The same divine power that created the heavens and earth, calmed the ocean, and raised the dead is available to every believer through the Lord Jesus Christ and is absolutely essential during spiritual attacks.

The Bible tells us to stand firm and resist the devil (Eph. 6:11; James 4:7). It does not say, "Arm yourself and go fight him," for the simple reason that the battle for our salvation has already been won at the cross. Once you are God's child, you are eternally secure; Satan cannot have your soul, or your eternal life (John 10:29–30). But his goal is to thwart the Lord's plan for you, and he can do a significant amount of damage. He is out to steal your peace and joy, cause confusion and anger, and encourage wrong relationships in your life. He will do anything he can to cheat you out of the blessings the Lord has promised. And the holier you attempt to live before God, the stronger the attacks are likely to be. Satan is after your testimony—he wants to ruin your witness and make you as ineffective as possible.

Would you say that yours is a holy life and that you are walking in obedience to God? If not, you may have yielded to some satanic attack, believed the devil's lie, and given yourself over to him in some way. What may have seemed like an innocent temptation at first can eventually exert a viselike grip on you. Christians are to be under God's control, but the enemy ultimately wants you under his influence, and he will do his best to destroy everything good in your life. Satan's objectives are very clear, namely, to draw believers away from God and cheat the Lord out of the glory He deserves. As long as the devil is around, we will suffer his assaults, so the question is not how to avoid satanic attacks, but how to overcome them.

Paul laid out the battle plan in the sixth chapter of Ephesians. First, we must identify the enemy (vv. 11–12); second, we are to dress in the full armor of God and stand firm (vv. 13–17). The next verse reveals the key to withstanding Satan's onslaughts: we must appropriate the strength of the living God. How do we get His power into our lives, to be unleashed in any and every circumstance? There is only one way: by prayer (v. 18).

It is through prayer that the Lord releases His energy, divine power, and protection, enabling us to live a godly, holy, and peaceful life regardless of our circumstances. It is only through prayer that our minds and spirits can discern what the average person cannot detect. Only through prayer can we sense forewarnings of Satan's attacks, which can be aimed anywhere—finances, family, relationships, or health. The one thing Satan hates above all else is the believer who knows how to persist in prayer and claim the promises of God. The enemy has no defense against persevering prayer, which crushes his might and sends him running. On the other hand, when we do not pray, we set ourselves up for defeat.

We have this power available to us, and yet we often fail to stand firmly against satanic attacks. Since our enemy knows the power of prayer, he will use distractions against us to get our minds focused on anything but prayer. He will do everything possible to keep us from spending time in communion with our heavenly Father. Satan wants us too busy to talk to the One who knows everything, loves us always, and desires to defend us in any situation.

Paul knew how essential it is to recognize prayer's role in protecting us against spiritual attack. Our heavenly Father sees the whole combat zone in which you and I live each day. He knows where we are in the battlefield and the nature of our weaknesses. He is also aware of what Satan is up to in our lives—every cunning device, exactly where he will attack, and who he will use in the effort.

If you are prayerless, if you don't cry out for His divine direction and guidance, and if you don't put on His armor by faith every day, the enemy is going to succeed. And more than likely, he will hit you where you do not expect it because that is his battle strategy.

The importance of prayer cannot be overemphasized. Your understanding of Scripture will be in direct proportion to your prayers. The holiness and righteousness of your life are directly related to your prayers. Your fruitfulness and usefulness to almighty God are also proportional to your communication with the Father. It is critical that you understand praying is not "Lord, bless me, bless him, bless her. Give me this; give me that." Those little, quick prayers are fine if you're "prayed up." Serious praying, however, is talking to your heavenly Father, who listens and desires to answer. It is about humbling yourself and acknowledging not only your need but also His presence, His holiness, and His righteousness. The source of our strength is the living God, and His power is channeled into our lives primarily when we listen and talk with Him.

Understanding exactly what it takes to release God's awesome power, Paul wrote, "With all prayer and petition pray at all times in the Spirit" (Eph. 6:18).

By "all prayer," he was referring to prayer in general, that is, requests, thanksgiving, praise, and intercession (prayer to God on behalf of others), all of which are important. Next, he used the word "petition," which speaks of a particular, singular request. God displays His power through prayer when we ask for something specific and He does exactly what we requested. But if we are praying only "Bless me, bless this, bless that," how can we know whether God has answered?

Paul also talked about praying at all times. We are most vulnerable to satanic attacks when we are not praying. Satan arranges a sequence of events in your life and mine to defeat us. He wants to get you too busy, distracted, or negligent to pray because once you are prayerless, you will soon become concerned and worried. Burdens will become heavier, and you will feel discouraged and weary. Eventually you will feel emotionally, spiritually, and physically weak. Then when you drop your guard, Satan will hit you. You simply cannot afford to be prayerless!

First Thessalonians 5:17 instructs us further with three powerful words: "Pray without ceasing." How can we pray at all times? To do so means to live in God-consciousness. Think in terms of a telephone. If you hang up, you have disconnected the call. "Praying without ceasing" means you do not hang up—you continuously stay on the line with God. That is how He intends for us to live. If I meet somebody I have been praying for and something good has happened in his life, I will say, "Thank You, God, for what You did for him." If I see evil going on, I will say, "God, I am trusting You to correct this situation." The truth is, we should be able to talk to the Father specifically all the time. "Praying always" means living in communion with the Father, in constant awareness of His presence.

The only way we can be strong enough to withstand the traps and counterfeits of the devil is by having a relationship whereby God is always speaking to our hearts and we are always talking to Him in return. You and I cannot be discerning unless we are praying as we ought. So, when you're driving down the expressway, what are you thinking about? Why don't you talk to God? When you wash the dishes and clean your house, what are you thinking about? You can talk to the Father. Talk to Him about everything. Satan wants you to think there are times when you do not need God. Since he hates it when you are on your knees, he will keep you too busy to pray.

Is your prayer life pitiful or powerful? No one else can put on your spiritual armor for you. If you want God's best in your life, get on your knees. Divine, supernatural power is available if you will cry out to God and claim it by faith. Your prayers release God's power into your life and make it possible for you to stand firm against every onslaught of the devil.

THE ARMOR OF GOD

Aggravations. Frustrations. Feelings of inadequacy. Moments of doubt and fear. Where do these emotions come from? Are they self-imposed? Or do we have another force working against us, someone who, if he could, would destroy our peace and give solid evidence to our fears?

We would be remiss to give Satan credit for everything that goes wrong in our lives. Certainly, the last thing we need to do as believers is to constantly focus our spiritual eyes on the enemy and his tactics. Joshua, Jehoshaphat, Nehemiah, Esther, and Daniel had one thing in common: they refused to dwell on Satan's intervention in their lives. Each faced impossible situations, yet he or she turned to God, who subsequently brought deliverance.

Although we do have a real enemy who seeks our destruction, we are not defenseless. We have the strength given to us by Christ Himself to overcome our adversary. This is our hope: that Christ overcame the deepest, darkest, strongest evil that Satan could muster. In His death and resurrection, Christ broke the power of sin and put an end to eternal death.

Satan can tempt us to sin, but we can say no to his enticements (1 Cor. 10:13). We are not pawns floundering within his grasp. We belong to the Son of God; we are His, and He is our eternal Savior. Jesus won the victory and proclaims the name of all who believe in Him before God's throne of grace. Nothing can separate us from His eternal love (Rom. 8:38–39).

On the other hand, the apostle Peter cautioned us to "be of sober spirit, be on the alert. Your adversary, the devil, prowls around like a roaring lion, seeking someone to devour. But resist him, firm in your faith" (1 Peter 5:8–9).

You may ask, "If Jesus Christ has won the victory, why are we still in the battle?" The reason is that we live according to God's timetable. He knows the exact moment of Satan's final defeat. The present victory is ours on a daily basis as we cling to Jesus Christ. However, we must claim that victory and learn to walk in the Spirit, as Christ walked while He was here on earth.

One of the principal reasons for Jesus' coming was to personally identify with us—our needs, heartaches, joys, and even failures. Though Christ never suffered defeat, He knew what it was like to be separated from the Father. On the cross, for a brief time, He was separated from God as He bore our sins. But death could not hold Him. Jesus canceled mankind's sin with His atoning blood and, in so doing, set the stage for Satan's final defeat. When we realize that God understands what we are facing and is willing to provide the strength we need, then trusting Him with even the smallest details becomes a natural part of life.

Until Christ returns, we are soldiers engaged in spiritual warfare, and we have the victory when we do battle in the power and name of the living God. Peter's words of warning to us are a signal not to turn and run, but to stand firm in our faith, trusting God and refusing to be drawn aside by the temptations and deceptions of the enemy. One of the best ways to defend against and overcome Satan's ploys is to understand your position in Christ. The book of Romans is foundational in this aspect.

The apostle Paul wrote, "For all who are being led by the Spirit of God, these are sons of God. For you have not received a spirit of slavery leading to fear again, but you have received a spirit of adoption as sons by which we cry out, 'Abba! Father!' The Spirit Himself testifies with our spirit that we are children of God, and if children, heirs also, heirs of God and fellow heirs with Christ" (Rom. 8:14–17).

Satan is an enemy to be respected and understood. Instead of submitting to God and His omnipotence, the devil rebelled and drew away one-third of heaven's forces with him. Christ's victory over Satan is total and complete. Try as he may, he can never snatch the victory out of God's almighty hand. If you are living for the Lord Jesus Christ, He will empower you to do God's will so you can find blessing and safety.

Paul told us to put on the armor of God when we battle our spiritual enemies:

Finally, be strong in the Lord and in the strength of His might. Put on the full armor of God, so that you will be able to stand firm against the schemes of the devil. For our struggle is not against flesh and blood, but against the rulers, against the powers, against the world forces of this darkness, against the spiritual forces of wickedness in the heavenly places. Therefore, take up the full armor of God, so that you will be able to resist in the evil day, and having done everything, to stand firm.

Stand firm therefore, having *girded your loins with truth*, and having put on the *breastplate of righteousness*, and having *shod your feet with the preparation of the gospel of peace*; in addition to all, taking up *the shield of faith* with which you will be able to extinguish all the flaming arrows of the evil one. And take the *helmet of salvation*, and the *sword of the Spirit*, which is the word of God.

(EPH. 6:10–17, EMPHASIS ADDED)

Though at times—especially in our present age—it seems we are in the midst of a horrendous physical battle, the real war is against the powers of spiritual darkness. Satan's goal has not changed over the years. The enemy knows his ultimate destiny, yet he will never give up his evil intent against the kingdom of God until Christ banishes him to the eternal lake of fire (Rev. 20:10). The only way he can do damage to the kingdom of God now is by enticing God's beloved children to yield to sin, thus damaging their fellowship with the Lord.

Satan will try to discourage you by filling your mind with an array of doubt and confusion, but you do not have to believe him. The message of the gospel of Christ is given to you as a sure authority. God's Word provides all the details you need to know about Satan.

Paul also admonished us to "stand firm"—a phrase that denotes extreme faith in the One who gives us life and strength. But the enemy of faith is pride—a sure road to spiritual defeat. In the ministry, I have seen many who have fallen because of pride, undone by their refusal to humble themselves before God and accept His plan for their lives. This is one reason why it is tremendously important to put on the entire armor that God has given to us.

The armor keeps us mindful of who is in control of our lives and who is our Advocate before the Father (1 John 2:1).

On our own, we cannot defeat or even resist the enemy. Only through the power of Jesus Christ do we have the ability to stand and claim what God has done through His Son. The victory took place at Calvary (Col. 2:13–15). However, if we demand Satan's forces to leave without using the name of Jesus Christ, we position ourselves for a prideful defeat. Pride also comes into play when we think we are in control of our lives: "God is opposed to the proud, but gives grace to the humble" (James 4:6).

Make a habit of claiming the armor of God each morning before you leave your house—a conscious act of submitting your life to the Lord as your final authority. Acknowledging your need for Him is a sign not of weakness, but of unshakable trust. When you place your faith in Jesus Christ, heaven is on your side.

Are you standing fully clothed in His armor, or do you rise in the morning, grab a cup of coffee, and run out the door? Do you think of Jesus throughout the day, hoping to make more time for Him in the evening, only to find other commitments taking His place?

Establish and commit yourself to time alone with God. Let the life of Jesus Christ be your example. Even before His day began—which was much busier than ours—Christ rose to be alone with the Father. Your life may be stretched to the limit. God knows what you are facing, and He will help you make time to be with Him if that is truly your heart's desire.

Whatever transpires in your life, the wisest decision you will ever make is the decision to spend time with the Lord on a regular basis. This teaches you to recognize Satan's movement and prepares you for battle when the enemy approaches. Paul told the Ephesians they were in a war, but clothed in the armor of God, they were assured of victory.

SIX

A MESSAGE PRECISELY
FOR YOU

When was the last time you heard God speak to you in your spirit?

I believe God desires to communicate with each of us on a daily basis—in fact, as often as we need to hear from Him, which may be several times in a day. He always has a message for us that is more timely than the daily news and more important than the message that any person on earth can give.

A woman once told me that her mother-in-law had died a few weeks earlier after a very painful experience with stomach cancer. I began to offer my sympathy when the woman interrupted me and said, "I'm glad this happened."

I was a bit taken aback. "You are?" I asked.

"Oh, yes," she said. "This wasn't a negative thing at all. It was the most positive experience in her life and certainly one of the most positive experiences in mine."

Most people would consider stomach cancer to be anything but positive. I was interested in hearing more of her story, which she was happy to tell.

"My mother-in-law was one of the most bitter, spiteful, difficult women I have ever met. I knew from the first minute she laid eyes on me that she was determined to be my enemy," she began. "In fact, my husband and I eloped so we wouldn't have to deal with her at our wedding ceremony. During the fifteen years that I knew her before her diagnosis with cancer, I never heard a kind word from her lips—except to our daughter. She had a soft spot in her heart for our daughter, but not for anyone else. She wasn't mean only to me, but to my husband, to her other two sons, and to everyone she encountered. Repairmen told me that they dreaded a call from her home, and even the kindest clergyman we know had a difficult time with her rebukes and sarcasm."

"She must have been a woman with a great deal of inner pain," I said.

"Yes," she replied. "I didn't realize how much inner pain she had, however, until after her diagnosis. Up to that time, I just figured she was a hateful, mean woman. I didn't take the time or make the effort to see beyond her façade."

"She may not have let you see inside her," I said.

"I believe that's right," she agreed. "She had a stone wall around her heart. And she kept this stone wall in place for several weeks after her doctor told her she had cancer. Initially, she was given only a few weeks to live. It was amazing to everyone who knew her and knew her condition that she lived nearly five months."

"And you believe that was the grace of God?" I asked.

"Yes," she said. "What happened was this. She refused all offers of help except those from my husband and me. We were the only ones she would allow to enter her home to fix meals for her and to change her bed and do her laundry. When the pain was intense, she'd ask us to read to her or to stay and converse with her to help take her mind off the pain. As the days went by and she saw that I was caring for her with love and concern—not with criticism or hate—she began to tell me her story. I began to understand why she was filled with such anger."

"Was it something from her childhood?" I guessed.

"Actually from her teen years," she said. "A woman in her church accused her of stealing funds that the youth group had collected for a ski trip. The accusations were made in a very hurtful and public way, and my mother-in-law was given little chance to defend herself or to reply to the charges. She hadn't taken the money, but ironically, about the same time she had found twenty dollars in a small coin purse in the gutter of a street near her home. She had spent the money, figuring that she was the beneficiary of finders, keepers. When she offered this explanation as the reason she had had more spending money of late, the woman refused to believe her story and not only called her a thief but a liar.

"My mother-in-law became so angry that she dropped out of church and turned her back on God. For years she had told me she was an atheist. After her diagnosis she modified that to say she didn't believe in God because if there was a God, He should be just and righteous, and there had been no justice on her behalf in this unfortunate situation."

"So she had been angry and bitter for decades," I said.

"Yes, for forty-nine years. The more she suffered with her disease, the more she concluded that there was no God of mercy or kindness. She couldn't explain away, however, the peace that my husband, daughter, and I felt in our hearts—or the kindness and love that we showered upon her. Bit by bit, she began to soften. She even started asking us to read some of the Psalms to her when she was in pain. We had a couple of conversations about heaven too."

"Did she accept the Lord as her Savior before she died?" I asked.

"Yes, but it happened in a way that I would never have anticipated," she said as tears welled up in her eyes.

"One day when I went over to fix dinner for her, our daughter went along. She said, 'Granny Lou, I love you. And Jesus told me to tell you that He loves you too.' I froze in my tracks. I steeled myself for what I felt sure would be my mother-in-law's reply, probably something like, 'That's nice for you to believe.' Instead, she said, 'I know He does, dear. He told me so Himself last night.'

"She looked up and I'm sure she read my face, which no doubt expressed great surprise and pleasure. She said, 'I saw Jesus last night. He came to the foot of my bed in a pool of bright light and said, 'Lou, I'm here to tell you that I love you. I want you to come live with Me.'"

"Wonderful!" I said.

She continued, "I was so stunned, all I could stammer was, 'That's great, Mother Lou.' She said, 'I know you probably think it's strange He would come calling on me like that, and I was pretty surprised myself. I asked Him, "How could you love an old hag like me?" He said, "You won't be an old hag when you are living with Me." And then He was gone.'

"Not long after that, she asked my husband to pray the sinner's prayer with her. And about a week later, she died. Just before she died, she said, 'I wasted a lot of years railing against God. Instead of my doing all the talking against Him, I should have done a little more listening to Him.'"

"What a tremendous testimony!" I said.

"My mother-in-law isn't the only one with a testimony," she said. "The Lord did a great thing in my own heart through this. I discovered in caring for my mother-in-law that I had failed to love as Christ loved. I repented of the hatred I had held toward my mother-in-law and asked God to forgive me and to help me love her as He loved her. He softened my heart and gave me compassion and tenderness toward her that I would never have believed were possible. I find myself looking at difficult people with new eyes. In fact, I'm considering taking a volunteer position with the hospice program. I believe the Lord still has things to teach me and ways to use me."

"I feel certain that He does," I said.

"One thing I know with certainty," she said as our conversation drew to a close, "God can cross *any* barriers we might put up. I'm grateful that He still had something to say to my mother-in-law. I have a new faith that He still has something to say to me too."

Yes, a thousand times yes! God does still have something to say to each one of us. He never reaches the place where He doesn't have a message that is precisely for us.

GOD DESIRES TO COMMUNICATE WITH YOU

When we think of communicating with God, very often we think about our talking to God. In conversing with people through the years about prayer, I've discovered that most people spend about 99 percent of their time talking to God—telling Him what they want Him to do, asking Him for things they want Him to give them, voicing their belief in His promises, even pleading with Him at times to do things in their lives that He has already done!

I've met people who have asked God on numerous occasions to save their souls. One young woman said, "I've been saved three times." And she could recount each occasion in vivid detail. She had "walked the aisle" at her church when she was a young teenager in response to a salvation altar call, then had given her life to Christ when she was a teenager attending a youth camp, and finally, had prayed to ask the Lord to come into her life during a prayer meeting in her college dorm room. A friend of mine asked her, "Which time worked?"

The young woman replied, "Each time I felt God forgiving me of my sins."

The fact was, God forgave her sinful nature and entered her life the first time she asked Him to do so. She was converted to Christ the first time she turned to God to receive His forgiveness.

The fact also is, God forgives you each time you come to Him and confess that you have sinned. He forgives you and then assists you in repenting of your sins.

Your salvation is a definitive work in your life the moment you accept that Jesus died on the cross for your sins. His indwelling Holy Spirit continues to convict you of areas that need changing in your life—habits that need to be dropped or acquired; attitudes that need to be altered; automatic responses that need to be transformed to line up with God's Word and the life of Christ. You don't need to plead with God to save you or to forgive you or to change you. He responds to you the moment you turn to Him to receive His love. And He then begins a renewal work that is ongoing in you the rest of your life.

People who repeatedly ask God to forgive them and to save their souls need to accept the certain fact that He has. They then need to forgive themselves and move forward in their lives.

Other people repeatedly ask God for things with an attitude of worry. They want to make sure God doesn't forget them. They aren't 100 percent certain that God is going to provide what they need. They spend most of their days struggling and striving to make sure they have not only enough material substance, but an abundance of material wealth. And then, they add a prayer, "Oh, God, please give me this, please give me that."

Jesus taught His disciples to pray, "Our Father in heaven . . . give us this day our daily bread" (Matt. 6:9, 11 NKJV). The concept of daily bread goes far beyond a loaf of whole wheat bread for physical nourishment. *Bread* is a term that refers to everything that is necessary for wholeness in life. It refers to the things we need physically, but also to the things we need mentally, emotionally, and spiritually. Jesus told His disciples on one occasion, "I have food [bread] to eat of which you do not know." When His disciples asked for an explanation,

He said, "My food is to do the will of Him who sent Me, and to finish His work" (John 4:32–34 NKJV).

When you ask the Lord to give you your daily bread, He intends that your request will mean, "Give me today what You know I need to carry out Your purposes for me on the earth. I trust You to meet all my needs."

Now you are to pray specifically for the Lord to defeat evil whenever and wherever you encounter it—in yourself or in others. That is the foremost role of petitioning the Lord in prayer. In Jericho, Jesus asked a man who was blind, "What do you want Me to do for you?" The man was obviously blind; nevertheless, Jesus asked. You are to tell the Lord specifically what you want Him to do to reverse evil, destroy evil, and defeat the enemy in your life (Mark 10:51 NKJV).

About your daily needs, however, you are not to worry. Jesus taught,

> Do not worry about your life, what you will eat or what you will drink; nor about your body, what you will put on. Is not life more than food and the body more than clothing? Look at the birds of the air, for they neither sow nor reap nor gather into barns; yet your heavenly Father feeds them. Are you not of more value than they? Which of you by worrying can add one cubit to his stature? . . . For after all these things the Gentiles seek. For your heavenly Father knows that you need all these things. But seek first the kingdom of God and His righteousness, and all these things shall be added to you.
>
> (MATT. 6:25–27, 32–33 NKJV)

Your communication with God is also to include praise and thanksgiving. You are to

> Enter into His gates with thanksgiving,
> And into His courts with praise.
> Be thankful to Him, and bless His name.
> For the LORD is good;
> His mercy is everlasting,
> And His truth endures to all generations.
>
> (Ps. 100:4–5 NKJV)

Great is the Lord, and greatly to be praised!

"With thanksgiving, let your requests be made known to God," Paul advised the Philippians (4:6 NKJV). You make your petitions with thanksgiving, fully expecting God to hear you and answer you *according to the will of heaven*.

But in all your praise and thanksgiving and voicing of requests, you must take time to listen. God desires to say something to you.

Two-Way Communication

Think about your relationship with someone you love. If you do all the talking in that relationship, it isn't truly a relationship, is it? True communication is a two-way street. You express yourself, and then you listen to the other person. He or she expresses something to you, and you respond. In that way, decisions are reached, consensus is built, agreements are forged, problems are resolved, secrets are shared, dreams and ideas are revealed, information is exchanged, attitudes are influenced, encouragement is offered, advice is given and received, and a sense of intimacy is developed.

If you spend all your time telling God about your problems and needs, your feelings, your hopelessness, your desires, you are missing out on hearing about God's desires, His feelings, and His dreams for your life and for the lives of others. You also will miss out on hearing about how God feels about you.

DO YOU WANT TO HEAR FROM GOD?

"Dr. Stanley," a man admitted to me, "I'm not sure I *want* to know how God feels about me." If that's your attitude, you likely are carrying a load of guilt.

Define and examine closely what you think God would be displeased about, ask Him to forgive you of that habit or past deed, and then go on in your life with a determination never to do that thing again. The feeling you have of condemnation is *not* God's feeling toward you. It is your response toward your disobedience of His commandments. The apostle Paul very clearly taught that the purpose of the Law is to bring you to just this point of conviction of sin.

When you line up your life against God's absolutes and His lasting commandments, you fall short. You know you have erred.

Anytime that you attempt to compare yourself and your achievements to God, you also fall short. Consider Romans 3:23: "For all have sinned and fall short of the glory of God." When you stand before the absolute perfection of God, you must admit your weaknesses, your failures, your inabilities, your shortcomings.

God does not change His nature in order to make you feel better about yourself. That is something human beings often try to do: alter their behavior so that other people will respond to them in ways that are warm and accepting. God does not change. Rather, God holds out to you His great love and His ideal for you—that you can be transformed by the power of His Holy Spirit working in you, so that you are enabled to do His will and walk in His ways. God's desire is *not* that you feel condemned or guilty, but that anytime you have these feelings, you turn to Him immediately to receive His forgiveness and experience His love.

God always feels love and forgiveness toward you, regardless of what you have done or how much you may have rejected Him in the past.

As a young minister drove me to the airport, we had an opportunity to talk. He told me that he still struggled with his perception of God. He said, "I've heard people whom I admire greatly tell me that God is a loving God— including you, Dr. Stanley—but I still have a picture of God as a stern judge. I guess I grew up thinking, *There's God, way up there, sitting in His judgment seat just waiting for me to do something so He can whack me.* It's hard for me to think of God as being very close or very touchable."

I said, "Tell me about your father."

As you might imagine, his father had been a very tough disciplinarian. "My father was hardly ever there," he said. "He traveled a lot in his work, and when he was home, Mom made sure that he punished us for things we had done while he was away. Dad had very strict rules, and he expected us to follow them even when he was gone."

"If that was the case," I said, "I'll guess that you dreaded your father's coming home."

"Yes," he said, "I suppose I did."

"But at the same time you wanted his approval?"

"Oh, yes," he said. "I thought my father was everything. I very much wanted my father's approval, but he was hardly ever there to see me do anything that he could approve. I think he made it to only one of my basketball games, and as I recall, I was so nervous he was there that I didn't do very well that night."

"Have you given God all the traits that you experienced in your earthly father?" I asked. "Have you made God just a bigger version of your dad?"

He thought for a minute and then said, "Yes, I think that's what I've done."

Since our time was short, I encouraged him to go back to his Bible and read about Jesus in Matthew, Mark, Luke, and John. "Jesus told His disciples, 'If you had known Me, you would have known My Father also . . . The words that I speak to you I do not speak on My own authority; but the Father who dwells in Me does the works. Believe Me that I am in the Father and the Father in Me' [John 14:7, 10–11 NKJV]. When we see Jesus, we are seeing the very nature and character of the Father at work."

I continued, "Get a clear picture of Jesus. With your spiritual eyes, see Jesus as He gently touched those who were sick. See Him as He picked up little children and held them and blessed them, even when other people clamored for His attention. See Jesus as He stopped to talk to people along the way. He always had time for people. He healed all who came to Him. He had close fellowship with people who were called sinners by the religious society."

As I talked about Jesus, I could see tears form in this man's eyes. "Get a clear picture of Jesus on the cross. He died so that others might come to know the Father as intimately as He knew Him—so that they might be one with each other and one with the Father. When you get a really vivid picture of Jesus, you'll have the right picture of God."

He nodded. I continued, "Would the Jesus that you know from the Gospels sit on a big throne high and far away from you, judging you harshly every time you made a mistake?"

"No," he said very softly. "He wouldn't."

"Then neither does God the Father," I said.

When you see God as standing in harsh judgment of you, you are projecting onto Him your feelings of guilt, judgment, and condemnation. You may very well be projecting onto God the failures and faults of your earthly father. Own up to your feelings, and ask God to help you get a true picture of who He is and what He is like. I believe He will reveal Himself to you. Own up to your failure and sins, and ask Him to forgive you and to help you change your ways. *He will!*

GOD'S MESSAGE OF LOVE FOR YOU

I believe there are at least three messages that God desires to communicate to each one of us on a daily basis.

The first message God wants to convey is this: "I love you." We may know that in a broad, general sense. Most of us would readily agree with the childhood chorus, "Jesus loves me, this I know." But on an ongoing daily basis, God has a unique way of expressing His love for us. We must have keen spiritual ears to hear this message.

A woman told a marriage counselor, "My husband never tells me he loves me."

The marriage counselor turned and asked the husband, "Is that true?"

The man replied very contritely, "I guess it is."

The counselor asked, "Do you love your wife?"

"I do," the man said. "I love her a lot."

"Are you afraid to tell her that you love her?" the counselor asked.

"No," the man said, "I'm not scared to tell her I love her."

The counselor asked, "Then do you know why you never tell her that you love her?"

He thought for a moment and said simply, "Well, I think the main reason is, she never stops talking long enough for me to say so."

Is it possible that the main reason you have never heard God tell you how much He loves you is that you have never stopped petitioning Him long enough to listen to His voice?

God desires to communicate His great love for you on a daily basis. He desires to tell you how much you mean to Him and how He delights in having a relationship with you.

I once talked to a young woman who was very much in love with the man who eventually became her husband. She said, "He does the nicest things to tell me he loves me."

"Like what?" I asked her.

"Oh, he leaves me little notes here and there. He might put a fresh rose in my mailbox or leave a loving message on my voicemail. Every day it's something different." Then she added, "I hope he never runs out of ideas!"

God never runs out of ideas about how to tell you in unique ways that He loves you. His love may come to you in the form of an unexpected blessing, a call from someone you haven't heard from in a while, a kindness extended to you by a total stranger, the opportunity to hear a favorite song, a hug from a child. Each day God has a new way of sending His love message to you.

God wants you to know several things about His love.

God Wants to Tell You That His Love Is a Gift

God wants you to know that His love for you is a "perfect gift" (James 1:17). There is nothing that you can do to deserve this gift or to deserve a greater expression of this gift. His love for you has always been, is now, and always will be an infinite love.

The only thing you can do in conjunction with His gift is to receive it and to thank Him for it. There is no earning His perfect gift; there is no exchanging it.

There was a situation in my life in which I told God precisely what I wanted Him to do to a particular person. I was hurt, frustrated, and impatient. I trusted God to be my avenger, but I wanted Him to do His avenging right away! He responded to me by speaking in my heart, *I can't do that.*

"Why not?" I asked.

Because My love for that person is as perfect as My love for you. If I didn't love that person as much as I love you, you couldn't trust My love. You couldn't count on My love always being there for you when you sin. You couldn't count on My love being there for you when you hurt others. But because I love this person as much as I love you, you can count on My love.

I learned through that experience that we can always trust a perfect love. Such love comes from God alone. He is the giver of this kind of love to each one of us.

God Wants to Assure You That His Love Is Everlasting

Moods change. Emotions fluctuate from day to day, sometimes from hour to hour. God's love for you has no variation. You have this word from the Lord: "I have loved you with an everlasting love" (Jer. 31:3).

Paul described God's everlasting love in this way:

> For I am persuaded that neither death nor life, nor angels nor principalities nor powers, nor things present nor things to come, nor height nor depth, nor any other created thing, shall be able to separate us from the love of God which is in Christ Jesus our Lord.
>
> (ROM. 8:38–39 NKJV)

You can't start God's love flowing toward you because it already is flowing toward you. You can't deter it, stop it, interrupt it, or change it. His banner over you is love, and it is always love. You didn't deserve it, and therefore, you can't do anything to "undeserve" it.

God's love toward you has nothing to do with *your* nature. It has everything to do with *His* nature.

God Wants to Tell You That His Sacrificial Love Is Available to All

God sent His only Son, Jesus Christ, to die as an expression of how much God loves us. God sacrificed His beloved Son on our behalf—on my behalf, on your behalf, on behalf of every person alive today. There is no higher price that could ever have been paid.

On a daily basis, God will bring people across your path whom you may find to be troublesome, irksome, or a nuisance. He does so as a constant reminder to you, "I love even him. I love even her." You continually are called to face the fact that you are more like those whom you dislike than you are willing to admit. You have flaws and failures and quirks that annoy or anger others. Only when you accept the fact that Christ died for you, *and* Christ died for every other person you encounter, can you begin to love others as Christ loves them.

A number of years ago, several of my friends told me how a particular man had ridiculed me. He had made it very public that he didn't like me or what I stood for. I categorized him as a braggart and a bully and pretty much wrote him off as someone I'd try to avoid if at all possible. In plain language, I decided that I didn't like him. Never mind that I didn't know him very well. I concluded that if even a small fraction of what I had been told he had said and done was true, then I didn't like him.

Some time later we were both on the same program at a major conference. I spoke and then he spoke. I sat and listened with no expression on my face, but with a heart of stone. As he spoke, however, something happened. God sovereignly poured His love for this man into my heart. I saw him as a man—a sinner who had been redeemed by Christ, just as I had been a sinner who was redeemed by Christ. I felt warmth and compassion toward him that I had never dreamed possible.

After the evening meeting, I ran into the man in the lobby of the hotel where I was staying. He asked if I would like to go with him down the street to a café to get a bite to eat before retiring for the night. I agreed. We had a wonderful conversation over our late-night snack. I discovered that I had been wrong about him in many ways. God had done some breaking and refining and pruning in his life. He had also done some in mine. We could relate to each other without any animosity whatsoever.

I learned a valuable lesson through that experience. God's love manifests itself in forgiveness—forgiveness that was purchased through sacrifice. What Jesus did for me on the cross, He did for my worst enemy. Therefore, I can't have that person as an enemy. This is what Jesus meant when He taught, "Whenever you stand praying, if you have anything against anyone, forgive him, that your Father in heaven may also forgive you your trespasses. But if you do not forgive, neither will your Father in heaven forgive your trespasses" (Mark 11:25–26 NKJV).

God Wants to Say to You That His Love for You Is Immeasurable

God's love for you is inexhaustible and beyond any form of measurement. It cannot be multiplied, added, divided, or subtracted. Although we can never fully comprehend the vastness of God's love, Paul encouraged the Ephesians to grow in their understanding of God's love:

> For this reason I bow my knees to the Father of our Lord Jesus Christ . . . that you, being rooted and grounded in love, may be able to comprehend with all the saints what is the width and length and depth and height—to know the love of Christ which passes knowledge; that you may be filled with all the fullness of God.
>
> (EPH. 3:14,17–19 NKJV)

As your relationship with God grows deeper, you will find that the Lord reveals to you more and more of His love. You no doubt will find yourself saying again and again, "Lord, I didn't know You could love a person that much. I didn't know it was possible to love like that."

We often discover this truth when other people hurt us. God loves us more than our pain hurts us. He covers our wounds with His love. No matter how much others might criticize us, reject us, or cause us harm, if we turn to God in our pain, He extends to us enough love to completely compensate for the pain. We turn to Him with a pound of pain, and He gives us back two pounds of love. He gives us enough love not only to heal us but to provide an overflow of love that we can extend to the very people who hurt us!

The Bible teaches that we are to speak well of our enemies and to do good to them. The expression of our love toward those who harm us will be equal to a heap of hot coals of conviction poured on their heads. In other words, our love will compel them to turn to God for mercy. In this way we overcome evil with good (Rom. 12:20–21).

There was a time in my life when I experienced a great deal of emotional pain in one particular relationship. It seemed that no matter what I tried to do, I did the wrong thing in this person's eyes. Time after time I went to God, throwing myself on His mercy and love, asking Him to heal my wounds and to help me respond to this person in the right way. And time after time, I felt His great love pouring over my heart like a healing balm. It was as if He wrapped me in His arms again and again so that He could hold me close and tell me He loved me.

The love God extended to me was in overflow proportions. One of my friends who knew what I was going through said to me, "I don't know how you can speak so calmly about this person. I don't know why you aren't filled with anger. Are you in denial?"

I said, "No, I'm not in denial about the circumstances. I hurt. But I do not hate. I have only love for this person. God gave me an overdose of His love in healing me of my pain, and it's impossible to feel hate when His love has been poured to the overflow point in your heart."

The love that God gives to us is divine love—His love, *agape* love. The love that I felt for this person who had hurt me was not on a human scale. It was an overflow of God's love. And friend, that's the best kind of love there is.

GOD'S MESSAGE ABOUT HIS PRESENCE WITH YOU

The second great message that God desires to communicate to you on a daily basis is that He is with you—regardless. Again and again, God speaks to your heart, "I'm here."

In communicating His presence to you, the Holy Spirit gives you several specific messages.

He Speaks Words of Affirmation

The Holy Spirit is 100 percent committed to building you up. The biblical term for this is *edification*—the building up for strength and ministry. The Holy Spirit affirms to you continually that "you belong," "you are worthy," "you are valuable."

Do you have somebody in your life who tells you without qualification or disclaimer, "I believe in you, your talents, your best future"? That person is showing unconditional love to you. The Holy Spirit has this same message for you. He *believes* in you.

One of the foremost assurances that the Holy Spirit gives you is that you are saved, you are a member of Christ's body. The Holy Spirit brings to your awareness verses of Scripture that affirm that you are saved by the atoning blood of Jesus Christ and that when you have believed in Jesus with your heart and confessed your faith in Him with your mouth, you are forever forgiven and assured of eternal life. The Holy Spirit affirms this truth to you. He says to you, "You are cleansed. You are forgiven. You do have eternal life. You do have a home in glory."

He Speaks Encouragement to Give You Boldness

John made this observation: "Love has been perfected among us in this: that we may have boldness in the day of judgment; because as He is, so are we in this world. There is no fear in love; but perfect love casts out fear" (1 John 4:17–18 NKJV).

When Peter and John were imprisoned for healing a man who could not walk and for using that miracle as an opportunity to proclaim the gospel, the authorities who were holding them eventually let them go with a stern threat that they should cease preaching about Jesus.

How did Peter and John respond? They made their way to their fellow believers, reported what the chief priests and elders had said to them, and then they all raised their voices to God with one accord and said,

> Lord, You are God, who made heaven and earth and the sea, and all that is in them. . . . Now, Lord, look on their threats, and grant to Your servants that with all boldness they may speak Your word, by stretching out Your hand to heal, and that signs and wonders may be done through the name of Your holy Servant Jesus.
>
> (ACTS 4:24, 29–30 NKJV)

Peter and John didn't pray against their enemies. They concluded, rather, that "both Herod and Pontius Pilate, with the Gentiles and the people of Israel, were gathered together to do whatever Your hand and Your purpose determined before to be done" (Acts 4:27–28 NKJV). They saw God's hand in their persecution; they saw their affliction as a means of extending the gospel. Therefore, they didn't pray to be released from persecution; rather, they prayed that they might speak even more boldly in the face of it.

When the devil roars against you, don't pray that the roaring will cease; rather, pray that you will have boldness to roar back your witness of the gospel of Jesus Christ with an even greater intensity! God says that He is with you—He will never leave you or forsake you. Furthermore, He is the God of all creation; He has all power and authority. He is on your side. He has a purpose that He will accomplish if you will only replace fear with love and stand strong in His presence.

He Gives You a Specific Word of Witness

Jesus taught His followers, "When they bring you to the synagogues and magistrates and authorities, do not worry about how or what you should answer, or what you should say. For the Holy Spirit will teach you in that very hour what you ought to say" (Luke 12:11–12 NKJV).

On a daily basis, you may not know how to respond to people who ask you questions about your faith. You may be taken by surprise by those who would try to tell you dirty jokes, or who make sarcastic comments against Christians and against God's Word, or who try to talk you into certain activities that you know are contrary to God's commandments. Sometimes people you consider to be friends will tempt you to do what you know not to do. What shall you say?

In these moments you can trust the Holy Spirit to be present with you. You can breathe a quiet prayer, "Help me, Lord. Give me Your words to say." And then you can speak what comes immediately to mind. You can trust the Lord that if you preface your comments with such a prayer, and genuinely are open to hearing what He has to say to you and through you, He will bear the consequences for your words. He will prompt you to speak what He wants you to speak, and He will cause the other person to hear what he or she needs to hear.

He Gives You Insight into God's Eternal Plan

Jesus foretold times of trouble to His followers. He warned His disciples, "They will put you out of the synagogues; yes, the time is coming that whoever kills you will think that he offers God service. And these things they will do to you because they have not known the Father nor Me" (John 16:2–3 NKJV).

Even as Jesus gave His disciples this prophetic word, He added, "When

He, the Spirit of truth, has come, He will guide you into all truth; for He will not speak on His own authority, but whatever He hears He will speak; and He will tell you things to come" (John 16:13 NKJV).

There is a big difference between facts and truth. Facts are rooted in details that tell who, what, when, where, and how. Truth, however, encompasses more than facts. It is rooted in *significance* and *meaning*. You can know the facts of an event or situation or experience, but only as you understand the meaning of the significance of what has happened can you come to know the truth. Ultimately, truth has an eternal, divine quality to it. All truth flows from God. All truth points to God. Your quest must be not to get only the facts in life, but to understand life's facts in the context of God's eternal purposes. You must seek to have His understanding and to know what things mean from His perspective.

Truth is what Jesus said the Holy Spirit would give you. He will reveal to you *why* certain things are happening, *how* they fit into the broader purposes of God, and *what* you might expect as a result.

When you are faced with puzzling situations or difficult problems, ask the Lord to reveal to you not only the immediate solution, but also the truth of the matter. Ask Him to tell why He has allowed certain things to happen and what He hopes to accomplish as a result—not only in your life, but in the lives of all others involved directly or indirectly. Jesus said that the Holy Spirit would be faithful in guiding you into all truth.

He Gives You Direction

God will reveal the purpose and meaning for things that happen in your life, and He desires to impart wisdom to know how to respond to the things that happen to you. James urged, "If any of you lacks wisdom, let him ask of God, who gives to all liberally and without reproach, and it will be given to him. But let him ask in faith, with no doubting" (James 1:5–6 NKJV).

God does not want you to live in a dark fog, never knowing which way to turn or how to respond to the circumstances that sometimes overwhelm you as tidal waves. No! He wants you to make sound decisions, rational choices, and well-founded plans.

Liberally

God doesn't play games with wisdom. He desires that you know fully what He desires for you to be and do. God has no desire for His people to stumble about in ignorance, wondering if they are acting in a way that is pleasing or displeasing to Him. The Bible is very clear in stating God's commandments and principles. It is very clear in stating God's covenants—what He desires to do for His people and what He requires of His people.

A man was asked, "Do you understand every verse in the Bible?"

"No," he admitted, "but I understand enough of it."

The person asked, "What do you mean 'enough'?"

"Well," the man said, "I understand enough to be troubled. You see it's not the parts of the Bible that I *don't* understand that trouble me—it's the parts that I *do* understand that trouble me. I understand enough of the Bible to know what I *should* be doing."

The vast majority of people are capable of understanding right from wrong. Their disobedience of God's Word is not the result of a failure to understand the Bible or even a failure to understand the dictates of the God-created conscience; rather, they haven't read the Bible, or they don't want to do what they know they should do.

1. *Guidance through His Word, the Bible.* If you have a question about the course of action you should take, turn first to your Bible. The Bible is God's foremost way of communicating with you. In the Bible, you have the complete revelation of God. He doesn't need to add anything else to this Book. Through the ages, the revelation of God was an unfolding truth by God about Himself. In Jesus, that truth was fulfilled. As Jesus said of Himself, He didn't come to change anything about the law or the commandments; He came to show us by His life's example how fully to live out God's plan in our lives and to obey His commandments (Matt. 5:17).

God's Word is for all people because it speaks to the basic human condition. The Bible addresses every emotion, problem of the heart, human relationship dynamic, aspect of the psyche, temptation, desire, heartache, joy, issue of faith, love, or hope that you can experience.

Ask God to speak to you through His Word. In response to your prayer, the Lord often will direct your mind to a particular passage of Scripture that you have encountered in your regular daily reading of the Bible. He will bring to your remembrance His truth on a matter.

If you don't hear from God about precisely where to turn in the Scriptures, begin to read the words of Jesus. (I suggest you read a Bible that has the words of Jesus printed in red ink; that makes it very easy to see what Jesus said.)

You may want to use a concordance to find verses related to a particular problem or question. Many times I have found that God doesn't direct me immediately to the passage that gives me guidance, but as I continue to read and study, God leads me step-by-step to the information that He wants me to see with new spiritual insight.

Eventually, you will come to an incident in Scripture, a passage, or even a single verse that is directly related to your concern, question, or problem.

Of course, you are wise not to limit your search of God's Word to times of extreme need or crisis. Read His Word daily: "This Book of the Law shall not depart from your mouth, but you shall meditate in it day and night, that you may observe to do according to all that is written in it. For then you will make your way prosperous, and then you will have good success" (Josh. 1:8 NKJV).

As you read the Bible daily, God directs you, challenges you, warns you, comforts you, and assures you. Daily reading is like preventive spiritual health care. It's better to divert a problem or to address an issue before it truly becomes a major concern. In daily reading, God refines you, bit by bit, slowly and yet continually transforming your thoughts and responses into those of Jesus.

The guidance that God gives to you in His Word is complete. It is a thorough answer. The more you read the Bible, the more you will begin to see how principles are connected and reinforced. The main themes and teachings of the Bible are repeated again and again—in different words, in different people, in different situations.

2. *Guidance from the Holy Spirit.* A second way that God speaks to you is through His Holy Spirit, who lives within you. The Holy Spirit brings a "witness" to your spirit that is usually yes or no in nature. The Holy Spirit speaks in your heart a no to everything that will bring you harm; He speaks a yes to everything that will bring you blessing. At times He qualifies His yes to you by

saying, "Yes, but first this," or "Yes, but wait." You have a knowing that some might call intuitive. You sense in your spirit His response.

You must ask Him for His guidance. You may make plans and then act on them without submitting them first for His approval and direction. Then when you find yourself in trouble or need, you say, "Why did God allow this? Why me?" The fact is, you never consulted the Lord first about what you were about to do.

You can never ask too many times of the Holy Spirit, "Should I do this—yes or no?" or "Should I say this—yes or no?" Generally speaking you will have a sense of enthusiasm and eager desire marked with great joy and freedom, or you will have a sense of foreboding, danger, caution, or need for silence.

I find that it is much easier to receive the direction of the Holy Spirit by asking for yes-or-no counsel than to ask Him the broad and undefined question, "What do You want me to do today?" You already have an idea about what needs to be done. Ask the Lord specifically if your wisdom on the matter matches His wisdom—yes or no.

3. *Guidance as you pray.* Very often, in imparting wisdom to you, the Holy Spirit will remind you of what God has said to you and done for you in the past. Sometimes He will give you very detailed words to say or very clear directions about where to go and what to do. At times He will guide you as you pray.

On countless occasions, I have not started out to pray for a certain thing, but as I have waited in silence for the Holy Spirit to bring to my mind various aspects of a situation, I find that He reveals things to me, and I feel prompted to pray in a direction I had not anticipated.

4. *Guidance through godly advice from other people.* In addition to speaking to you through His Word and through the Holy Spirit, God uses other people to speak to you. Some may be total strangers. Others may be members of your immediate family or friends. He uses pastors, teachers, and Bible-study group leaders.

As you open yourself to hear God's word from other people, make certain that the word they give to you is in total alignment with God's written Word. God doesn't forget what He has already said, and He doesn't contradict Himself. If a word is from God, it will be consistent with what God has already revealed through Scripture and in the life of His Son, the Lord Jesus Christ. Also make certain that the person who gives you counsel has no ulterior personal motive. When you are confused, in pain, or in dire need, you are much more subject to manipulation than you might be at other times. Make certain that the person doesn't want something from you, isn't trying to manipulate you for selfish purposes, or isn't seeking personal praise and glory for the counsel given.

God's word through other people will never be anything that might harm another person. If someone advises you to take action that will damage or destroy another person's reputation, relationships, spiritual growth, or property, don't take that advice. God's word is for your ultimate and eternal good but also for the ultimate and eternal good of all His children.

Listen for two or more witnesses. The Lord may direct you to two or more passages of the Bible that convey the same meaning. He may bring a total stranger across your path who speaks a word that is very close to what you heard from your pastor in last Sunday's sermon. He may use a scriptural song that you hear on the radio to confirm what a friend counseled you to do. God gives His wisdom *liberally*. He desires to make Himself known to you and to reveal the full extent of what He desires for you.

Without Reproach

God never offers His guidance to you with the attitude, "You are stupid for asking this," or "You ought to know better." God never shames you for not having His wisdom. The heavenly Father doesn't impart His wisdom with reproach; rather, He instructs you as a patient teacher instructs a cherished student.

If you don't understand God clearly, He will speak to you again and again—using one method and then the next—to get His message across to you. As long as you seek to follow His guidance, He continues to send you His messages of wise counsel.

Reproach is a tool of the enemy. Satan says, "You'll never be a good person," "You've sinned to the point that God can never forgive you," "You've made so many mistakes that God can't use you anymore," "You're never going to get this right," "You can't give up this bad habit so quit trying," or "You are unworthy of God's love."

The devil lies to you about your ability to receive and understand God's wisdom, or your ability to enact it in practical ways in your life.

The reproach of the enemy often couches itself in terms of timing: "If you don't take action right now, you'll miss out," or "If you act now, people will think you are impetuous; wait a while." The reproach is this: you can't know God's timing.

A part of God's wisdom imparted to you will be not only *what* to do, but also *how* to do it and *when* to do it. Be sure to wait for the Lord to give you His full counsel on a matter. He will reveal to you the methods you are to use, even the tone of voice you are to use, and He will show you when to act. David knew this well. Time and time again he inquired of the Lord about what to do, how to do it, and when to take action. He said, "My soul, wait silently for God alone, For my expectation is from Him" (Ps. 62:5 NKJV).

There are times when the Lord will tell you to wait. There may be things that the Lord needs to do in another person's life before He can fulfill His plans in your life. There are other times when the Lord will tell you, "Act now. Don't delay." Be sensitive to His timing. The Lord wants you to be effective and successful in carrying out His will. He does not believe you are incapable of discerning His methods and timing.

Once you have heard from God, do what He tells you to do without doubting and without hesitating.

He Speaks Words of Peace to Your Heart

Even as the Lord gives you boldness, He gives you calm. Have you ever experienced this in your life? You knew what had to be done, and you knew you were the person to do it, and along with the courage you felt, you also felt a great sense of inner calm that, come what may, you had to act. That's the peace of God, which is always attendant with God's abiding presence. It's a peace that says, "I know God is in charge of my life and this moment. Come what may, I belong to the Lord, and He is present with me."

Paul wrote to the Philippians these words of comfort:

Be anxious for nothing, but in everything by prayer and supplication, with thanksgiving, let your requests be made known to God; and the peace of

God, which surpasses all understanding, will guard your hearts and minds through Christ Jesus.

(PHIL. 4:6–7 NKJV)

Keep in mind that Paul wrote that letter from a Roman prison. He had been in Roman custody for years. He never knew from one day to the next what his fate would be—from Rome's standpoint. Paul always knew, however, what his fate would be from God's standpoint.

He had confidence that God was in charge and that God would continue to be in charge until his last breath on this earth, and even then, God would continue to be in charge of his life. Therefore, Paul could make his requests to God with thanksgiving; he could ask for what he desired and, at the same time, thank God that God was in charge and God's will would be done. The ability to pray with thanksgiving gave Paul a deep peace, a total lack of anxiety or worry.

Do you know a person who is always fretting, always worrying, always upset about what to do or what will happen? That person may even be you.

The antidote for worry is a greater awareness of God's presence. When you feel anxiety rising up in you, ask God to make His presence known to you. Let Him know that you are trusting in Him. Tell Him what you would like to see happen, but add to your petition thanks for what God has done in your life in the past and praise for who God is. The more you thank and praise God, the greater calm you will experience. He is the Lord of all! All things do come from Him! He is our Provider, our Deliverer, our Savior, our Redeemer, our Rock, our Fortress, our Trust, our Life. He is the King of the universe, and He is still on His eternal throne.

And then, having made your petition known to God with thanksgiving and praise, choose to think about something other than your problem. It is no accident that Paul followed up his words about being anxious for nothing by saying,

Whatever things are true, whatever things are noble, whatever things are just, whatever things are pure, whatever things are lovely, whatever things are of good report, if there is any virtue and if there is anything praiseworthy— meditate on these things.

(PHIL. 4:8 NKJV)

Turn your attention away from your problem and toward the things that are truly good. Turn your mind to the solutions and answers that God has given you in the past. Turn your mind to His blessings and His promises. Focus your mind on His goodness and His love for you.

And then Paul advised, "The things which you learned and received and heard and saw in me, these do" (Phil. 4:9 NKJV).

Having prayed with thanksgiving and praise, and having turned your mind toward what is of God and from God, you must then begin to do what God leads you to do. Paul said, "Do what I have done." And what did Paul do? He worked; he prayed; he gave his witness; he taught the Scriptures to those who wanted to learn. He stayed very busy doing good things that were of benefit to himself, others, and ultimately, the kingdom of God.

That pattern of praying, focusing on the positive, and doing good is one that Paul said will cause you to be keenly aware that "the God of peace will be with you" (Phil. 4:9).

He Tells You His Presence with You Is Abiding

How often can you ask God for boldness, insight, or direction? As many times as necessary. He is always available. The Holy Spirit does not make periodic visitations to your life. No—He *abides* with you. He dwells within you. Jesus said, "He who abides in Me, and I in him, bears much fruit" (John 15:5).

You can trust God to give you boldness and wisdom that are effective. You'll bear fruit. You'll get the job done that God wants done. Along the way, you'll have an understanding of what God is seeking to accomplish in you and through you. You'll have the peace and calm of His presence. The Holy Spirit does not come and go from your life. He is with you *always*.

GOD'S MESSAGE TO YOU ABOUT HEAVEN

God has a third message for you, and the message is about your future and your ultimate destiny.

One of God's greatest acts of love toward us is the creation of heaven as our eternal home. God doesn't merely love us enough to create us and give us several decades of life on this earth. He loves us for all eternity. He intends to spend forever with us.

Jesus said to His disciples,

Let not your heart be troubled; you believe in God, believe also in Me. In My Father's house are many mansions; if it were not so, I would have told you. I go to prepare a place for you. And if I go and prepare a place for you, I will come again and receive you to Myself; that where I am, there you may be also.

(JOHN 14:1–3 NKJV)

Isn't it wonderful to know that Jesus is preparing a place just for *you*? If Jesus is preparing it, it's bound to be good—even beyond your highest expectations. A man told me, "I don't know what kind of place Jesus is preparing for me, but He's been preparing it for nearly two thousand years now and it only took Him seven days to make the world, so whatever kind of place it is, I know it's going to be far more wonderful than anything I could ever imagine!" Paul no doubt felt that way when he wrote to the Ephesians, "Now to Him who is able to do exceedingly abundantly above all that we ask or think" (Eph. 3:20 NKJV).

Paul wrote very specifically to the Colossians about heaven:

We give thanks to the God and Father of our Lord Jesus Christ, praying always for you, since we heard of your faith in Christ Jesus and of your love for all the saints; because of the hope which is laid up for you in heaven, of which you heard before in the word of the truth of the gospel.

(COL. 1:3–5 NKJV)

What Is the Hope of Heaven?

First and foremost, it is the hope of being with God for all eternity. It is the hope of everlasting life in the direct presence of your Creator.

Second, it is the hope that your life will come to full fruition. All that you have done, said, and been in this life will be revealed and judged by God. For the believer in Christ Jesus this judgment is nothing to be feared. Rather, it is something to anticipate with joy. Heaven is the place where you will be rewarded for your faithfulness.

This hope of heaven has a purifying effect on your life. When heaven and the rewards of God are kept in sharp focus before you, you have an increased desire and commitment to live as God intends for you to live—you want to give your best effort to saying and doing all that God asks you to say and do. The hope of heaven compels you to grow, yield to God's transforming work in your life, and become the person He has destined you to be. When you look around, you easily can become discouraged and feel as if you have failed to succeed according to the standards of the world. According to the standards of life in your heavenly home, you have a sense of encouragement and a feeling that you *are* succeeding according to God's standards.

Third, the hope of heaven is a life that is totally separated from evil. In heaven, there is no shadow, no darkness, no negative presence. In John's vision of heaven, he heard a voice from heaven proclaiming, "God will wipe away every tear from their eyes; there shall be no more death, nor sorrow, nor crying. There shall be no more pain, for the former things have passed away" (Rev. 21:4).

Whatever you envision as being of highest quality, most noble character, and brightest beauty, that is what you will experience in heaven, for you will be in the presence of God and those who are filled with the Spirit of God, without any influence of sin or the weaknesses of the flesh.

THE REASON TO KNOW ABOUT HEAVEN

God desires to say more to you about heaven. How do I know that to be true? Because there is much about heaven that God desires to see each one of us bring to this earth through our prayers, words, and actions.

Jesus taught His disciples to pray,

Your kingdom come.

Your will be done

On earth as it is in heaven.

(MATT. 6:10)

What exactly are you praying? If you don't have an understanding about heaven, and about God's rule of heaven, God's methods in heaven, God's purposes in heaven, how can you know if God's will is being done on this earth?

We are not destined to live solely on this earth. Our true home is heaven. We are citizens of heaven, and therefore, we are to abide by the higher laws and commandments of heaven. We are only travelers through this life. Paul called us "fellow citizens with the saints" and "ambassadors for Christ" (Eph. 2:19; 2 Cor. 5:20). We are Christ's emissaries on this earth—our true loyalty is to heaven.

God desires to reveal more to you about your eternal home so you will know better how to live in your temporary home—this earth.

What Are Some of the Hallmarks of Heaven?

Praise

John told us in his revelation that the throne of God is surrounded continually by those who praise God. They cry day and night,

"Holy, holy, holy;

Lord God Almighty,

Who was and is and is to come! . . .

You are worthy, O Lord,

To receive glory and honor and power;

For You created all things,

And by Your will they exist and were created."

(REV. 4:8, 11 NKJV)

When you praise God on earth, you are rehearsing something that you will be doing forever. Surely a major part of your bringing heaven to earth is accomplished through and manifested by praise.

The Exaltation of Jesus

Those who offer praise in heaven also proclaim the worthiness of Jesus. They cry out about our Lord,

> You are worthy to take the scroll,
> And to open its seals;
> For You were slain,
> And have redeemed us to God by Your blood
> Out of every tribe and tongue and people and nation,
> And have made us kings and priests to our God;
> And we shall reign on the earth. . . .
> Worthy is the Lamb who was slain
> To receive power and riches and wisdom,
> And strength and honor and glory and blessing! . . .
> Blessing and honor and glory and power
> Be to Him who sits on the throne,
> And to the Lamb, forever and ever!
>
> (Rev. 5:9–10, 12, 13 NKJV)

Your purpose as a Christian on this earth is to exalt Jesus, who said, "As Moses lifted up the serpent in the wilderness, even so must the Son of Man be lifted up, that whoever believes in Him should not perish but have eternal life" (John 3:14–15 NKJV). He also said, "I, if I am lifted up from the earth, will draw all peoples to Myself" (John 12:32 NKJV).

Jesus was prophesying His death on the cross, but the fact is, when you call people's attention to the cross and to the sacrifice that Jesus made there, He draws sinners to Himself as their Savior. Your purpose is to do the exalting of Jesus. Again, this is something you will be doing throughout eternity. This is a way you bring heaven to earth.

Humility to Serve and Authority to Reign

John said of God's servants in heaven, "And His servants shall serve Him. . . . And they shall reign forever and ever" (Rev. 22:3, 5 NKJV).

Part of what you do in bringing God's kingdom of heaven to earth is realized when you serve others—when you meet their needs, affirm them, teach them God's ways, and minister to them the gifts of the Holy Spirit as He pours these gifts through you as His vessel. You serve others when you proclaim the gospel of Jesus to them and make them disciples of the Lord, eager to obey His commands and follow in His footsteps. Your service to others is to be open and pure, without any shadow of ill motive.

Every servant has a master. Paul wrote to the Ephesians that the Master is in heaven (Eph. 6:9). You are to be quick to do His bidding.

As you serve, you are also to reign—not over people, but over evil. With Christ's love motivating you and the Holy Spirit empowering you, you are called to serve people and have dominion over the powers of Satan. So many people get this backward—they are ruling over people and serving Satan. Your role as a believer in Christ and disciple of the Lord is the exact opposite. You are to model for others the way that Jesus lived His life—a life of daily ministry to those in need, and a life of total victory over the power of the devil. You are to have full power and authority over the enemy, calling on the name of Jesus as you withstand the devil's assaults, resist his temptations, and endure any trials he may send your way (Eph. 6:9–10; James 4:7; 1:12).

There is much more that the Lord seeks to reveal to you about heaven, but this much is certain: the Holy Spirit's guidance of your life is in full accord with the "operations manual" of heaven. He has heaven in mind as your destiny, and His efforts are all aimed at guarding your steps and guiding your way so that you walk a straight path to your eternal home.

GOD IS ALWAYS SPEAKING—WILL YOU LISTEN?

God has much to say to you each day—about His great love, about the way He desires for you to live and experience His presence, about your ultimate destination. The question you must ask yourself is, *Am I listening?*

God is always speaking. The problem in your communication with God does not lie with Him. It lies in your lack of interest, your inability to hear

Him clearly, and your failure to take the time to listen to all that He longs to say to you.

In telling you of His love for you, God gives you motivation to face life with faith and enthusiasm.

In telling you of His plans, providing His guidance, and imparting His presence, God gives you a great sense of security and purpose.

In telling you of your future home, God gives you His goal for your life.

With love in your heart, ideas and plans and truth in your mind, and a goal for your efforts, you can't help having hope! You are eager to hear more of what God has to say. And the good news is that God always has more that He desires to share with you, to reveal to you, and to impart to you so that you might be comforted, guided, and perfected.

SEVEN

ARE YOU LISTENING?

Samuel was one of the mightiest prophets of the Old Testament. It's no coincidence that his first assignment from God necessitated that he learn how to hear God's voice. In 1 Samuel 3:4–10, Samuel, who had been entrusted to the care of Eli the Priest, was lying down one evening when the Lord spoke:

> The Lord called Samuel. And he answered, "Here I am!" So he ran to Eli and said, "Here I am, for you called me!" And he said, "I did not call; lie down again!" And he [Samuel] went and lay down. And the Lord called yet again, "Samuel!" So Samuel arose and went to Eli, and said, "Here I am, for you called me." He [Eli] answered, "I did not call, my son; lie down again." (Now Samuel did not yet know the Lord, nor was the word of the Lord yet revealed to him.) And the Lord called Samuel again the third time. So he arose and went to Eli, and said, "Here I am, for you did call me." Then Eli perceived that the Lord had called the boy. Therefore Eli said to Samuel, "Go, lie down; and it shall be, if He calls you, that you must say, 'Speak, Lord, for Your servant hears!' So Samuel went and lay down in his place. Now the Lord came and stood and called as at other times, "Samuel! Samuel!" And Samuel answered, "Speak, for Your servant hears." (NKJV)

Isn't that a beautiful way to answer God, "Speak, for Your servant hears"? Eli taught Samuel how to listen to God, and if we are going to be men and women of God today, we must learn how we can hear what God is saying to us. We do so in a number of ways that I will discuss briefly here.

EXPECTANTLY

If we are going to listen to God, we must come to Him expectantly. We must anticipate His speaking to us. Jeremiah 33:3 exemplifies this eagerness when it quotes God, "Call to Me, and I will answer you, and show you great and mighty things, which you do not know" (NKJV). Throughout Scripture we have the promise that God will indeed speak to us, but if we come to Him doubting His ability to speak, we will have a difficult time listening. Expectantly believing the promises of God is expressing faith, without which "it is impossible to please Him" (Heb. 11:6). We should all have great expectations when it comes to hearing Jehovah speak.

Expectancy is based on reliability. When Elijah confronted the 450 prophets of Baal and the 400 prophets of the Asherah, he did so with a boldness that seemed to border on downright insolence. After mocking the false prophets who were unable to call down fire from heaven to consume the prepared sacrifice of oxen, Elijah took his turn. You can almost imagine the smug grin on his face as he readied himself to call upon the God of Israel.

Before he did so, however, he had someone pour four large pitchers of water on the wood and oxen. For good measure, he had them drench the wood with four more pitchers, and just in case anyone thought it wasn't wet enough, he added another four, so that the "water ran all around the altar; and he also filled the trench with water" (1 Kings 18:35).

Was he expecting God to answer? You bet he was. He knew who the living, true God was because he had already seen God predict and execute drought. He had already witnessed His power at work in bringing the widow of Zarephath's son back to life. He had seen God's provision for her in supernaturally replenishing the bowl of flour and the jar of oil.

Elijah expected God to answer because He had faithfully responded in the past. Elijah's God is also our God, and His reliability hasn't altered one iota.

QUIETLY

The psalmist wrote, "Be still, and know that I am God" (Ps. 46:10). If we are to listen to God, we must be quiet and let Him do the talking. Too many of us, when we pray, simply read off a list of requests, then get up and walk off. Instead of listening to God, we only report our requests to Him. How can God speak to us if we don't take time to listen? Quietness is essential to listening. If we are too busy to listen, we won't hear. If we spend night after night watching television, and then try to listen, we will find our minds jammed with carnal interference. It takes time and quietness to prepare to listen to God. "My soul, wait silently for God alone, For my expectation is from Him" (Ps. 62:5 NKJV).

That is why so many people through the centuries have sought seclusion in deserts, mountains, or monasteries. There the noise of civilization vanishes and the voice of God doesn't have quite so much competition. Such silence, however, can be found in the quiet of a living-room sofa late at night or at the kitchen table early in the morning. The place isn't important. The decibel scale is. God's voice is still and quiet and easily buried under an avalanche of clamor.

PATIENTLY

God will not tell us some things instantaneously. We will hear some special revelations only after having waited a season of time. One of the reasons is simply that we're not always ready. Because of that, God will sometimes withhold information until we are prepared to listen.

We must be willing to listen to Him patiently because these times may draw out and stretch our faith. He has promised to speak to our hearts so we can expect Him to, but He is not compelled to tell us everything we want to know the moment we desire the information.

We'd like to say, "Lord, here's my order today. Please give me an answer before I get up off my knees." It may be weeks later before God speaks to us about this, not because He has forgotten, but because in the process of waiting,

He is changing and preparing us to hear His message, which we may not have received had He spoken instantaneously.

ACTIVELY

To hear God we must actively wait and meditate upon His Word. Colossians 3:16 declares, "Let the word of Christ dwell in you richly in all wisdom, teaching and admonishing one another in psalms and hymns and spiritual songs, singing with grace in your hearts to the Lord" (NKJV).

If we only know the Word selectively and dwell on one particular favorite subject, we fail to seek the whole counsel of God. The way we become wealthy and overflowing with the truth of the Word is to meditate upon Scripture, search it out, digest it, and apply it to our hearts.

Faced with one of the most difficult decisions in my life, I asked God to speak to my fearful, doubting heart. I was reading chapter 41 in the book of Isaiah when I came to the latter part of verse 9, and it was as if God said, "Now, Charles, 'You are My Servant, I have chosen you and have not cast you away: Fear not, for I am with you; Be not dismayed, for I am your God. I will strengthen you, Yes, I will help you, I will uphold you with My righteous right hand'" (vv. 9–10). I meditated upon that passage day and night for weeks, continually being reminded of His call to fearlessness and His assurance of divine help. "For I, the LORD your God, will hold your right hand, Saying to you, 'Fear not, I will help you'" (v. 13 NKJV).

When the moment of crisis came, I was filled with an awesome sense of peace. That passage had permeated my very being. I felt that I was seeing my situation from God's viewpoint, relying upon His promise and His power to perform it. Once again I understood what Paul meant by the peace that surpasses all understanding.

At another time in my life, the Lord had brought me back to Psalm 81 in my morning meditation for several weeks. Verse 6 kept grabbing my attention: "I removed his shoulder from the burden; His hands were freed from the baskets" (NKJV). I knew God was trying to speak to me through that passage, but I was not sure what He was saying. The more I read and meditated, the more I began to realize that He was preparing me for a change. At the time, I was pastor of a large church in a big city. We had a Christian school, which was growing rapidly, and I was heavily burdened because so much of the responsibility for it rested upon me.

After I spent several weeks meditating upon that passage and claiming it as a promise of relief, the Lord sent me a staff member who literally removed my shoulder from the burden and freed my hands from the baskets. She assumed full responsibility of the school, and I was free to give my time to the church.

God is so precise in His instructions and promises given through His Word. Meditation upon God's Word is one of the most wonderful ways we can listen to the voice of God for divine guidance.

CONFIDENTLY

We must be confident that when we listen to God, we will hear what we need to hear. It may not always be what we wish to hear, but God communicates to us what is essential in our walk with Him.

Would we withhold information from our children that they would need to possess in order to be obedient to our instructions? Would we tell them, "Here's what I want you to do," and then not provide them with information? Certainly not. The Lord Jesus said, "If you then, being evil, know how to give good gifts to your children, how much more will your Father who is in heaven give good things to those who ask Him!" (Matt. 7:11 NKJV).

DEPENDENTLY

As we come to God, we must come in recognition that we are totally dependent upon the Holy Spirit to teach us truth. If we come to Him with a prideful attitude, it will be difficult for the Holy Spirit to instruct us. In 1 Corinthians 2:7–11 Paul wrote:

> But we speak the wisdom of God in a mystery, the hidden wisdom which
> God ordained before the ages for our glory, which none of the rulers of this

age knew; for had they known, they would not have crucified the Lord of glory. But as it is written:

> "Eye has not seen, nor ear heard,
> Nor have entered into the heart of man
> The things which God has prepared for those who love Him."

But God has revealed them to us through His Spirit. For the Spirit searches all things, yes, the deep things of God. For what man knows the things of a man except the spirit of the man which is in him? Even so no one knows the things of God except the Spirit of God. (NKJV)

There's no way for us to hear from God apart from the ministry of the Holy Spirit. When God speaks through others or through circumstances, it is the work of the Spirit.

Jesus said in John 16:7, "Nevertheless I tell you the truth. It is to your advantage that I go away; for if I do not go away, the Helper will not come to you; but if I depart, I will send Him to you" (NKJV). And in John 16:13 Christ explains, "For He [the Spirit] will not speak on His own authority, but whatever He hears He will speak; and He will tell you things to come" (NKJV).

We each have a living, divine receiver within us in the person of the Holy Spirit. That is why Paul added in 1 Corinthians 2:12, "Now we have received, not the spirit of the world, but the Spirit who is from God, that we might know the things that have been freely given to us by God" (NKJV). Prayer isn't God up there and us down here; it is the Holy Spirit speaking within us, bearing witness to our spirits that we may know the mind of Christ. In fact, we do have the mind of Christ, but how do we appropriate that for ourselves at any given moment? By believing at that moment, by faith, that the Holy Spirit living within us will answer our petitions, speak to our hearts, and give us directions.

To receive God's directions we must have a right relationship with Him. That relationship means that we must be filled with His Spirit, and we must learn to walk in His Spirit, not grieving the Holy Spirit of God (Eph. 4:30). If we grieve God by saying yes to sin and quench the Spirit by saying no to God, how can the Holy Spirit who is both receiver and communicator to our spirits declare God's revelation? One of the primary reasons people do not hear anything when they talk to God is because they are not living in the Spirit. Their lifestyle is one of quiet rebellion against God.

One of the reasons God commands us to be filled with the Spirit is that He not only empowers us for service but also is essential to our hearing God. If the Spirit is quenched and grieved, He cannot deliver the message of God because we are not listening. If we refuse to hear what the Holy Spirit says to us, then our praying is useless babbling into heaven and God does not hear it. How we live makes a difference as to what we hear. A believer can live what most would characterize as a normal Christian life and still be in error, because he is not listening to the Spirit. We can never get enough education, enough experience, to live independently of the Holy Spirit. He must give us the mind of Christ, or we do not possess it. He is not going to speak until we admit that apart from His genuine work in our lives, we are helpless to receive anything from Him.

We cannot make God tell us anything one split second before He is ready. We can fast and pray and weep and give, but that doesn't impress Him at all. The only way is to come humbly before Him, dependent upon the abiding, effective work of the Holy Spirit within us.

OPENLY

We must come to God openly. 2 Timothy 3:16 is a familiar passage in which Paul wrote, "All Scripture is given by inspiration of God, and is profitable for doctrine, for reproof, for correction, for instruction in righteousness" (NKJV).

To listen openly means to be willing to hear God correct us as well as comfort us, to hear God convict us as well as assure us. We may be looking for a word of comfort from God when He may have a word of correction. If we come to Him only for comfort and prosperity, only for what is soothing to the ear, then we will not always hear what God has to say.

If we are unwilling to hear the correction, before long our need for correction will dramatically increase. As we listen to Him, humbly depending upon the Holy Spirit, God will bring to our minds areas that need to be corrected. We must accept both the positive and the negative.

Many of us have gotten on our knees before God and He spoke to us, but He didn't say what we wanted to hear. Even in the correction God has a positive goal in mind, and that is to prevent us from making disastrous mistakes and ruining our lives. When we come to Him with a mental spiritual sifter, picking out only what we want to hear, we will not hear accurately.

ATTENTIVELY

Listening to God demands our full attention. If He speaks through His Word (through His Spirit, through others, and through circumstances), then we must live every day attentively and alertly.

Someone might say something in passing that gives us a godly warning or admonition. God intended for it to drop into our spirits, nurture the truth, and bring it to life, letting it bud and blossom into correction and comfort. However, we must be attentive to produce such spiritual fruit. We must have our spiritual antennas fully extended. We must be vigilant to discern the voice of God in the circumstances of our lives each day. We must constantly ask, "What is really happening? What does this particular circumstance mean?" As Christians we cannot divide our lives into secular and spiritual compartments. Our whole walk is spiritual because Christ is life. Of course not everything we do, think, or say is spiritual, but our walk is spiritual because we are new creations in Christ Jesus. Thus in everything God allows in our lives, we must always look for His fingerprint. We must listen for the voice of God in every sound.

CAREFULLY

Hebrews 4:12 tells us about the power of the Word. It says, "For the word of God is living and powerful, and sharper than any two-edged sword, piercing even to the division of soul and spirit, and of joints and marrow, and is a discerner of the thoughts and intents of the heart" (NKJV).

In this verse, God informs us that everything we hear is to be sifted through the Word. Before we accept anything into our lives, we should filter it through Scripture and eliminate anything that contradicts Scripture. If it is contrary to the Word of God, it should be purged. That is why we must listen to Him carefully, because the Word of God reveals the innermost intentions and motivations of our lives. The Word of God pulls back the veil so that we can see the reality of all that is about us. The light of the Word illuminates everything enabling us to discern the truth from error. Whatever we hear we must thoroughly evaluate against the absolute standard of His truth.

SUBMISSIVELY

We need to listen to God submissively, because sometimes when He speaks to our hearts, we will not like what we hear. When the Lord tells us something we don't want to hear, we may not react in total obedience. But God doesn't get hostile over our rebellious spirits; that's not His response. He knew us before we ever came to listen to Him, and He knew exactly how we would respond. He may be grieved by our negative reaction, but He doesn't send down a squadron of angry angels to destroy us. He knows we will struggle with certain things.

When Jesus came to the Garden of Gethsemane, He was already committed to the Father's will. However, He struggled with the Father to determine whether there was another way to accomplish God's purpose. He struggled with separation from the Father while at the same time He was committed to God's will. There will be times when we come to God, listen to Him, and then grapple with what we hear. We may not be consistently disobedient to what we hear, but sometimes we may not understand how or why God is going to perform it. We may be as submissive as we know how at that moment, but still wrestle with what He says. Submission must ultimately accompany listening if we are to fully hear God. It is essential if we are to follow Him.

I recall a man who had just come out of the air force after World War II. He had been a skilled flight instructor and was expecting to join a major airline and spend the rest of his life as a commercial pilot. It would have been a good-paying job and one where, he felt, he could be a witness for Christ.

The Lord had other ideas. As he pondered several offers, the man was asked by a longtime friend to join him in evangelism work. He didn't like the idea and told God so. When the time came to give an answer to the airlines, however, he declined and went into full-time ministry, where he successfully labored for thirty years.

He told me there were many times when he watched jets fly overhead and he dreamed of piloting. He continued to receive lucrative offers to return to flying, but he turned them all down because he wanted to be submissive to God. Because of that yieldedness, he accomplished God's purpose in life, walking in the works He had ordained, not in his own well-laid scheme.

GRATEFULLY

When we come to the Father, we should have a grateful attitude. We should be grateful the Father would love us enough to send His only begotten Son to the cross; grateful for the crucifixion; grateful for our salvation; grateful that God has plucked us out of the kingdom of darkness and put us into the kingdom of light. As Paul explained in Philippians 4:6 and 7, "Be anxious for nothing, but in everything by prayer and supplication, with thanksgiving, let your requests be made known to God; and the peace of God, which surpasses all understanding, will guard your hearts and minds through Christ Jesus" (NKJV).

Out of the billions of people who make up this universe, God is interested in you. He possesses intimate knowledge of you in His incomparable, indescribable mind. When you come to Him, you should draw near with a thankful heart, because you do not come in contact with a heavenly Father who speaks to the masses, but one who speaks to individuals. That should invoke your unlimited gratitude.

REVERENTLY

A reverent heart should be the foundation of hearing God. We should be in awe that we can speak to the God who hung the sun and world on nothing, the God who created all the intricacies of human life.

We should be humble that this same omnipotent God is quietly willing to listen to us, while simultaneously giving direction to the vastness of the universe. His total, concentrated, and undisturbed attention is focused upon us individually. That ought to humble us and create within us a reverence that acknowledges God for the mighty Creator He is.

EIGHT

SITTING BEFORE THE LORD

Just the mention of the word *meditation* conjures up various and sundry images, all somewhat foreign to the Western mind. Somehow or another, contemporary believers have removed the word from the biblical vocabulary. Its usage now has been confined primarily to the practice of Eastern religion and, thus for the Christian, cast into an almost obsolete and forbidden sphere. This abandonment is at our great peril, because meditation and its scriptural application are of immense value if we are to listen accurately to God.

Perhaps no other man has pursued this godly endeavor more fervently and fruitfully than King David. Many of the psalms are the results of his quietly waiting and reflecting upon God. As a "man after God's own heart," David first had to know the mind and heart of God. To a large extent, David accomplished this through the persistent practice of godly meditation. A vivid illustration can be found in 2 Samuel 7. In this chapter we see that David has reached a place of rest in his reign. His war campaigns are no longer on the drawing board, and he is now contemplating building a temple for the Lord. The prophet Nathan gives an encouraging message of God's faithfulness to David and the Lord's plan for constructing the temple. David's response to Nathan's communiqué is found in 2 Samuel 7:18, "Then King David went in and sat before the LORD; and he said: 'Who am I, O Lord GOD? And what is my house, that You have brought me this far?'" (NKJV). Notice the phrase, David "sat before the LORD." Now he wasn't sitting in a chair as we would. He was kneeling and sitting back on his heels, listening, and talking to the Lord. David was meditating.

In his book *Knowing God*, author J. I. Packer gives as good a working definition of meditation as I have seen:

> Meditation is the activity of calling to mind, and thinking over, and dwelling on, and applying to oneself, the various things that one knows about the works and ways and purposes and promises of God. It is an activity of holy thought, consciously performed in the presence of God, under the eye of God, by the help of God, as a means of communion with God. Its purpose is to clear one's mental and spiritual vision of God, and to let His truth make its full and proper impact on one's mind and heart. It is a matter of talking to oneself about God and oneself; it is, indeed, often a matter of arguing with oneself, reasoning oneself out of moods of doubt and unbelief into a clear apprehension of God's power and grace. Its effect is to ever humble us as we contemplate God's greatness and glory, and our own littleness and sinfulness, and to encourage and reassure us—"Comfort" us in the old, strong Bible sense of the word—as we contemplate the unsearchable riches of divine mercy displayed in the Lord Jesus Christ.[1]

Meditation was nothing new to David because he had long known what it meant to meditate. We read in the Psalms how often he listened and talked to the Father out in the fields. Even when he was running from Saul and dodging javelins, David took time to meditate upon God. Since meditation is the one activity that should be the daily priority of believers, it is the one discipline Satan will doggedly keep us from observing. When we examine the rewards and the results of meditation, however, we will soon realize it can't be secondary. It has to be primary.

Many believers think that meditation is only for ministers or other spiritual leaders. They do not see its role in a secular world where strife and competition reign. It seems alien to persons who have to get up and hit the expressway at 7:30 A.M., be in noisy offices during the day, and then battle the traffic home, where they then must deal with domestic difficulties. Yet it is in the midst of such constant turmoil that the believer stands in great need of the quieting effects of meditation, so that he may distill God's voice from the roar of everyday living.

God gave the practice of meditation not just to preachers, but to all His children so that we might better relate to Him. Personal, private meditation begins when we get alone with the Lord and get quiet before Him. It may be for five minutes, it may be for thirty minutes, it may be for an hour. The important thing is that we get alone with the Lord to find His direction and purpose for our lives.

Personal and compelling guidance is only one of the benefits of meditation. Psalm 119:97–100 lists some of the other rewards of meditation, such as wisdom, discernment, keen insight, and heightened obedience.

Joshua 1:8 is a wonderful Scripture on the blessed benefits of concentrated thinking: "This Book of the Law shall not depart from your mouth, but you shall meditate in it day and night, that you may observe to do according to all that is written in it. For then you will make your way prosperous, and then you will have good success" (NKJV). Meditation is God's way of crowning our lives with His success and prosperity of soul, spirit, and body. It is also a catalyst to obedient living.

I want to share four principles that will guide you into meaningful meditation. These principles will be liberating truths that will cause you to hear the voice of God in a fresh, invigorating manner.

REVIEW THE PAST

Reviewing the past is an excellent way to begin our time of meditation, because as we do, we will see patterns that God has woven into our lives. One of the first steps that David took in 2 Samuel 7:18 was to recall God's blessings: "Who am I, O Lord GOD? And what is my house, that You have brought me this far?" (NKJV). David remembered his fight with Goliath. He remembered the years spent running from Saul, the battles he had won. Now that he had peace in his life, he had the privilege of savoring God's wonderful works.

When we meditate, we should focus on how God has operated in our lives in the past. We should look for His hand in all of our dealings. As we do, we can see His hand of correction, comfort, and exhortation, and we can better distinguish His moving in our lives at the present time.

REFLECT UPON GOD

Reviewing the past should be followed by reflecting upon God. Listen to what else David said: "And yet this was a small thing in Your sight, O Lord God . . . Now what more can David say to You? For You, Lord God, know Your servant. For Your word's sake, and according to Your own heart, You have done all these great things, to make Your servant know them" (2 Sam. 7:19–21 NKJV).

As we begin to reflect upon God, we should consider three facets: His greatness, His grace, and His goodness. When we meditate on the greatness of God and His names—Jehovah, Yahweh, Elohim, Everlasting, Infinite in Power, Absolute in Faithfulness—our gigantic mountains of trouble and heartache shrink in comparison. In the light of the presence and greatness of God, nothing is impossible in our lives. Our burdens dissipate in His very presence.

Focusing on difficulties intensifies and enlarges the problem. When we focus our attention on God, the problem is put into its proper perspective, and it no longer overwhelms us.

Jeremiah Denton was a prisoner of war in North Vietnam for seven horrendous years. As one of the highest-ranking American captives, he was subjected to particularly grueling torture, spending almost his entire incarceration in solitary confinement. In such a barren, brutal situation, it would be hard not to focus on the pain and tedium. Yet, Denton not only survived but also came back and was elected a United States senator from Alabama.

How did he survive? He stated on many occasions that an essential survival skill was quoting passages from the Bible. Internalized Scripture became the unseen sword that enabled him to fend off the cruelest weapons of the enemy. By inwardly focusing on the power of God to sustain and strengthen him, he was able to rise above the squalor of his lonely existence.

REMEMBER GOD'S PROMISES

As David continued to meditate on the Lord, he said: "And now, O Lord God, You are God, and Your words are true, and You have promised this goodness to

Your servant" (2 Sam. 7:28 NKJV). David recalled God's promises in establishing his name and family on an everlasting basis. When we kneel or sit before God and meditate upon Him, it's beneficial to review His mighty promises.

In Scripture, He has promised us peace, He has promised us provision, He has promised us protection. These promises belong to each of His children. When we meditate upon God and remember the promises He has given us in His Word, our faith grows and our fears dissolve. David understood that. Many times, in the caves hiding from Saul and with six to twenty thousand men searching for him, David quietly shifted his attention to God. Under the stars or in the darkness of the caves, David focused his attention on God who had equipped him to slay Goliath and had given him swiftness of body and keenness of mind. He remembered God who had allowed him to avoid the penetrating point of Saul's javelin. As he fixed his inner man upon God, his fears and frustrations were soothed by the presence of God.

MAKE A REQUEST

As we sit before the Lord in meditation, we shouldn't just listen; there is a time to make a request too. In 2 Samuel 7:29 David asked, "Now therefore, let it please You to bless the house of Your servant, that it may continue before You" (NKJV). What a tremendous request! He didn't just ask God to bless his family; he boldly asked for God's everlasting favor. And God answered his prayer.

On one occasion I was meditating upon the Word, and I came to Philippians 4:19: "And my God shall supply all your need according to His riches in glory by Christ Jesus" (NKJV). Suddenly I stopped. I began to meditate upon that verse. Without previous thought upon the subject, I prayed for God to provide a large sum of money. I didn't even have a purpose for it. I was burdened to ask for it and to expect it. Several days went by and my burden grew heavier, and all the time I wondered why. Without warning, I had a rather large financial need. Within a matter of hours, God supplied the finances to meet that need. He had burdened me to ask even before I knew I had a need! He had already set in motion to supply a need I didn't even know would exist.

REQUIREMENTS FOR MEDITATION

If we are to have a profitable time of meditation, we can't just rush in, jot down one or two prayer requests, quickly pray, and then go on to dinner. That's not what God wants. He wants us to sit before Him.

Meditation isn't a spontaneous occurrence. Certain disciplines must be put in play in order for us to receive the full benefits of its application. Certain requirements must be heeded if the biblical practice of meditation is to be more than just wishful thinking.

These are the principles that have aided me in personal meditation.

A Season of Time

When we think about meditating on the Lord, the first requirement is a season of time. The length of time, whether it's five minutes or an hour, will be determined by our purpose. If we are in deep distress about a subject, the period will be lengthened. If we simply want to be quiet, it may be a matter of minutes. Psalm 62:5 enjoins us to "wait silently for God alone, For my expectation is from Him" (NKJV).

When we tell God we don't have time for Him, we are really saying we don't have time for life, for joy, for peace, for direction, or for prosperity, because He is the source of all these. The essence of meditation is a period of time set aside to contemplate the Lord, listen to Him, and allow Him to permeate our spirits. When we do, something happens within us that equips us to carry out our duties, whether as a mother, a clerk, a secretary, a mechanic, a carpenter, or a lawyer. Whatever we do, the time of meditation is God's time of equipping us in preparation for life.

It is amazing what God can do to a troubled heart in a short period of time, when that person understands the meaning of meditation. We live in a hurried and rushed world, and it's not going to slow down. So each of us must ask, "How am I going to stay in the rush of it all and hear God?" I'm convinced that the man who has learned to meditate upon the Lord will be able to run on his feet and walk in his spirit. Although he may be hurried by his vocation, that's not the issue. The issue is how fast his spirit is going. To slow it down requires a period of time.

The most important lesson parents can teach their children is the practical importance of prayer and meditation. In doing so, they give their children a lifetime compass. When children learn early to listen to God and obey Him, and when they learn that He is interested in what interests them, they develop a sense of security that no other gift will give them. God is always available, no matter what the circumstances. He will always be there when parents are unavailable.

The only way to teach your children to spend time with the Lord is by example. They need to hear you praying, walk in on you praying, listen to you share how God is speaking to you. They will soon realize that if God hears the prayers of Mom and Dad, He will hear theirs as well. You could not give your children a greater heritage than praying parents.

Stillness

If we're really going to meditate upon the Lord, stillness is a key. Psalm 46:10 says, "Be still, and know that I am God" (NKJV). We'll know God best when we not only set aside time for Him but also learn to be still before Him.

Stillness brings us to the point where we can concentrate. It's difficult to fix our thoughts upon God as we barrel the expressway or stand in the midst of noisy friends. We often miss God's most beautiful interventions in our lives because we are so distracted by other things that we can't see or hear Him. We are not sensitive before Him. We haven't learned to be still in His presence.

When we become still before the Lord, gradually the competing elements of life ebb away. God's benevolent goodness, greatness, and grace come to the forefront of our minds and our problems begin to diminish.

Seclusion

Mark wrote of Jesus: "Now in the morning, having risen a long while before daylight, He went out and departed to a solitary place; and there He prayed" (Mark 1:35 NKJV). If the Lord Jesus Christ, who was perfect in His relationship with the Father, felt it necessary to leave the twelve disciples whom He loved the most and seclude Himself before God, then shouldn't we make provisions for such solitude?

Everybody needs to be alone at times. It's wonderful for husbands and wives to love each other and to want to be together, but there are times when they need to be apart. When each one meditates in solitude before God, nothing will bring the couple closer to intimacy with each other.

God wants you alone sometimes because He wants your absolute, undivided attention. For example, suppose your spouse was always with four or five people twenty-four hours a day. It wouldn't take very long before you would grow rather annoyed at that problem. So, too, God wants you to have a private time with Him, free from the competition of others. He loves just plain, simple, exciting you. He wants you all to Himself to put His loving, divine arms around you.

God doesn't hug two people at a time; He hugs us one at a time. He loves us one at a time, but unless we are willing to get alone with Him, our minds will always be divided. Private meditation allows the Lord Jesus Christ to have each of us all to Himself. His private workings are often His most precious.

Silence

Oftentimes God wants us to sit before Him in quietness. He doesn't want us to do all the talking. As Isaiah 30:15 says: "In quietness and confidence shall be your strength."

For some people, meditation is best described as a one-way conversation. They have no real relationship with God because they do all the talking. To have God speak to the heart is a majestic experience, an experience these people may miss if they monopolize the conversation and never pause to hear God's responses.

If we quiet ourselves before Him, God can interject His thoughts into our thinking. If we are silent for a few moments, He may bring a favorite passage of Scripture to mind, He may reveal an absorbing truth, or He may bring peace to our inner beings—or He may do all three. We should sit before Him in silence and allow Him to pour Himself into us.

Silence and seclusion before God allow Him to speak to our hearts clearly, positively, and unmistakably. Though God may not speak to us audibly, He will move in our spirits and impress our minds. We will know God has spoken to us. God saved us to glorify Him, and He developed a relationship with us so that we can love and understand who He is.

Self-Control

When we meditate, we may feel as if nothing is happening outwardly. Just because we can't detect God's functioning overtly doesn't mean that God is not at work. Just as Paul had to learn to keep his body under control (1 Cor. 9:27), every believer should consider self-control a necessary discipline.

As we begin to meditate, we may have to labor mentally a bit to focus our attention on God. If that sometimes is a problem, we can turn to a psalm and say, "Lord, I have a hard time keeping my mind on the subject at hand. I want to get immersed in this psalm and get my attention on You."

In a few moments you can stop reading and begin to think just about Him. As you do, become lost in His grandeur. There can be nothing better, more productive, or more rewarding in your life than to become lost in great thoughts about a great God.

Proverbs 8:34 exclaims, "Blessed is the man who listens to me, Watching daily at my gates, Waiting at the posts of my doors" (NKJV). Notice the word *daily*; that means the believer must take deliberate steps each day to bring his mind, body, and life under control so that he can spend time waiting and listening for God to speak.

Some people feel that certain body postures can aid in the practice of meditation. Others prefer to sit quietly with the palms of their hands raised upward to the heavens to receive gifts from above. Still others opt to kneel or even lie prostrate on the floor. I would encourage each individual to discover the posture he is most comfortable with, keeping in mind that God is, above all else, interested in the position of our hearts, not our bodies.

Submission

James wrote: "Humble yourselves in the sight of the Lord, and He will lift you up" (James 4:10 NKJV). If we are rebellious in our hearts and insist on having our own way, we won't meditate. Rebellion is the antithesis of submission, and if we are to hear Him adequately, our minds and hearts must be totally surrendered to Him. Yieldedness is vital in listening to what He has to say.

When we refuse to deal with the problem God has pinpointed, we don't lose our standing with Him. We are still saved, our relationship is the same, but our enjoyment of His fellowship is broken. Do you suppose it is possible that the primary reason we don't spend more time alone with God is we don't want to face the certain type of music He keeps sending our way? It is a song, which says, "Give up. Surrender. Yield. Let Me love you to the maximum of My potential, so that you will reach the maximum of your potential."

Now let's discover the rewards of spending time alone with God, thinking about Him, adoring Him, and praising Him.

A NEW PERSPECTIVE

When we meditate upon the Lord, we see things from a different perspective. The things that worry us lose their grip. The things that weaken us, God turns into strength. Our viewpoint of others and ourselves, of our tasks and our problems, even of our enemies, changes because we see them from God's viewpoint. Our inward look at problems or situations is replaced by a heavenly view, because we learn that we are seated in the heavenly places in Christ Jesus. Meditation brings us to a position in which we can see ourselves in the light of God's truth.

David declared in Psalm 36:9, "In Your light we see light." There is something about having God shed His enlightenment on a subject that causes us to see clearly His truth. Paul prayed that the Ephesians might be given a "spirit of wisdom and revelation in the knowledge of Him" so that "the eyes of your understanding [may be] enlightened" (Eph. 1:17–18 NKJV). We cannot rightly see ourselves or God without His revealing participation.

The pressures in our lives begin to dissipate when we are secluded, silent, and still before the Lord. God pulls the plug in the pressure tanks of our lives, and our anxieties begin to drain. When we first begin to meditate, our frustration levels are usually at full, but the longer we sit focusing upon Him, the emptier the reservoirs of tension become. Biblical meditation causes something to happen to our spirits, in our souls and our emotional beings, even in our human bodies. Our physical tiredness is somehow lessened. Isn't it strange that we will sit down to watch television for three to four hours a night, just to get relaxed, when the Divine Relaxer can do it in a few minutes? Focusing attention on God can help believers go to sleep, peaceful and relaxed, despite the difficulties of the day.

Peace

Jesus said, "My peace I give to you" (John 14:27). Christ who lives within us comes to the forefront of our lives. He becomes the all in all.

A Positive Attitude

As God substitutes peace for pressure, a positive attitude replaces a negative one. We can't wait to get up the next morning to see what God is going to do in our lives. When we spend time with God, our old selfish selves move out of the way and let the radiant Christ within us blossom and grow.

Personal Intimacy

When we sit before the Lord, it's like the experience we had when we met that special person for the first time. As we talked and shared our hearts, our joys, and our hurts, we grew intimately interested in each other.

As time passed, we realized that we could live with that person for the rest of our lives. It's the same with God. He never wants us to think of Him as distant or detached. Through the Holy Spirit, God lives intimately with each of us. He is embedded within the deepest core of our lives, and He desires fellowship with us so that He can pour His life into us. But, He can't do that if we fail to spend time meditating upon Him and learning who He is.

Purification

As an expression of His love and devotion to us, God will often put His finger on areas of our lives that are conspicuously wrong. Because He loves us, He wants to cleanse us so that we might be filled with His life and joy.

That is when we either run away or develop our relationship with Him. When we are willing to sit before Him and let Him expose our hearts, something happens. He prunes from our lives what isn't clean. However, if we rationalize our problems when He points them out, we will spend less and less time meditating, because we won't want to face God in that area of our lives.

If we don't want to be alone with God, it may be because He is dealing with particular points in our lives that we simply don't want exposed. We will not let Him love us.

When two people who live together intimately have something wrong in their relationship, they don't really have to tell each other. Both of them know it. When we are quiet before the Lord, and He wants to do something in our lives and things are not right, we stymie our growth by not yielding to Him. We work against the very God who is on our side, working for us, encouraging us, and building us up. So whatever He brings to mind, the best thing is to admit it, confess it, repent of it, and deal with it. That is the only way to keep the sweet fellowship of meditation.

Ongoing personal purification was one of the chief attributes that made David a man after God's own heart. We all know that he was far from perfect. His record as a murderer and adulterer would eliminate him from any pulpit in America, yet Jesus referred to Himself as the "Offspring of David" (Rev. 22:16 NKJV). How could David commit such gross iniquity and still obtain such divine affirmation?

I believe it was because David was zealous to confess and repent whenever God pinpointed David's sin and confronted him with it. Psalm 51 has been the soulful prayer of many a believer who has willfully or blindly offended God, as David's remorse was laid open before God.

When he wrongfully numbered the children of Israel in a census, he quickly admitted his wrongdoing. "And David's heart condemned him after he had numbered the people. So David said to the LORD, 'I have sinned greatly in what I have done; but now, I pray, O LORD, take away the iniquity of Your servant, for I have done very foolishly'" (2 Sam. 24:10 NKJV). Rather than run from God's searching, probing light, David humbled himself before the Lord, confessing his transgressions and asking God to cleanse him.

A Passion for Obedience

As we kneel before God and He pours Himself into us, we in turn give ourselves in devotion to Him. The result is that God places within us a passion for obedience. We want to obey God. Nobody has to prod us. We don't have to hear sermons to make us obey Him. Obedience is now part of our inner beings.

We can be tired, weary, and emotionally distraught, but after spending time alone with God, we find that He injects into our bodies energy, power, and strength. God's spiritual dynamics are at work in our inner beings, refreshing and energizing our minds and spirits. There is nothing to match meditation in its impact upon our lives and the lives of others.

An unschooled man who knows how to meditate upon the Lord has learned far more than the man with the highest education who does not know how to meditate. Education not backed with meditation is doomed for failure. When we make time alone with Christ a priority of our lives, it affects and influences every single facet of our lives. Of all the things Christ wants for us, loving Him and focusing our attention on Him are the most important. Then we can follow Him and receive all He has prepared for us.

I am always moved when I read one special verse in the fourth chapter of Acts. Let me describe the situation leading up to it. Filled with the newly discovered power of the Holy Spirit, Peter and John had been ministering powerfully. Thousands had been saved and great numbers added to the fledgling group of Christians.

Peter and John were arrested by the Sadducees and brought before Annas the high priest, Caiaphas, John, and Alexander, all of high-priestly descent. They placed Peter and John squarely in the center of their contemporaries and asked about the nature of the disciples' work.

Picture it for a minute, won't you? Peter and John, two large, cedar-rough fishermen with a minimum amount of education, stood before a room full of highly educated, influential, skilled, religious rulers.

The outcome of the confrontation is electrifying. Immediately, Peter took the offensive, pushing the Sadducees into the proverbial corner. He attacked with power and persuasiveness. His hearers were startled. Luke recorded their amazement in the potent language of Acts 4:13: "Now when they saw the boldness of Peter and John, and perceived that they were uneducated and untrained men, they marveled. And they realized that they had been with Jesus" (NKJV).

Though the rulers referred to the two men's association with Jesus, the principle holds true for us today. The amount of time we spend with Jesus—meditating on His Word and His majesty, seeking His face—establishes our fruitfulness in the kingdom. Meditation is simply a matter of spending our time in rich fellowship with our personal Lord and Savior. Do people recognize us as "having been with Jesus"?

PART THREE

GOD FREES YOU FROM FEAR AND ANXIETY

NINE

WHY WE LOSE OUR PEACE

There is only one way to experience an abiding peace that transcends circumstances. The answer is "by faith." By faith we ask and then trust God to be present in our lives. It is as though we have put a sum of money in the bank, and by faith we write checks because we know that there are funds already deposited to cover our withdrawals. We have asked God to accept and forgive us and to be present in our lives with His abiding peace, and then we go out and live expecting Him to do the very thing we trust Him to do.

So the foundation for living in God's peace is faith—an active, confident trust in His presence and power to sustain and comfort you—which frees you from fear and anxiety no matter what the circumstance you face. There are, however, certain issues that can rob us of our peace. Let me mention a few of them.

SUDDEN FEAR

Here's a sweet story told to me by a woman who learned this truth the hard way:

When she was a child, her mother had prepared her for the first day of kindergarten. Her mother had taken her to the school and shown her the classroom. She had introduced her to her teacher. She had walked her to the bus stop where the bus would pick her up and drop her off in the afternoon.

My friend said, "On the first day of school, my mother said to me before she walked me to the bus stop, 'Remember, Jesus is right there with you all day. He knows right where you are.' And then she added, almost as an afterthought, 'He knows where you need to be, and He will help you get there.'"

"Well," my friend said, "when the school bus pulled up to the school, it drove right past the kindergarten rooms. I could see my classroom, and as soon as I got off the bus, I headed toward it. I didn't get more than a few steps before a teacher stopped me. She said, 'You can't go that way.'

"I said, 'But I can see my room.' The teacher said, 'No, you have to go this way to get there.' She pointed in the opposite direction from the classroom to a fairly large group of students who were walking together. She nudged me toward them.

"I had no idea where I was. Mom hadn't shown me that part of the school. I was just a little girl in a very big group of children walking down one hallway and then the next. I was scared. I kept saying to myself, 'Jesus is right here with me. Jesus knows where I am. He knows where I need to be, and He's going to help me get there.' I kept saying those sentences over and over as I kept walking.

"Along the way groups of students left the main hallway and went to various classrooms. I was more and more confused, but I kept walking with the main group of students. Finally there were only a few of us still walking together. The others were third graders, and when they turned away from the main hallway to go to their rooms, I found myself walking alone, still saying to myself, 'Jesus is right here with me. Jesus knows where I am. He knows where I need to be, and He's going to help me get there.'

"I looked up . . . and there was my room and my teacher! I was never so relieved in all my life!

"The next day, I had a little more confidence. I knew Jesus was with me and He knew where I was, and He would help me get to my room. I had peace. By the end of the first week, I had the routine learned!"

And then my friend said these words I'll never forget: "People all my life have asked me why I seem to be so confident, even in situations I've never experienced before, including some scary and troubling times. I think it goes back to that first day of school. Mom told me that Jesus was right there with me. She told me Jesus knew where I was, knew where I was supposed to be, and that Jesus would help me. I didn't doubt her. I believed in the truth of God's presence with me, and I never stopped believing.

"I've walked down the hallways of life with peace and confidence ever since. I may feel a little lost at times. I may not know all I should know. But I know that I'm connected to the Way and the Truth, and He'll get me to where He knows I'm supposed to be."

There's the truth in a nutshell. She kept remembering her mother's words and trusted that Jesus was there to help her and give her peace—in spite of the fear she felt so strongly as she sought to navigate in a big, strange place.

Some people are so accustomed to responding to every little dip and rise of life with fear and small doses of panic that they can't even imagine there's another way to respond. They are so upset by change of all types that it never even dawns on them that they can live with greater emotional stability.

Say no to fear. Instead, practice a life of trust. Every day begin with the affirmation, "I trust You, Jesus. I count on Your peace and presence today."

THE ENEMY

We can be attacked by our enemy, the devil, who may use various means to cause us to doubt and lose faith in our God. He often does this by priming the pump of doubt with questions—for example, "If God is with you, then why has this happened?" On occasions like this, you have to stand up to the devil, the one who is the ultimate source of any fear that paralyzes you or any anxiety that lingers and hinders you.

I sometimes speak out loud to the devil, the evil power that seeks to thwart the plan of God in our lives. I tell him forthrightly, "Devil, you will not have my peace. I refuse to live in fear and worry. I will trust God." In the Scriptures, we are urged to resist the devil, and when we do, he must flee from us (James 4:7). So, at moments of fear and anxiousness, resist him in the name of Jesus!

SIN

It is very important for us to repent of any sin that may become an obstacle to our receiving and enjoying the peace of God. Check your own heart for any sin that may be resident—anything that counteracts God's peace. Sin always creates such an obstacle.

A person can pray repeatedly for God's peace and believe in his heart for God's peace. He can remind himself of the promises of God and quote them too. But if that person continues to harbor sin in his life and willfully chooses to continue to rebel against God, he will not experience true peace. Even what seems to be a simple matter, like not forgiving someone who offended you, can create havoc in your spirit. The convicting power of the Holy Spirit will continue to compel you to face up to what you know is a sin before God. And until you do so, you will have a restlessness and anxiety deep within. The more a person asks God for peace, the more that inner turmoil is likely to increase.

Peace and rebellion cannot coexist!

The only recourse is to confess the rebellion to God, surrender that area of life to Him, and ask Him for help in turning away from that sin and resisting all temptation to return to it. Then God's peace can flow in your life again.

GIVING UP PEACE

So often in times of crisis we lay down our peace. Yes, we actually give it over to someone else. I had what for me was a very traumatic incident some time ago. I remember the incident well. As I came to my car, it was evident that someone had broken into it, and my briefcase was missing. "No! No! No!" The words came out of my mouth almost involuntarily. I could hardly believe what I was seeing—the front seat was empty and one of my most precious possessions was gone.

My briefcase contained my Greek New Testament, which I felt fairly certain the robber could not read, and a couple of other books and papers that were probably insignificant to the thief. All those items were fairly easy to replace, and I felt very little pain over the loss. The briefcase itself was fairly old, so I didn't feel much pain over its loss either, but what pained me was this: In my briefcase was my favorite Bible. It was the one I had preached from for years. I had marked various notes and dates throughout the Bible. It was something of a biographical sketch of the way the Lord had spoken to me through the years. I felt as if a major "record" of my life had been taken.

And that wasn't all. The Bible had been a gift from my mother.

For about three months, I felt as if I had lost my best friend. I wasn't angry as much as I felt grieved. Someone had intruded into my life—including my spiritual life—and had taken something very valuable to me. In moments like this—moments of loss, of unwarranted accusation against your character, or of personal rejection—it is so easy to fall into the trap of losing your peace.

On a number of occasions through the years when I have felt troubled, anxious, or frustrated, I blamed other people for "stealing" my peace. I was wrong. The truth is, nobody else should ever have been blamed for my loss of peace. In each and every case, I was the one who laid it down.

Hear me very carefully on this point. Nobody can take your peace from you. If you have lost your peace, you have lost it for one main reason: you have surrendered it.

Time and again I hear people say that they are distressed or troubled in spirit by something that happened or something that was said or done against them. I hear variations of "if only she," "if only he," and "if only circumstances had been different" statements. Again, the truth is that no circumstance, situation, person, or organization can steal your inner peace.

We lose our peace because we lay it down. We give it up. We concede it. We abandon it.

LOSING FOCUS

We can allow the myriad of bad-news situations we hear and read about every day to cause us to lose our correct focus. Instead of having our minds set on God and trusting Him for His peace and presence, we allow our thoughts to get sidetracked and galvanized by the negative news and circumstances we see and hear.

Just think about how the COVID-19 pandemic has caused life to change throughout the world. As I write this in the fall of 2020, long lockdowns and social distancing rules have caused us to reinvent a great deal of how we conduct our lives, families, churches, and businesses. Along with social and political unrest, the fluctuating economy, wildfires, hurricanes, earthquakes, and all the other news bombarding us on a daily basis, we can become completely overwhelmed, restless, discouraged, and confused.

Even so, coping with an ever-changing news cycle seems to have become part of our daily lives—producing a deep sense of foreboding and fearful anticipation that hangs over us and continually steals our focus. Although it is both wise and godly to be diligently watchful and take reasonable measures when such events occur, it is neither necessary nor Christ-honoring to become obsessed. And what I have observed during such times of worldwide adversity is that many are in danger of becoming consumed by circumstances they can do absolutely nothing about—the health, weather conditions, economies, and movements of whole nations that are beyond any one person or group of people to influence.

And it isn't always major events that devour our attention. Bad news may be far more personal or private but just as threatening to us. We may hear bad news from a physician about our health or the health of a loved one. We may hear bad news about a couple that has separated or divorced, about a child who has run away, about a job that has been lost, or a financial enterprise that has filed for bankruptcy. When we see and hear of such terrible news, it is so easy for us to become focused on the negative, to become paralyzed by fear, and sometimes to project that some of these negative possibilities could happen to us so we, too, may become victims. Let me suggest some questions for you to consider if you feel your peace is slipping away or you have become focused on the negative aspects of life.

Question #1: Have You Stopped Thanking and Praising God?

People who lay down their peace often have stopped praying with thanksgiving and praise. Followers of Jesus need a vibrant prayer life. As the gospel song says, they need to "stay in touch with God." They must avoid talking with God only about what they think they need, and regularly live with a thankful heart—giving thanks always in all circumstances for all things. There is a direct correlation between the degree people pray with faith, praise, and thanksgiving, and their confidence in prayer, their assurance that God hears and answers their cries to Him.

Question #2: Are You Limiting God by the Way You Think?

Imagine a circumstance that you consider to be bad. Use whatever descriptive words you want to use—hard, difficult, agonizing, strenuous, debilitating, horrific, sorrowful, perturbing, penetrating, or painful. Is there a problem too awful or too hard for God to handle?

If your answer to this question is anything other than "no," your understanding of God is too limited or small. The well-known devotional writer Oswald Chambers wrote, "When it begins to dawn on my conscious life what God's purpose is, there is the laughter of the possibility of the impossible. The impossible is exactly what God does."[2] He had it right. With God the impossible is possible, so there is nothing too big for our God. We do not want to be charged with having a God that's too small, do we?

Our God is a great and limitless God. He dwells in eternity and operates in infinity. He has all things within His understanding and all things under His control.

Question #3: Are You Dwelling on Negatives?

Most people who lay down their peace later admit they had begun dwelling on the negative aspects of life. Rather they should have harnessed their minds to dwell on and appreciate the positive, good things of life.

The temptation to dwell on the negative aspects of life is profound. I mentioned earlier how debilitating this can be to the life of our souls. Interestingly, this tendency to negatively focus often begins in our homes and institutions: fathers criticizing their children with little or no praise to balance their assessment, supervisors telling their employees what they are doing wrong far more than telling them what they are doing right—and the same is true for teachers, doctors, lawyers, and accountants. Much of the information these profession-als give us tends to deal with errors, negative situations, breaches of law, and numbers that cannot be reconciled.

It is not uncommon for a person to go through an entire day and not hear one encouraging statement from another human being.

If you feed your heart and mind a continual diet of negativity, your faith will begin to erode. If you do the same with those with whom you live and work, they, too, will become negative, self-deprecating, and critical of them-selves and others. This is what you and they will be thinking and saying:

"What's the use?"

"Why try?"

"Nothing goes my way."

"The world is going to pieces."

"Nothing is secure or safe anymore."

"People are just out to get me."

The more a person thinks along any of these lines, the more depressed, distressed, and oppressed that person is likely to feel!

Question #4: Are You Allowing Negative Emotions to Linger in Your Heart?

There are times when we are hit from the blind side by an accident, trag-edy, sickness, or undesirable situation. There are also the internal impulses and desires that can cause us twinges of inner anguish or need. There are times when we suddenly find ourselves in a difficult situation that we had not antici-pated. There are moments when we hear or see devastating news that causes us momentarily to feel as if the rug has been pulled out from under our feet.

Anxiety occurs. Panic erupts. Fear strikes.

When those moments occur, we can do one of two things. We can either open the door and invite those negative, unproductive emotions to settle into our hearts, or we can take action immediately to regain our peace and confidence!

Now, anxiety, panic, and fear are normal human responses to a sudden accident, tragedy, crisis, a deeply unsettling situation, or bad news. These responses are nearly instinctual. They are "automatic." There is no fault in feeling these emotions. They are part of God's built-in warning system to us so we might take action to seek protection or preservation of life. They are something of a fight-or-flee reaction to what we perceive to be threatening. Every person feels moments of anxiety, panic, or fear at times.

The error comes when we accept these emotions, whether with open arms or begrudgingly, and allow them to linger and gradually find a resting place in our hearts. If we do that, these emotions become chronic or long-lasting. They become our "state of being," not just a temporary response. They become our prevailing attitude and mind-set. Rather than allowing negative "stuff" to capture our hearts, we need to do what Jesus did and taught.

Question #5: Are You Forgetting Jesus' Example?

I find it fascinating that Jesus, our Master, was a realist. Jesus never called those who followed Him to live in denial or to live with their heads in the sand. To the contrary, throughout the Gospels Jesus confronted problems. He acknowledged the fierce temptations of the devil and the controlling power of sin at work in the world. He didn't take His disciples off to a monastery in a remote place to escape the world. No! He called His disciples to be "in the world" and yet not "of the world"—in other words, not to be ruled by the world's evil systems or governed by human tendencies.

Jesus knew He and His disciples were living in a troublesome time. He called them to face trouble head-on, but He called them to do it by following His example. So He told them not to keep worrying about tomorrow—whether they would have clothes to wear or sufficient food to eat. He reminded His followers that their heavenly Father looked after the sparrows and clothed the "lilies of the field" and He would, no doubt, do the same for them!

The assurance of Jesus is that because God is with us, we do not have to give in to, sink beneath, or become defeated by troubles. We can face them, confront them, challenge them, deal with them, and in the end overcome them! What consolation this should bring to our hearts.

Jesus taught His followers that all troubles are passing in nature. Sickness and trouble are for a season and for a reason. Storms arose and prevailed—both in the natural on the Sea of Galilee and in the supernatural lives of those possessed and oppressed by the devil—for a season and a reason. Jesus' very life was for a season and a reason. Even His death and burial in a tomb were only for a season and a reason!

The passing nature of troubles is something Jesus calls us to recognize. His challenge is to endure, to persevere, to learn, to grow, and to overcome. I use the little phrase "for a season and a reason" because I think it explains accurately the issue. Jesus knew that God permits things to happen in our lives only for a certain period of time and for a particular reason.

I believe an even more accurate way of translating His "Let not your heart be troubled" would be "Don't let your heart be troubled any longer." And why should we be troubled and lose our peace if we remember our Lord's example of living confidently, knowing that His Father was watching, directing, caring for, and loving Him and His followers on a daily basis? God will do the same for us.

TEN

OVERCOMING FEAR

Many people think the opposite of fear is hope, or courage, or strength. The true opposite of fear is faith. And when fear causes paralysis, it not only quenches one's peace but it attacks the foundation of that peace—namely, our faith. Peace goes out the window when fear is present. In many polls taken since the beginning of the COVID-19 pandemic, evidence shows that large segments of our population are living in fear—fear of leaving home, of traveling, of impending doom, of strangers, etc. The other side of the coin is, of course, the majority of these fearful people are not experiencing peace—the calmness of soul, the elimination of anxieties, and the serenity necessary to conduct one's normal affairs in a steady, fear-free manner.

Much of fear is rooted in doubt that God will be present, provide justice or help, or be capable of dealing with the crisis at hand. Faith says, "Yes, God is here. Yes, God will provide. Yes, God is capable of all things!"

Much of fear is rooted in threats—sometimes threatening words, sometimes threatening behavior. Faith says, "I will not be traumatized by threats. I will act wisely, not fearfully. I believe God will prevent whatever the threat is from ever coming to pass. And if the threat does come to pass, I believe God will help me deal with whatever is thrown at me."

When Saul, king of Israel, realized that God had taken His hand of anointing and blessing from him because of his arrogance and disobedience, and had placed it upon the young man David, he was furious. He began a campaign to find David and kill him—to remove this threat from his life. On the other hand, David felt threatened by Saul's army and on several occasions feared for his life, but the Scriptures tell us that David was strengthened by God's promises to protect him and one day make him king of Israel.

In our modern world we often read of people who, in spite of intimidation by disease, accident, or danger, pressed ahead to uncertain outcomes—rejection, defeat, and, yes, sometimes victory. Arctic explorers, Olympic athletes, missionaries, venture capitalists, and philanthropists come to mind. So threats do not have to stymie and cripple us.

Some years ago, I felt threatened by the potential backlash that could occur when I announced that my wife was seeking a divorce. In many churches, for the pastor's marriage to be in trouble is tantamount to his being identified as a moral failure. I had great inner concerns when the announcement was made.

When I told the board of my church, they responded by saying, in essence, "You've been here for us during difficult times. Now we're going to be here for you during this difficult time. You've been here for us when we needed you, and now we're going to be here for you because you need us."

I felt great encouragement when various board members told me that they knew the kind of man I am. They knew my character and my devotion to the Lord. They knew that I lived what I preached to the best of my ability. They would stand with me regardless of what eventually happened.

Our challenge in times of threat is not to focus on what might become a reality, but rather, to focus on what we can count on being true!

Many people are living under a dark cloud of threat today. Some are experiencing the threat of disease, some are facing the threats of injury to their children, and some are hearing threats related to the loss of their job.

The answer to all these types of threat is faith in what we know to be true about God and about His love and care for us and His ability to provide for all we need—especially His peace, which can help carry us through anything.

THE NATURE OF OUR FEARS

Once when I was about fifteen, I was down at a creek by myself. There was a big rock there that we used to dive off of, and for some reason that day I decided that I'd dive off and then stand on my head in the water. I dived, got myself perfectly balanced in a headstand underwater, and then I couldn't seem to get myself unbalanced. The current kept me in an upright position, my head at the bottom of the creek bed, no matter which way I moved. I panicked, thinking, I'm going to drown! Somehow I had the sense to push up and tumble forward and, as quickly as possible, get my head out of the water so I could breathe.

That kind of fear is a normal, natural, instinctual fear associated with physical survival.

Identify your fears. What do you fear most?

Death? Being alone? Old age?

Do you fear being rejected or criticized, or losing someone you love?

Do you fear poor health or perhaps the possibility of developing a particular disease?

Do you fear a tragedy involving a child or spouse?

Fear can sometimes lurk in our hearts in such a subtle way that we don't even identify the feeling we have as fear. It may be that we have a sense of foreboding, an uneasiness, or a feeling of dread.

Let's take a look at several of the biggest and most common fears we all face.

Fear of Sin's Consequences

Fear is a normal and universal response to our knowing we have sinned and become separated from God. Fear of this type is the first emotion we find in the Bible. In the third chapter of Genesis we read that Adam and Eve heard God walking in the garden in the cool of the day, and they hid themselves from God's presence. God called to them, and Adam replied, "I heard Your voice in the garden, and I was afraid because I was naked; and I hid myself" (Gen. 3:10 NKJV).

A recognition of our own sin always makes us feel exposed and vulnerable to God's judgment. There is a fear of being "found out" and chastised.

God actually built the emotion of fear into our human nature so that we might flee danger. His intent was that Adam and Eve flee from the presence of Satan, the serpent who came with temptations in the Garden of Eden. That is the rightful purpose and function of fear—to cause us to turn and walk away from the devil's temptations any and every time they come.

Fear of Danger and Harm

Since the fall of man in the garden of Eden, fear was not only to be the emotion a person felt in the presence of Satan, but also the first emotion a person felt in the presence of anything associated with death, destruction, or danger. It is the first emotion we are to feel in the presence of evil of any kind, from any source. In our fear we are to take precautions or adopt a defensive posture in anticipation of an assault or, if possible, flee the scene—commonly known as the fight-or-flight reaction.

So we have a number of natural, normal fears—such as the fear of falling, the fear associated with coming in contact with a burning stove, or the fear of crossing a busy freeway at rush hour. These are fears that help protect us and preserve life. They turn us away from harm and pain and help us avoid injury, not only physically but emotionally and spiritually.

I have a very healthy fear of snakes. I've had that fear since I was in my twenties. I was walking one day with a member of the church where I was the pastor, and suddenly he said, "Stop. Don't take another step." It was early in the morning, and the shadows were crossing the path we were walking. I looked ahead, and there in the shadows I saw what he had already seen. A rattlesnake was coiled as if preparing to strike.

I stood absolutely still, too frightened to even blink or speak in reply, until that snake uncoiled itself and slithered off to the side of the path.

Was that a normal response? Yes, it was. Has that fear of snakes contributed to my being alive today? Very likely. As much time as I have spent in wilderness areas in my life, my fear of snakes no doubt has kept me from harm on a number of occasions. I give snakes plenty of opportunity to get out of my way!

Normal and positive fears are not only related to natural phenomena or creatures. They are also related to internal human attitudes. For example, it should be the norm for a person to fear taking a hallucinogenic drug, to the point where that person refuses to experiment or try that drug. It should be the norm for a young person to fear engaging in sex apart from marriage, not only because of the danger of unwanted pregnancy or contracting a sexually transmitted disease, but also because of the emotional danger of finding oneself feeling rejected, lonely, ashamed, and guilty for disobeying God's commandments. It should be the norm for a person to fear getting into a car that is about to be driven by a person who has been drinking alcohol. It should be the norm for a person to fear the consequences that may come from committing a crime. Fear can be an agent of protection for our physical lives and the well-being of our souls.

God never intended, however, that we be afraid of Him or afraid of our future in Him. When we read in the Bible about having a "fear" of the Lord, that term fear actually refers to great reverence, honor, or awe. It is an awe rooted in our awareness that God governs all things and is absolutely righteous in all His judgments. An awesome awareness and reverence of the glory of God produce humility and obedience.

God also never intended that we live in fear that keeps us from seeking a deeper relationship with Him or that keeps us from going about normal daily life or fulfilling the responsibilities we have to others. The apostle Paul wrote to Timothy, his coworker in the ministry, saying, "God has not given us a spirit of fear, but of power and of love and of a sound mind" (2 Tim. 1:7 NKJV).

Any fear that keeps you from being a witness for the gospel, makes you cower in weakness before other people, keeps you from reaching out in love to those in need, or keeps you from behaving in a rational manner is not a normal fear God intends for you to have!

Fear of Evil

Spiritual dangers are just as real as physical dangers. It is good for a person to be fearful in evil situations.

Many years ago, I traveled with a group of seventeen people from my church in Ohio to do missions work for two weeks in Haiti. While in Haiti we watched a man performing a dance. As he danced and whirled his machete in our direction, I suddenly felt a horrible presence of evil all around us. Momentarily, I was filled with fear for my physical safety and the safety of the people with me. My immediate response to this fear was anger, and out of that anger I began to pray and intercede for our safety.

This fear was rooted in the spirit realm. It was a fear I've come to recognize as a fear that any Christian should feel in the face of pure evil.

Why do I say it is a good thing to feel fear of evil? Because that fear can and should drive you to pray, to trust God to deliver you from the power of evil, and to get as far away from evil as possible!

Fear of Disobeying God

It is also good to have a fear of disobeying God. That fear can and should compel a person to obey!

One of the times I was most afraid in my life was the time I was first elected president of the Southern Baptist Convention. I felt very inadequate, and I really didn't want the position. It was a time of much division and heartache among the fifteen million or so Southern Baptists, and although some of the leaders of the convention wanted me to run for the office, I told God and these men and women that I did not want to.

The night before the nominations, I was in a meeting with a group of preachers and one missionary woman. This woman boldly said to me, "Charles Stanley, get on your knees and repent. You are God's choice to be president. Get on your knees and repent!" I fell to my knees immediately! I prayed, but I still resisted in my heart.

I told God repeatedly that there were men who were much more qualified for the job. I told Him that there were men better suited in temperament for the position. I reminded the Lord about how much animosity other people in the denomination were feeling toward me. I asked Him to call somebody else.

The morning of the nominations, I awoke with a firm decision in my heart that I wasn't going to allow my name to be put into nomination for the presidency. As I prepared to leave the hotel room, I reached out to put my hand on the doorknob, and God spoke to my heart, *Don't put your hand on that doorknob until you are willing to do what I tell you to do.* I fell to my knees at the end of the bed, sobbing. I knew I had to do this, or I would be in disobedience. I told the Lord once again that I really didn't want to do this, but at the same time, I knew I had to agree to be nominated. I remember thinking, *Maybe the Lord just wants to humble me, and that will be the end of it.*

I went over to the place where a number of pastors and other church leaders were in a prayer meeting. I said to a friend of mine, "I think you ought to do this." He said, "I'm not going to do it." The Lord spoke in my heart, *Tell them*, and I heard myself saying, "I'll do it." Immediately, I became gripped with overwhelming fear. I felt as if I were falling off a mountaintop, headed for a crash on the rocks far below. Other people in the room, however, began to pray with great rejoicing. I finally concluded, "Okay, Lord, I'm doing what I believe You have told me to do." And in coming to that conclusion and affirmation, fear left.

After the votes were counted, amazingly to me, I won the election.

No sooner was I elected than a group of men set out to destroy my reputation and keep me from being an effective leader. That didn't bother me. I wasn't afraid of that. Once the issue was settled, it was settled for me. I put all my efforts into being the best president I knew how to be, with God's guidance and strength.

I learned in that experience that faith in God is always more powerful than fear. I also learned that an ongoing trust in God can keep fear from becoming a dictating, domineering emotion.

Real or Shadow Fears?

The fears I have described above are normal, and in many ways helpful. They are real fears.

Shadow fears, however, are those that are not real. They reside only in our imaginations or our minds. If they persist or grow, they can result in a person's developing a "spirit of fear."

A spirit of fear enslaves a person's mind and heart. The person who has a spirit of fear—which may be anything from a serious phobia to a paralyzing or crippling fear that keeps that person from functioning normally in relationships with other people—is a person who becomes a slave to fear. Such a person won't go certain places, engage in certain activities, or speak out in certain situations because he or she fears great loss, injury, persecution, or retribution.

The first goal many of us have when dealing with fear is determining if the fear we feel is legitimate or if it is a shadow fear.

Researchers who have studied fear have concluded that there is virtually no difference in our physiological reaction to these two types of fear. The physiological response of a person who comes into contact with a live bear is almost identical to the physiological response of a person who sees dimly in the shadows a person who is dressed up to look like a bear.

The same holds true for fears rooted in our emotions. Fears related to our feelings of self-worth or self-esteem are especially damaging. For example, the person who fears rejection tends to respond to other people out of that fear whether or not the fear is justified. And the results or consequences are the same, whether or not the assessment is valid!

Some shadow fears come from bad teaching. Fears about whether one will get to heaven often develop because people have been taught incorrectly about God's power to forgive or about God's gift of eternal life. Fears about God often materialize when people have been taught the wrong things about the true nature of God.

Other shadow fears arise because of prejudices or from the bad influence of parents when we were young children.

Fear—like anxiety—can be slavish, crippling, and paralyzing. It

- clouds the mind—stifles thinking and snuffs out creativity.
- causes tension in the body, which often leads to temporary emotional paralysis or a failure to act.
- weakens our confidence and boldness, especially in declaring the goodness of God or the good news about Jesus Christ as Savior.
- keeps us from praying, and especially from praying boldly and with faith.
- keeps us from reaching the full potential that God has for us in every area of our lives.

A fear that constricts or limits us does not fit who we are to be as sons and daughters of the almighty God.

The key questions we must ask in determining whether a fear is normal, real, and helpful or if it is debilitating, enslaving, and paralyzing are these: What does God say about this fear? Does He say that this is something I should fear? Or does He say that He is sufficient in all ways to meet my needs so that I don't need to fear this thing, this relationship, this action, this possibility, or this situation?

SEVEN STEPS TO OVERCOMING FEAR

There are steps we can take to overcome fear.

1. Acknowledge the Fear You Experience

Acknowledge that you are fearful. Ask God to help you identify the fear—to name it, define it, and bring it to the surface of your conscience so you can talk about it and confess its presence to the Lord.

Don't deny that you feel fear. Don't think that you are too "mature" to be afraid. We never become so spiritually mature that we do not feel fear—either the natural and normal fear that helps in our preservation and protection, or spiritual attacks of fear. Fear can grip any of us.

David, who had experienced the power of God to protect him and preserve his life in numerous situations, still wrote:

> My heart is severely pained within me,
> And the terrors of death have fallen upon me.
> Fearfulness and trembling have come upon me,
> And horror has overwhelmed me.
> So I said, "Oh, that I had wings like a dove!
> I would fly away and be at rest.
> Indeed, I would wander far off,
> And remain in the wilderness."
>
> (Ps. 55:4–7 NKJV)

Don't just accept a fear in your life as something harmless. The reality is that fear keeps you from going some places God desires you to go. It can keep you from doing some things that God may desire you to do.

Acknowledge your fear. Face up to it.

2. Ask Immediately for God's Help

Go to your heavenly Father immediately to ask Him to help you conquer your fear. Ask the Lord to cleanse your mind of fearful thoughts. Ask Him to protect your mind from gripping fear. Ask Him to prepare you to counteract fear in positive, strong ways.

The psalmist wrote:

> I sought the LORD, and He heard me,
> And delivered me from all my fears.

(Ps. 34:4 NKJV)

3. Determine the Root Fear

Ask God to help you identify any emotions that may be linked to fear, such as:

greed: fear of not having enough

rejection: fear of not being accepted

guilt: fear of being found out

lack of confidence: fear of failure

anger: fear of not getting your own way, losing control or esteem

jealousy: fear of not having what you believe is rightfully yours

indecisiveness: fear of criticism, fear of making a wrong decision

A pastor I know told me about a woman who was very afraid of going outside after dark, even though she lives in what many would consider to be a very safe neighborhood. She is afraid even to go out to her car in the driveway or to turn off the sprinklers in the yard.

He asked her why she thought she had this fear. She didn't know. She said she had always been afraid of the dark. I could relate at that point. As a boy I was very afraid of being alone in the dark.

The pastor probed further, "But why do you think you are afraid of the dark?"

She said, "I guess because I think something bad could happen to me in the dark, and I wouldn't see it coming in time to protect myself."

"Do you think you are totally responsible for protecting yourself in the dark?" the pastor asked.

"I never really have thought about that," the woman said.

The pastor went on, "Do you think it is possible that God desires to protect you, His child, when you are alone in the dark?"

"Well, yes," she said, and a tear began to flow down her cheek.

The pastor said to me, "This woman came to realize that the fear beneath the obvious fear was a fear that God might not always be there for her. We went through about a dozen passages in the Bible that assure us of God's constant presence with those of us who have accepted Jesus as our Savior.

"She finally said, 'I'm not afraid of the dark! I'm afraid God is negligent! I've got to start seeing God as standing right by my side all the time, and especially in the dark.'"

The truth is, God is always by your side.

Your ability to see Him present with you, just inches away from you and walking with you stride by stride, may very well be the key to your walking in faith, not fear.

4. Go to God's Word

The Bible has dozens of "fear not" verses. I especially like Isaiah 41:9–13 as a passage of Scripture that confronts fear:

> You whom I have taken from the ends of the earth,
> And called from its farthest regions,
> And said to you,
> "You are My servant,
> I have chosen you and have not cast you away:
> Fear not, for I am with you;
> Be not dismayed, for I am your God.
> I will strengthen you,
> Yes, I will help you,
> I will uphold you with My righteous right hand."
>
> Behold, all those who were incensed against you
> Shall be ashamed and disgraced;
> They shall be as nothing,
> And those who strive with you shall perish.

You shall seek them and not find them—
Those who contended with you.
Those who war against you
Shall be as nothing,
As a nonexistent thing.
For I, the LORD your God, will hold your right hand,
Saying to you, "Fear not, I will help you." (NKJV)

Read that entire chapter aloud to yourself—in fact, read it repeatedly if you need to. Let the words sink deep into your spirit.

Read and memorize verses that deal with fear. Psalm 56 is a wonderful psalm for those who are fearful that their critics or enemies will destroy their work, reputation, influence, or property.

Be merciful to me, O God, for man would swallow me up;
Fighting all day he oppresses me.
My enemies would hound me all day,
For there are many who fight against me, O Most High.

Whenever I am afraid,
I will trust in You.
In God (I will praise His word),
In God I have put my trust;
I will not fear.
What can flesh do to me?

All day they twist my words;
All their thoughts are against me for evil.
They gather together,
They hide, they mark my steps,
When they lie in wait for my life.
Shall they escape by iniquity?
In anger cast down the peoples, O God!

You number my wanderings;
Put my tears into Your bottle;
Are they not in Your book?
When I cry out to You,
Then my enemies will turn back;
This I know, because God is for me.
In God (I will praise His word),
In the LORD (I will praise His word).
In God I have put my trust;
I will not be afraid.
What can man do to me?

Vows made to You are binding upon me, O God;
I will render praises to You,
For You have delivered my soul from death.
Have You not kept my feet from falling.
That I may walk before God
In the light of the living? (NKJV)

Psalm 91 is a tremendous psalm that addresses feelings of fear:

He who dwells in the secret place of the Most High
Shall abide under the shadow of the Almighty.
I will say of the LORD, "He is my refuge and my fortress;
My God, in Him I will trust."

Surely He shall deliver you from the snare of the fowler
And from the perilous pestilence.
He shall cover you with His feathers,
And under His wings you shall take refuge;
His truth shall be your shield and buckler.
You shall not be afraid of the terror by night,
Nor of the arrow that flies by day,

Nor of the pestilence that walks in darkness,
Nor of the destruction that lays waste at noonday.

A thousand may fall at your side,
And ten thousand at your right hand;
But it shall not come near you.
Only with your eyes shall you look,
And see the reward of the wicked.

Because you have made the LORD, who is my refuge,
Even the Most High, your dwelling place,
No evil shall befall you,
Nor shall any plague come near your dwelling;
For He shall give His angels charge over you,
To keep you in all your ways.
In their hands they shall bear you up,
Lest you dash your foot against a stone.
You shall tread upon the lion and the cobra,
The young lion and the serpent you shall trample underfoot.

"Because he has set his love upon Me, therefore I will deliver him;
I will set him on high, because he has known My name.
He shall call upon Me, and I will answer him;
I will be with him in trouble;
I will deliver him and honor him.
With long life I will satisfy him,
And show him My salvation." (NKJV)

Focus on passages in which various individuals in the Bible faced fear. Note the way God dealt with them and how He directed them. For example: Moses felt fear about returning to Egypt (Ex. 3). Esther felt fear in confronting Haman (Est. 3–5).

Memorize verses that speak to God's desire for you to walk in faith. Saturate your mind with passages that build up your faith.

5. Praise the Lord

As you read and speak God's Word, accompany the truth of God's Word with your vocal and frequent praise.

Here are three of my favorite passages to use in confronting fear:

> The LORD is my strength and song,
> And He has become my salvation.
>
> (Ps. 118:14)

> The voice of rejoicing and salvation
> Is in the tents of the righteous;
> The right hand of the LORD does valiantly.
> The right hand of the LORD is exalted;
> The right hand of the LORD does valiantly.
> I shall not die, but live,
> And declare the works of the LORD.
>
> (Ps. 118:15–17 NKJV)

> I will extol You, my God, O King;
> And I will bless Your name forever and ever.
> Every day I will bless You,
> And I will praise Your name forever and ever.
> Great is the LORD, and greatly to be praised;
> And His greatness is unsearchable.
>
> (Ps. 145:1–3 NKJV)

6. Take a Positive Step

Jesus often asked those He delivered or healed to take a positive action as part of their deliverance or healing. A paralyzed man, for example, was told to pick up his pallet and leave the pool of Bethesda. A blind man was told to go wash in the pool of Siloam.

I believe it is very important for a person to confront fear by taking a positive step in faith. Do something that gives you an experience in which God can reveal to you that He is greater than the fear you have felt.

I heard about a woman who had an irrational fear of walking on the grates in the sidewalks of San Francisco. She had a fear that one of them would collapse as she stepped on it and that she would go tumbling into the space below. She asked the Lord to deliver her from this fear, and in her spirit she felt the Lord speaking to her, "Go for a walk with Me." She went out on the street, knowing the Lord wanted her to walk on every grate that she encountered. Seven grates later, she returned to her apartment and again felt in her spirit the Lord speaking to her, "I am walking with you wherever you walk."

Most people know the story of David and Goliath. But one of the important facts of that story that many people overlook is this: David ran toward Goliath. He ran in faith based upon God's previous deliverance of him from a bear and lion. He ran in confidence, knowing God had given him the ability to both run fast and use a sling well. He ran with wisdom, knowing he had chosen exactly the right stones.

As you look back over your life, you no doubt can recount many instances in which God has been with you in fearful circumstances. He has delivered you before. He has given you certain abilities and strengths. He promises in His Word to impart wisdom to you if you will only ask. At times you need to confront a frightening situation in a very direct and practical way. Run toward that thing that is causing fear, trusting God even as you go. The words of David are good ones to memorize: "I come to you in the name of the LORD of hosts . . . This day the LORD will deliver you into my hand . . . The battle is the LORD's" (1 Sam. 17:45–47 NKJV).

7. Make a Decision

Come to a firm decision that you are not going to live in fear. Make a choice to believe God—yes, believe Him more than you believe your own emotions.

You may not get to the point of complete faith and trust immediately. The growth of faith takes time and testings, seeing that God is faithful in situation after situation, crisis after crisis, hurtful circumstance after hurtful circumstance. Our faith and confidence in the Lord grow as God reveals His faithfulness to us over time. You can begin, however, to act on your decision to have faith by saying to the Lord every time fear strikes, "God, You are in control of my life, not just some of the time, but all the time."

Also make a decision that you are not going to be afraid of God. My concept of God as a child was that God was a stern judge sitting up in heaven just waiting for me to make a mistake so He could punish me. I tried hard to please Him, and much of the time as a child I didn't think I did a very good job. I lived in fear that God would place a terrible disease on me or I'd die in a gruesome accident. I imagined something terrible, really bad—the most bloody and awful judgment!

Now when I think about my loving heavenly Father, my thoughts are the exact opposite. I don't see Him as a judge but as my sustainer, protector, provider, and preserver of life. I know that He will forgive me if I sin and that I am eternally secure in my salvation. I know that His desire for me is always something that will lead to my eternal good.

Make a decision that you are going to believe in God, who loves you, provides for you, cares for you, is always available to you, and is in control of your life at all times. Make a decision to trust Him.

As you do, I have no doubt that God can melt away your crippling fears so you can truly experience the depth of His abiding peace.

ELEVEN

GIVING UP ANXIETY

When traffic on the freeway has come to a dead stop, and you've already been late to work two times this month . . .

When the daily news reports that thousands more people have contracted a deadly virus . . .

When the stock market has dropped five hundred points . . .

When you find drugs in your son's bedroom . . .

When you suspect that your unmarried daughter might be pregnant . . .

When the doctor says that he needs to run some more tests, and he isn't smiling as he says so . . .

The normal and natural response is anxiety. It's a feeling of being hit with something unexpected. Anxiety begins in our emotions, not our minds. It is a response to something we perceive or feel to be negative, and more specifically, something that we believe to be an attack against us.

ARE YOU DISTRACTED OR UNCERTAIN?

Anxiety is a problem we all face at one time or another. The Greek word for *anxious* in the following passage from the Sermon on the Mount means "distracted." It is a word that refers to uncertainty. That's what anxiety produces in us. It gives us a feeling of, What next? It is a feeling that the rug has been pulled out from under us and we have no idea if we are going to fall, how hard, in what direction, or onto what!

The word *anxious* is also translated as "worry" in the Bible. For many people, worry has become a way of life. They live in a state of uncertainty and worry. If that describes you, I encourage you to read again the words of Jesus. His command to you is very plain. In the Sermon on the Mount, Jesus said,

> Do not worry about your life, what you will eat or what you will drink; nor about your body, what you will put on. Is not life more than food and the body more than clothing? Look at the birds of the air, for they neither sow nor reap nor gather into barns; yet your heavenly Father feeds them. Are you not of more value than they?
>
> (MATT. 6:25–26 NKJV)

This is not a suggestion. It is a command.

You may say, "But I can't help feeling anxious, I have always been a worrier!" I've heard that from many people through the years. My response is, "Oh, yes you can."

There's nothing about a circumstance that automatically creates anxiety. Anxiety occurs because of the way we respond to a problem or troubling situation. Your ability to choose is part of God's gift of free will to every human being. You can choose how you feel, you can choose what you think about, and you can choose how you will respond to a circumstance.

Several years ago, a friend of mine shared an experience about a choice she made. Her elderly father, a widower, had moved into her home, and 99 percent of the time the relationship was a very positive, mutually enriching one. She recalled, however, that one day her father had been particularly cranky. Nothing had suited him, he had been verbally critical about several things, and she became irritated in return with his pessimism and negative outlook.

Then she told me, "We were getting ready to leave the house on errands and I looked up to see my father walking out the door and I thought, *That's my father. I love him. He's old and he's not going to be with me very much longer— even if he lives another ten or fifteen years, that's not very long.* I thought about how much I would miss my father when he was no longer with me, and I made a decision. It was a conscious, intentional decision. I said to myself, *I'm going*

*to choose to love him and enjoy being with him every day for the rest of my life or
his life. We're going to live in peace.*

"I immediately began to treat my father with kindness and understanding,
and within a matter of hours he had apologized for his bad mood and admitted
that he really hadn't been feeling well for several days. From that day on, we
had a wonderful relationship."

Yes, you can choose how you feel and how you will respond!

No situation automatically causes anxiety. It certainly isn't God's purpose
for you to feel anxious. He doesn't allow situations in your life so you will have
anxiety. No! God may allow a situation in your life to develop stronger faith,
grow and mature, or change a bad habit or negative attitude. But God does not
set you up for anxiety. He is always at work to bring you to a place where you
will trust Him more, obey Him more fully, and receive more of His blessings.

CONCERN IS NOT THE SAME AS ANXIETY

We must be careful not to confuse concern with anxiety. It is normal for a
Christian to have deep concerns. Concern motivates us to intercede and to take
godly actions toward meeting the needs of others. Concern, yes! Anxiety, no!

Concern is rooted in caring. We are to be concerned, for example, about
our families, our health, doing a good job in our work—because we care about
the well-being of our families, our personal well-being, and the success of our
work. Concern involves wanting to see things done well so that God receives
glory from our lives.

Some concern is also rooted in obedience. There is no place in the Scriptures
where we are given license to be irresponsible. We are to live out God's commandments in our daily lives. We are to live honest and moral lives—paying
our bills, telling the truth, giving a full day's effort for a full day's wage, and so
forth. Living a responsible life involves a certain amount of concern rooted in
a desire to be obedient to the Lord.

A concern rooted in caring or in obedience, however, is not the same as anxiety.

If your child walks into the house and has injured her ankle, you have a genuine right and responsibility to be concerned about whether her ankle is sprained or broken. Concern will lead you to action and to seek medical advice. Or consider the person who walks in to work one day, and his employer says, "We no longer need your services." Fired. Out of his office and onto the street in one day.

"Well, that's a good time for anxiety!" you may say.

Not according to God's Word. Concern, yes. Concern about continuing to provide for your family or yourself, concern about how and where to find another job, concern about what steps to take first . . . most definitely, yes. But to fall apart emotionally, become filled with fear, feel paralyzed, or allow strong thoughts of bankruptcy and homelessness and a bleak future to overtake one's mind . . . absolutely not! That's anxiety.

Concern is productive. It is forward-looking and positive.

Anxiety is the opposite—it is counterproductive, stuck in the present, and negative.

Concern motivates us to take action. Anxiety paralyzes us.

Concern may very well be marked by tears, expressions of sorrow and sympathy, empathy, thoughtful reflection, and quiet time for meditation. In the end, however, concern leads us to make decisions. It leads us to the point of saying, "I choose to trust in God. I choose to seek His plan and purpose in this. I choose to take the action He leads me to take."

Anxiety tends to be marked by hand-wringing, uncontrollable crying, deeply furrowed brows and slumped shoulders, sleepless nights, nervous twitches, and endless pacing. Anxiety is a treadmill that tends to keep a person in a state of fear and negativity, and without peace.

THE RESULTS OF ANXIETY

Here are seven highly negative results associated with anxiety:

1. Anxiety Divides a Person's Mind

Many people live with a degree of stress that results from what I call a "divided mind." The person is working on one task, is engaged in a meeting with one group, or is involved in a conversation with one person, but in the back of that person's mind and heart, another problem or situation has center stage.

A cancer patient once said to me, "My first thought every morning and my last thought every night, and every third or fourth thought all day long is, *I have cancer.*" I feel certain that people who are fighting a major problem of any kind have times when that situation fills their minds much of the day.

A divided mind keeps a person from fully concentrating on the tasks at hand. Nagging worries or unsettling feelings distract him, causing him to live in a state of semi confusion at all times.

A woman told me about her husband's mental illness. I asked her, "How did Bill's mental illness affect you?"

She said, "I never knew which Bill was going to be waiting for me when I got home. Would it be the sweet and loving Bill, or would it be the angry, sullen, silent Bill?"

"Did this impact your work?" I asked.

She said, "I nearly lost my job because I couldn't concentrate at work. It didn't matter if I was in a meeting or working alone at my desk, my thoughts tended to gravitate toward his situation. His refusal to get professional help or take the medicine prescribed for him, and what this was doing to our relationship. I couldn't help but dwell on what might happen to our marriage. I also wondered if his illness was something that our baby daughter might inherit biologically. I was preoccupied with thoughts about what I might do, should do, could do, and mostly by the helpless feeling that I might not be able to do anything to help.

"Since I couldn't concentrate fully, I just didn't do my best. I made careless mistakes. In the end, I was passed over for a promotion. It was then I woke up and thought, *Something has to happen here. If Bill isn't going to get help, I at least can get help for myself. I need to regain my peace.*"

2. Anxiety Lowers a Person's Productivity

If a person has a divided mind, it is only logical to conclude that such a person will be less productive. He won't be able to sustain an effort and will be less likely to see any project through to a quality completion. Not only is the person less productive, but he or she is usually less efficient too. The quality of work tends to suffer.

3. Anxiety Leads a Person to Make Unwise Decisions

The person who cannot focus on a task is a person who generally cannot complete his required "homework" on a project, cannot perceive all facets of a problem, and cannot listen at length or with sufficient concentration to those who might give sound advice. The result is often poor decision making and problem solving. Bad choices and decisions are a setup for failure, which only leads to greater anxiety. The highly anxious person is often emotionally paralyzed to the point at which he can't make any decision, and thus, he doesn't move forward in his life. He lives in a cloud of apprehension and confusion.

4. Anxiety Drains a Person's Energy

Prolonged anxiety is exhausting. It wears out your immune system and alters certain chemical systems in your body so that you are depleted of vitamins and minerals that help you maintain a good energy level.

5. Anxiety Produces Physical Ailments

Scientific and medical researchers have shown through the years that anxiety produces numerous negative effects in the human body, including headaches, stomachaches, intestinal disorders, constriction of blood vessels resulting in high blood pressure and a greater likelihood of heart attacks and strokes, and biochemical disorders that put hormonal systems out of balance, which can result in multiple diseases.

In fact, some of our nation's premier medical schools are stating unequivocally that through faith and prayer, elements of anxiety, stress, and fear are positively reduced in patients with the result that many experience healing more rapidly.

6. Anxiety Alienates Other People

When a person is less focused or distracted, it becomes more difficult to communicate with him. Such a person often is fidgety and frustrated, quick to blame and to criticize others, and quick to become angry. Poor communication is very damaging to friendships, marriages, and parent-child relationships. The result can easily be that other people feel alienated, unwanted, or undesirable.

7. Anxiety Depletes a Person's Joy

The person who lives with prolonged anxiety is a person who usually feels robbed of joy. Anyone who worries continually or who continually feels overwhelmed by life is a person who has less hope and is less capable of appreciating or enjoying pleasurable moments. There always seems to be a problem lurking in the back of his mind or deep in his soul. Peace and joy cannot coexist with anxiety.

Given all these negative effects, our conclusion must be that a troubled soul is not God's plan for us! God's Word plainly says, "Do not fret—it only causes harm" (Ps. 37:8 NKJV).

WHAT ABOUT PANIC ATTACKS?

"Panic attack" is the term sometimes used when anxiety spins your emotions out of control. Your heart begins to race, you may begin to sweat profusely, become dizzy or light-headed, or feel as if you're falling apart.

I have had such an experience. It was sheer horror. I can understand now why some people turn to drugs when they feel the way I felt at that time. The feelings of anxiety and unrest, along with extreme fatigue, seem to deepen. I felt as though things inside me were spinning out of control and that I was coming apart at the seams. In my desperate hours I cried out to God—like a little boy calling for his daddy after a bad dream. His presence surrounded and sustained me through that difficult season.

If you don't know the Lord, what are you going to do to calm your heart and mind? If you don't know the Lord, and you face a sudden tragedy or load of stress that seems about to swamp you, what will you do to ease your emotions? It's easy to turn to drugs or alcohol or something that you hope will give you a momentary escape.

The good news is that those who truly know the Lord don't need to walk down the path that leads to chemical addiction. They can cry out to God, "Hold me! Help me! Don't let me go!" And the more they cry out to God with a sincere heart, the more God will impart to them His presence to drive away the anxiety, slow down the world that seems to be spinning out of control, and give them genuine peace.

Our loving heavenly Father holds on to us. He hears our cries. He embraces us with His everlasting arms. He holds us tightly in His comfort of us. The closer we cling to Him, the quieter our spirits become.

WHAT SHOULD WE IMMEDIATELY DO WHEN ANXIETY STRIKES?

What should we do when anxiety strikes? First and foremost, we must ask God to give us His peace and His answers. A man I once knew suddenly felt some unusual sensations in his leg. This discomfort continued, so he sought medical advice. After a series of tests, his doctor told him he had a virulent and rare form of cancer.

He was devastated by the news. An athlete in vibrant health (or so he thought), he saw his future crumbling before him. Anxiety began to grip his mind. He began to imagine all the worst possible scenarios, but thankfully, his friends gathered around him and sought to give him support and encourage his faith. They urged him to consider that God's presence and peace were available to him.

Fortunately, he was healed and then regularly helped other cancer victims as they struggled on their own journeys. He had peace, and sought to pass it on to others. He found the secret to peace when worry and anxiety loomed across his path. How should we proceed?

Very specifically, we must ask God to deal with the problems that are filling both our conscious and subconscious minds. This is not likely something we do just once. It is something we may have to do many times throughout the day.

We must ask the Lord to help us focus all of our thoughts and energy on the immediate situation at hand.

Say to the Lord, "You are in control of this situation. I trust You to deal with this troublesome person or persons, or these circumstances. Help me to give my full attention to the task that You have put in front of me right now. Calm my heart, focus my attention, infuse my mind with Your ideas and creative solutions, and give me the strength to be diligent until this project or meeting is completed."

As Anxiety Subsides . . .

As the immediate force of an anxiety attack subsides, you need to settle this issue in your life: Is God my loving heavenly Father at all times, always seeking my eternal best, or not?

The key to overcoming anxiety is to get your thinking right about God. The fact is, God is sovereign. He created everything and has absolute control over every aspect of His creation. He is all-powerful, all-knowing, and ever present.

He knows absolutely everything about your situation. He knows how to produce wholeness out of brokenness. He knows how to build strength out of weakness. He knows how to heal what is sick. He knows how to bring reconciliation and love out of estrangement and hate.

Furthermore, He loves you with an unconditional, unfathomable, immeasurable love. He knows everything about you, and loves you still.

A loving heavenly Father who is in total control, all-knowing, and ever present whom you can trust. And trust is what causes anxiety to disappear.

THE CHOICE IS YOURS

You can fall into a downward spiral of anxiety. Or you can say, "Heavenly Father! I bring this to You. It's beyond my control or influence. I feel helpless in this situation, but You have the power to change it. You love me perfectly. I am trusting You to handle this in the way You see fit. I know that whatever You have planned for me is for my good. I look forward to seeing the way You choose to express Your love and wisdom and power." Friend, this is the way of peace—the road out of anxiety and worry.

TWELVE

DEALING WITH THE
CAUSES OF ANXIETY

"Are you going to be ready?"

For years I would answer "yes" to that question preachers commonly are asked. "Yes, of course I'm going to be ready to preach a good sermon on Sunday." But deep down inside, I had self-doubts.

One of the things I felt anxious about nearly all my adult life was that I wouldn't be ready to preach on Sunday. I prayed. I studied diligently. I trusted God. But then I prayed some more and studied harder. And then . . . I prayed still more and studied still harder. I lived with the anxiety about the next sermon until the moment I stood up to preach it. Afterward, I'd begin to worry about the next Sunday's sermon. Fortunately, with God's help, I eventually had victory over that lifelong cycle of anxiety and experienced relief.

For the most part, we are the ones who determine how long we will be anxious. Thus the need for anyone who consistently experiences anxiety attacks and an ongoing sense of being distraught and worried to have a complete physical checkup. Too often, however, we fail to deal with the issues that entangle us, and we allow worry and anxiety to settle permanently in our souls. The result is that we lose our peace.

As I experienced, if we permit negative and worry-filled thoughts to take root in our hearts, we can create a general state of anxiety. This way of thinking can become established within us and lead to negative attitudes that can last for years.

People have told me from time to time, "I'm just a worrier." Or they have told me about someone they know well, "He's always a little uptight," or "She tends to fret a lot." Some people refer to this continually anxious state as being "high-strung" or "always wound tight." If anxiety has become the norm for your life, however, you need to take a look at the reasons for that feeling. They are generally related to deep inner needs. Those needs tend to relate to one or more of the following.

THE INNER NEEDS THAT CAUSE LONG-TERM ANXIETY

A Lack of Self-Worth

A person who feels a lack of self-worth has lost sight of his or her value to God, our heavenly Father. Again, let me remind you of what our Lord said:

> Look at the birds of the air, for they neither sow nor reap nor gather into barns; yet your heavenly Father feeds them. Are you not of more value than they?
>
> (MATT. 6:26 NKJV)

I think Jesus was saying to those listening to Him that a person with low self-worth does not see his or her needs as being worth as much as the needs of the little sparrows that are continually under God's watchful eye.

So many of us do not think God is capable or desirous of meeting our needs on a daily, hourly, minute-by-minute basis. We don't see ourselves as being worthy of the care He bestows on a little bird in the yard.

I've had people say to me, "God doesn't care about my car breaking down." Yes, He does.

"God doesn't care about the leaky pipe in my bathroom." Yes, He does.

"God doesn't care whether I get a raise at work." Yes, He does.

God cares about every detail of your life, and His plan is to provide for you fully.

There are several reasons why we tend to see ourselves as being unworthy of His love, but do you remember His plan? Jesus sacrificed Himself for you and me. Nothing God could ever do would be a greater display of the truth that He considers you to be worthy of loving, nurturing, and blessing.

A Desire for Total Control

A second deep inner cause of anxiety is a desire to control all things to our benefit, including things over which we truly have no power. I believe this desire for power and control often springs from a lack of trust in God, who alone can control every aspect of our lives.

There are many things people do today in an effort to take charge of their lives—from taking vitamins to exercising daily, from eating five servings of fruits and vegetables to getting sufficient sleep. Now those things are beneficial, and I routinely engage in good nutritional and exercise habits. But I do so not to extend my life, but rather to give good quality to every hour I live.

A life riddled with anxiety produces the opposite of energy, vitality, increased productivity, and an abundance of life. As noted in the previous chapter, anxiety has been linked to numerous ailments and conditions, from heart attacks and strokes to high blood pressure, from digestive tract disorders to nervous breakdowns, from an increase in accidents at home and at work to less efficiency and less focus on any given task. You've never heard of people "worrying themselves to life"—no, the phrase we often use is that a person is "worried to death." In truth, anxiety can kill a relationship, destroy the fun of any event or experience, and detract greatly from a person's willingness to embark on new challenges and opportunities.

People worry about so many things they can never control. Your anxiety will not make a bit of difference in tomorrow's weather . . . it won't make another person love you . . . it won't allow you to relive a single second of yesterday.

Let God do what only God can do. Trust Him to act on your behalf out of His infinite love and mercy toward you.

Concern for What Others Think

We have a multibillion-dollar clothing industry in the USA, and it is built upon the premise that looking good is important. We seek to dress well because we are concerned about how others think we look. It is true. We get anxious about our appearance and our performance in life. In other words, many of us worry about how we stack up, and that is another cause of deep inner anxiety.

We work harder with longer hours and overschedule our lives in an effort to impress others with our productivity and performance or at least to satisfy our own internal need for success.

Yet Jesus tells us that our heavenly Father's opinion about who we are is all that truly matters. If He approves of us, that's all the approval we need. He gives us our identity and an inner beauty that far surpasses anything related to what we might wear, own, drive, or live in.

As for performance, what more does our heavenly Father expect of us than that we do our best? We are responsible to prepare carefully, and then to step out and work hard!

For many years I was afraid of disappointing God by not performing up to His high standards (whatever those were), but now I know we cannot disappoint God.

A person can disobey God—either willfully or unknowingly—but he cannot disappoint God. A person can sin or rebel against God, and reap God's consequences for that sin as a means of chastisement. But a person cannot disappoint God.

Stop to think about it for a moment. A God who can be disappointed is a God who loves conditionally—a God who loves us when we perform well, and then withdraws His love if we perform badly. The truth of God's love is that His love is unconditional. He loves us at all times with an infinite, overwhelming, merciful, gracious, passionate love! God's embrace of love doesn't change based upon our performance. On occasion we may feel inadequate and incapable of successfully completing an assignment, but that doesn't have to be a permanent, continuous feeling for us. God can and will help us.

He may whisper to our hearts, "I can help you do better than that. I created you to do better than that. I desire that you do better than that." Even as He whispers these messages to our hearts, He is holding us close and valuing us beyond measure. God never withdraws His presence or His love from His children.

My fear of failure was rooted in a lack of understanding God's unconditional love. It was rooted in my lack of knowing that God at all times considered me worthy and valuable. It was rooted in my lack of awareness that I could never disappoint God and God would never reject me or withdraw His presence from me.

Have you come to the place in your life that you truly know God loves you, and that nothing you do or say puts you beyond the realm of God's infinite, unconditional love? If you know with certainty this great love of God, then you also know that while you may disappoint yourself or others, you cannot disappoint God. He will never leave you, forsake you, or turn away from you.

Our part is to trust God and acknowledge Him in all things. His part is to lead and guide us in the paths He wants us to pursue.

Striving to Follow the World's Pattern

The world tells us that we will feel secure and be free of all anxiety if we just have enough money in our bank accounts, our investment portfolios, or our retirement accounts. That just isn't true. There's no lasting security in money, stocks, bonds, or any other form of financial investment.

The world tells us that we will feel secure if we just get our home mortgages fully paid. Not true. No house is ever fully secure against natural disaster, fire, or vandalism.

The world tells us that we will feel secure if we just follow a certain health regimen. Not true. Even very physically fit and apparently healthy people have accidents, contract infectious diseases, and are subject to life-threatening illnesses.

The world tells us that we will feel secure and be free of anxiety in our careers if we are promoted to positions that are high enough in the company or we achieve a certain degree of fame. That also isn't true. Any movie actor or actress will tell you that you are only as famous as your last successful movie or play. Any business executive will tell you that in today's business world, CEOs, top executives, and upper-management employees are sometimes more likely to lose their jobs than many lower-on-the-ladder employees.

The truth is that the world has no magic solution for 100 percent security in any area of life. Only Jesus can give a person the confidence of security deep within.

A man said to me once, "Well, back to reality . . . I dread going back to the office."

I asked, "Don't you enjoy your work?"

"No," he admitted. "I really don't. I like the product we manufacture and I like the money I earn and I like the people I work with . . . but I don't enjoy the tasks and the pressure and the responsibility I face from day to day."

"Why don't you find a job you would enjoy getting up and doing every morning?"

He looked at me as if the thought had never even once crossed his mind. "I've got too much at stake in my current position," he said with a great weariness in his voice. "At my age, I doubt that I could be hired at a decent salary by any other company."

"Have you ever stopped to think what you might like to do if you didn't work at the job you presently have?"

His eyes brightened. "Sure," he said. But then his shoulders slumped and the light went out of his eyes. "But that's only a daydream. Maybe I'll get to do that in another ten years when I retire."

I felt sorry for this man as I watched him leave. To think of awaking each morning and going through the motions of a job only for the money seems like sheer drudgery. Such a job is a burden, not a blessing. And the greater the burden associated with any responsibility, the greater the tension, frustration, and anxiety. Furthermore, there's plenty of opportunity for regret to settle in. If this man doesn't begin to pursue the God-given dreams that reside deep in his heart, he's going to find himself saying in the future, "I regret I spent my life doing what I did. I wish I had taken a different path." He will especially feel that way if he develops health problems that keep him from pursuing his dream when he retires in ten years.

If you are stuck in a job or a situation that is overly tedious, boring, exhausting, or that involves constant struggle—make a change! I'm not talking about having a tedious day or a boring week or a tiring couple of weeks as you bring a project to conclusion. Every job has certain moments and periods that are more demanding than others. I'm talking about a job that has very little exhilaration and joy associated with it—a job that seems to drain you without giving back much satisfaction or fulfillment. A job with no internal reward, only an external paycheck, is not a job worth the time and energy of your life.

Ask God what He would have you do, and start getting the information and training for doing that work. Begin to develop the necessary skills for your "dream job." Put out applications for employment in that field.

If you believe you are in the job God has given to you, but you find it a constant drain on your emotions, energy, and creativity, ask God to help you develop a new attitude toward your work. Ask Him to show you His higher purposes for your being where He has placed you. Begin to see your job as a God-given opportunity.

Living in the Tomorrow

One of the foremost causes of anxiety is a desire for the good things of the future to arrive. Today many children live in this distraction—they long to be grown up, or to "finally" be a teenager, or to get out on their own. Other people fear the future. Generally, those who have a negative view of God's trustworthiness and of life in general have a desire to get into tomorrow so they can get the bad stuff of today behind them. They are worried about what will happen in the near future or the distant future, and they miss out on the fullness of today because they are anxious about tomorrow.

A person may say:

"Suppose I don't get into the college of my choice . . ."
"Suppose I don't get the job I want . . ."
"Suppose I get fired . . ."
"Suppose the person I love doesn't love me back . . ."
"Suppose the people who are invited to my party don't show up or don't have a good time . . ."
"Suppose something comes up to keep me from leaving for my vacation on time . . ."

Friend, the God who is in control of today is also the God who is fully in control of tomorrow. He has already prepared for what will happen to you! He has already provided what you will need tomorrow. He has already anticipated the problems you will face tomorrow and set into motion everything required to resolve those problems.

You cannot predict tomorrow. You cannot fully prepare for all contingencies. You cannot fully provide for all you'll need in your future. God not only can, He already has! God is never caught off guard. He is never taken by surprise. He never comes up short. So you do not have to live with anxiety about the future. The peace-filled heart is the one that recognizes, "My times are in His hands."

God desires that we view our troubles, whether present concerns or those looming in the future, from His perspective. We are not to deny them or seek to escape them, but rather to regard them as trials and tribulations that we must overcome.

God never expects us to put up with constant anxiety. He intends for us to confront those situations that make us anxious, to face up to the anxiety we have allowed to fill our hearts, and to come to grips with the agitation we feel inside. He intends for us to resist the tendency to worry or become fearful and to refuse to lay down our peace no matter what the devil sends our way.

I don't know that a person ever becomes immune to anxiety. But I am confident of this: It would take a lot to make me anxious now. When I look back over my life, I realize that things that once upset me don't bother me as much now. Things that once caused me to feel anxious don't cause anxiety now. I also know that the more a person trusts God to meet his deep inner needs, the more his faith is going to grow, and the quicker he will be able to trust the Lord in all situations.

I encourage you today . . .

- Refuse to allow anxiety to become a "state of being" in your life.
- Believe God when He says you are worthy of His constant care.
- Yield total control of every area of your life to God.
- Refuse to be caught up in what others think of you.
- Refuse to be trapped into operating according to the world's systems.
- Get your priorities in line with God's priorities for you.
- Choose to live in today, not tomorrow.

And you will find yourself living with a growing, deep inner peace, free from fear and anxiety.

PART FOUR

GOD PROVIDES A WAY THROUGH PAIN AND SUFFERING

THIRTEEN

THE POWER OF PERSPECTIVE

Several years ago, a good, very godly friend of mine lost his wife to cancer. It was devastating. We had prayed and prayed for her recovery, but there was no sign of God's healing hand. Jim sat by his wife's side all day, every day. Anything he could do to make his wife more comfortable, he did gladly. And yet he remained powerless to do the one thing he desired most of all—to heal his wife.

I had heard Jim pray. I had seen him hurt. His faith had not been shattered; yet his wife eventually died. Although he eventually recovered from the heartbreaking loss, the question remained: Why did this happen? What was the point? What was accomplished? Why was grief so unfairly imposed upon such a God-fearing family?

Jim and his family were certainly not the first to ask such painful and complex questions. And they were well aware of that. In anticipation of questions raised by circumstances such as these, God has given us in the gospel of John a narrative that helps us gain the perspective needed to survive tragedies such as that faced by Jim.

The problem with studying any familiar passage is that we rarely allow ourselves to feel what the characters must have felt. Why should we? We usually know what happens in the end.

Unfortunately, this familiarity with the Scriptures often robs us of their intended results. It is hard to feel the fear David must have felt when he faced Goliath when we know from the outset that he comes out the victor. We miss the sense of isolation Moses must have felt as he fled Egypt for his life. After all, he ends up a hero. So as you approach this familiar narrative in John 11, try to forget the end of the story, even though we discussed it briefly in chapter 4. Instead, do your best to put yourself in the shoes, or maybe the sandals, of the people involved. If you read what happens but neglect to consider what must have been felt, you lose some of the richest insights of this story.

"HE WHOM YOU LOVE IS SICK"

Now a certain man was sick, Lazarus of Bethany, the village of Mary and her sister Martha. And it was the Mary who anointed the Lord with ointment, and wiped His feet with her hair, whose brother Lazarus was sick. The sisters therefore sent word to Him, saying, "Lord, behold, he whom You love is sick."

(JOHN 11:1–3)

The household of Mary and Martha is one in which Jesus and His disciples had been given hospitality whenever they had been in the area of Judea. Apparently, Lazarus was a wealthy man, and he used his wealth to support the ministry of Christ. The fact that Mary and Martha sent for Jesus as soon as Lazarus became ill is evidence of their faith in His power. No doubt they thought, *If Jesus is willing to heal total strangers, certainly He will jump at the opportunity to heal one who has been a friend.* But such was not the case.

But when Jesus heard it, He said, "This sickness is not to end in death, but for the glory of God, so that the Son of God may be glorified by it." Now Jesus loved Martha and her sister and Lazarus. So when He heard that he was sick, He then stayed two days longer in the place where He was.

(JOHN 11:4–6)

These verses make absolutely no sense, humanly speaking. That is why I love this story, because most adversity makes about as much sense from our perspective. It is clearly stated that Jesus loves this family; then He makes no move to relieve their suffering. I can relate to that. Whenever the bottom drops out, I go scrambling to the verses in the Bible that remind me of God's love—yet at times it seems God is unwilling to follow through with any action.

We need to pause here because at this point in the narrative we have our greatest struggles. I am referring to that time between the point we ask God for help and the point at which He does something. It is so easy to read, "He then stayed two days longer." But the delay was like an eternity for Mary and Martha. The Scripture informs us that they knew the general area and how long it would take Him to make the trip to Bethany. So they waited. And as the hours dragged on, they watched their brother grow weaker and weaker.

Finally the day arrived when, according to the normal traveling time, Jesus should arrive. No doubt they took turns sitting with Lazarus. That way one of them could go out to the road to look for Jesus. I can imagine Mary or Martha asking all the men and women coming from the direction of Perea if they had seen a group of twelve or so men headed that way. As they would shake their heads no, the sisters' hope burned a little lower. "Why didn't He come? Maybe He never got the message? Maybe He left Perea without sending word back to us? Where is He? After all we have done for Him, it is the least He could do." And yet He failed to come when they expected Him.

Lazarus died. Maybe Mary came in early one morning to check on him and found him dead. Perhaps it was in the afternoon when both Mary and Martha were at his side that he breathed his last breath. Whatever the situation, both women felt that hollow, helpless feeling that always accompanies death. It was over. He was gone. Soon their thoughts turned to Jesus, *Why didn't He come? How could He know what we were going through and yet stay away?*

These, no doubt, are some of the questions you have asked as you have cried out to God in the midst of the adversity in your life. How can a God of love stand back and watch my friend and his wife suffer and not do anything about it? How can He watch from the balcony of heaven as women are physically or sexually abused? How can He watch husbands walk out on their wives and children? Does He know what is going on down here?

Once again, this narrative is helpful. Jesus knew exactly what was going on. He knew what Mary and Martha were going through. He knew his friend's condition was worsening. And He knew the moment Lazarus died:

> And after that He said to them [the disciples], "Our friend Lazarus has fallen asleep."
>
> (JOHN 11:11)

Yet He did nothing! Keep in mind, Lazarus was not some guy off the street. He had invited Jesus into his home. Lazarus had expressed faith in Christ and His ministry. He was a good man. He certainly had more faith than most of the other people Jesus had healed. Some of them did not even know who Christ was (John 9). But Jesus was nowhere to be found when Lazarus needed Him most. To add insult to injury, Jesus had the nerve to say to His disciples,

> "Lazarus is dead, and *I am glad* for your sakes that I was not there."
>
> (JOHN 11:14–15, EMPHASIS ADDED)

Jesus was "glad"? How could He say such a thing? Two of his best friends go through emotional turmoil; another friend dies of an illness; and Jesus says He is glad? What could He have possibly been thinking? What was going through His mind?

My friend, the answer to that question is the key to unlocking the mystery of tragedy in this life. To understand what was going on in the mind of Christ and in the economy of God in a situation like this one is to discover the universal principle that puts together and holds together all of life—both now and for eternity. Christ had a goal in all this, a goal so important that *it was worth the emotional agony* Mary and Martha had to endure. It was worth risking the destruction of their faith. It was even worth the death of a faithful friend. What Jesus, in conjunction with His heavenly Father, had in mind was so incredible that even through the pain surrounding the whole event Jesus could say, "I am glad this has happened." In other words, "Men, what you are about to see is so fantastic that it is worth the pain and death of My beloved friend." If they were like us, they probably thought, *What could be worth all of this?*

"IF YOU HAD BEEN HERE"

Now Bethany was near Jerusalem, about two miles off; and many of the Jews had come to Martha and Mary, to console them concerning their brother. Martha therefore, when she heard that Jesus was coming, went to meet Him; but Mary still sat in the house. Martha then said to Jesus, "Lord, if You had been here, my brother would not have died." . . . And when she had said this, she went away, and called Mary her sister, saying secretly, "The Teacher is here and is calling for you." And when she heard it, she arose quickly, and was coming to Him . . . Therefore, when Mary came where Jesus was, she saw Him, and fell at His feet, saying to Him, "Lord, if You had been here, my brother would not have died."

(JOHN 11:18–21, 28–29, 32)

Mary and Martha, for all their time spent with the Son of God, were still human to the core. They wanted to know one thing: "Jesus, where in the world have You been?" They had no doubt that Jesus could have healed their brother; Martha even indicates that she believes there is still hope (John 11:22). But the fact that He had seemingly ignored their plight had left them confused and frustrated. Why did He delay?

When Jesus therefore saw her weeping and the Jews who came with her also weeping, He was deeply moved in spirit and was troubled, and said, "Where have you laid him?" They said to Him, "Lord, come and see." Jesus wept. And so the Jews were saying, "See how He loved him!"

(JOHN 11:33–36)

At this juncture any doubt about Jesus' love and concern for Lazarus is laid to rest. "Jesus wept." Yet His overt concern about His friend Lazarus adds another layer of mystery to the story. If Jesus was so concerned, why did He not come to Lazarus's aid? Why did He let him die?

Once again we are faced with what appears to be an unsolvable mystery. It becomes apparent that whatever Christ had in mind, whatever He was trying to accomplish, it was worth sacrificing the emotions of the ones He loved as well as His own. Jesus wept when He arrived to find Lazarus dead. Think about it. His knowledge of the future did not keep Him from identifying with the sorrow of those around Him.

ASKING THE RIGHT QUESTIONS

If anything is clear from this story, it is that some things are so important to God that they are worth interrupting the happiness and health of His children in order to accomplish them. That is an awesome thought. To some, it may seem like an indictment of the character of God. But this principle will become clearer through the pages and chapters that follow. Whether some persons can fit this idea into their theology or not, the fact remains that the Son of God allowed those He loved to suffer and die for the sake of some higher purpose.

Some individuals may think such a statement implies that we are merely pawns to be moved about and even abused at God's whims. But remember, "Jesus wept." He was moved with emotion at the sight of Mary and Martha's sorrow. He was touched by the love they had for their brother. He was not emotionally isolated from the pain suffered by those whose perspective was different from His own.

When you hurt, God hurts. Regardless of what He may be in the process of accomplishing, regardless of how noble His purposes may be, He is in touch with what you are feeling. He is not like the football coach who sneers at his players when they complain of their pain. He is not like the boxing coach who whispers into his fighter's ear, "No pain, no gain." Neither is He like the parent who laughs and says to a child who has lost a first love, "Don't worry. You'll get over it."

Through all the pain and adversity God may allow us to face, two things are always true. First, He is sensitive to what we are feeling:

For we do not have a high priest who cannot sympathize with our weaknesses.

(Heb. 4:15)

Jesus wept over Lazarus. He weeps over our sorrow as well.

Second, whatever He is in the process of accomplishing through our suffering will always be for our best interest. The degree to which things actually work out for our best interest is determined by our response. As we trust God through our adversity, when all is said and done, we will sincerely believe it was worth it all.

"How?" you might ask. "How could what I am going through at home work out for my best interest? How could God ever use the death of my spouse (or child)? What could possibly be worth the isolation and hurt I am feeling now?"

When I was a little boy, I used to ask some of those same questions. My father died when I was seven months old, so I grew up without a dad. I remember watching my friends with their fathers and wondering why I couldn't have one too. It didn't make sense. My mom had to work long, hard hours in a textile mill. By the time I got up in the morning to go to school, she was already at work. I had to learn to fix my own breakfast and dress myself for school by the time I was six years old.

By the grace of God, my response to all of that was different from that of many young men who lose their fathers. Instead of rebelling against God for taking my dad, I decided at a very young age that I would look to Him to be my Father. My dad's death did not cause me to turn away from God; rather, I turned toward Him. I learned early in life about the daily sufficiency of Christ. I learned how to pray. I learned how to walk by faith. The untimely death of my father was actually the catalyst God used to teach me the most important lessons of life—the lessons that have allowed me to survive intense rejection as an adult both on a professional level and personal level. But at the age of seven or eight I could not see what God was up to. It made no sense at all then. There was nothing to compensate for the loneliness I felt. In fact, it has taken me more than forty years to make sense out of the adversity I faced as a child. And the lessons continue.

Not too long ago, my son, Andy, said to me, "You know, Dad, Becky and I probably reaped the real benefits of your not having a father when you grew up."

"What do you mean?" I asked.

"Well," he said, "when it came time to raise your own kids, you didn't have a pattern to follow. You had to be completely dependent upon the Lord for everything."

As I thought about it, he was right. When I realized how committed they are to the Lord, and when I thought about how different they are from many preachers' children, I was even able to thank the Lord for not giving me a father. If that was what it took to prepare me to raise my own children, *it was worth it all!*

A SICKNESS NOT UNTO DEATH

What, then, did Jesus have in mind by delaying His return to Bethany, thus allowing Lazarus to die? What was so important that He was willing to allow His close friends to go through the agony of watching their brother die? The answer to that question gives us a great deal of insight into the character and economy of God. Jesus Himself provided the answer when He was first informed of Lazarus's illness and then again when He stood at the tomb.

> The sisters sent word to Him, saying, "Lord, behold, he whom You love is sick." But when Jesus heard this, He said, *"This sickness is not to end in death, but for the glory of God, so that the Son of God may be glorified by it."* Now Jesus loved Martha and her sister and Lazarus.
>
> (JOHN 11:3–5, EMPHASIS ADDED)

> And so they removed the stone. And Jesus raised His eyes, and said, "Father, I thank You that You always hear Me; And I knew that You have heard Me always; but because of the people standing around I said it, *so that they may believe that You sent Me."*
>
> (JOHN 11:41–42, EMPHASIS ADDED)

From the very beginning, Jesus had two specific purposes in mind. His purpose was not to cause Lazarus to die. Neither was it to cause Mary and her sister mental and emotional anguish. On the contrary, His goals in all that happened were to bring glory to God and to cause others to believe in Him. The opportunity to accomplish these two things was worth the pain and suffering Mary, Martha, and Lazarus had to experience. To Christ, this opportunity to publicly display the power of God was worth risking the rejection of some of His closest friends. It was even worth the death of a loved one.

BUT FOR THE GLORY OF GOD

To glorify something is to so arrange things as to focus attention on it or bring it honor. We glorify a picture when we hang it at a focal point in a room. We may further glorify it by shining a light on it. We glorify a singer when we put him or her on a stage and focus our attention on the performance. When we stand and applaud at the end, we are, again, glorifying the performer.

Jesus said that the purpose of this seeming tragedy was the glorification of Him and His Father. Lazarus died so that for a short moment in time the focus of attention might be God and His Son. Jesus was so given over to seeing His heavenly Father glorified that He was "glad" Lazarus died if that was what it took. This was not out of character for our Savior. He spent His whole life in an attempt to focus the attention of man on His Father. He did everything with that purpose in mind. At the end of His earthly ministry He summed up His life's work by saying,

> I glorified You on the earth, having accomplished the work which You have given Me to do.
>
> (JOHN 17:4)

As much as Jesus dreaded the cross, He knew that His own death was a part of His Father's plan to draw attention to Himself. Yet knowledge of what He would accomplish through His death and resurrection in no way erased the pain of the cross. Neither did it minimize the emotional anguish of watching His followers abandon Him at the moment He needed them most. When He uttered the words, "Yet not My will, but Thine be done," He in essence said, "Whatever it takes, regardless of the sacrifice, let it be done!" He then went to the cross determined to bring His Father glory, even at the expense of His own life.

MANY BELIEVED IN HIM

The second purpose behind Jesus' delay was that many might put their trust in Him as the Messiah. More important than keeping everybody healthy was moving people to faith. So Christ purposefully waited until it was too late so that He might perform a miracle of such magnitude that many would put their faith in Him. And that is exactly what happened (John 11:45). Just as He allowed those He loved to suffer for the sake of those who had not believed, so He will allow us to suffer today. Nothing gets the attention of an unbeliever like a saint who is suffering successfully. It is easy to talk about Christ when everything is going fine. Our words take on a great deal more significance when they are spoken from a life filled with pain.

I can hear the skeptic now, "Are you saying that God would allow me—His child—to suffer for the sake of some unsaved person?" That is exactly what I am saying. But keep in mind, it was His Son who prepared the way. If almighty God saw fit to allow His own Son to suffer unjustly that we might be saved, why should we think it below us to suffer so that others might believe?

The late Dr. Barnhouse had an experience during his ministry that illustrates this point perfectly. He was conducting a week of services in a church. The pastor of the church and his wife were expecting their first child. During the week, Dr. Barnhouse would kid with the pastor about being so uptight.

On the last night of services the pastor did not show up. Dr. Barnhouse assumed he was at the hospital with his wife, so he went ahead with the service. Toward the end of the service he noticed that the pastor slipped in quietly and took a seat on a back pew. When the service was completed, the pastor made his way to the front, dismissed everyone, and asked Dr. Barnhouse if he could see him in his office.

"Certainly," he said and followed him to the back.

As they shut the door behind them, the pastor wheeled around and blurted out, "Dr. Barnhouse, our child has Down syndrome. I haven't told my wife yet. I don't know what I'm going to tell her."

"Friend, this is of the Lord," Dr. Barnhouse said. And then he turned to this passage in the Old Testament:

And the LORD said to him [Moses], "Who has made man's mouth? Or who makes him dumb or deaf, or seeing or blind? Is it not I, the LORD?"

(Ex. 4:11)

"Let me see that," the pastor said. He read it again.

As the pastor studied the passage, Dr. Barnhouse said, "My friend, you know the promise in Romans 8. All things work together for good—including this special child—for those who love the Lord."

The pastor closed his Bible. Slowly he walked out of the office and went straight to the hospital room of his wife. When he arrived, she said, "They won't let me see my baby. What's wrong? I've asked to see my baby, and they won't let me."

The young pastor took his wife by the hand and said, "Who has made the dumb or deaf or seeing or blind? Is it not I, the Lord? Darling, the Lord has blessed us with a child with Down syndrome."

She cried long and hard. Then as she began to settle down, she said, "Where did you get that?"

"From God's own Word," he said.

"Let me see." Then she read it.

Meanwhile, news of the birth swept through the hospital. This information was of special interest to the switchboard operator in the hospital. She was not a Christian. In fact, she was a cruel woman who enjoyed seeing Christians crumble. She was convinced that under pressure, there was really no difference between Christians and everybody else. When the pastor's wife called her mother to give her the news, the operator listened in—expecting the young mother to go to pieces.

"Mother, the Lord has blessed us with a child with Down syndrome. We don't know the nature of the blessing, but we do know it is a blessing." There were no tears, no hysteria, no breakdown.

The operator was shocked. But when she absorbed what she heard, she began telling everyone. Soon the entire hospital was buzzing with the story of the pastor and his wife's response. The following Sunday the pastor was back in his pulpit. In the congregation, unknown to him, were the telephone operator and seventy nurses and staff members from the hospital. At the conclusion of the service the pastor offered an invitation.

"If you have never met Jesus Christ, I want to extend to you an invitation to do so."

That morning thirty nurses from the hospital came forward receiving Christ. All because of one special child and the faith of the young pastor and his wife.[3]

Would God allow this child to be born with a handicapping condition for the sake of thirty nurses? Absolutely. Just as He allowed a man to be born blind that His Son might heal him. Just as He would allow one whom He loved to die in order that he might be raised. And just as He allowed His own Son to be murdered in order that many might receive eternal life. God allows suffering so that others might come to faith in His Son.

THE ROLE OF PAIN

It has been said that where there is no pain, there is no gain. This phrase applies not only in the realm of athletics, but in the spiritual realm as well. The pattern we see in Christ's earthly ministry and in His personal pilgrimage bears this out. Suffering is the means by which God brings glory to Himself and to His Son. Although suffering is usually the last thing to be considered useful, it is God's most useful tool. Nothing compares with suffering when it comes to bringing God glory, for nothing else highlights our dependence, weakness, and insecurity like suffering.

But suffering is also the way God brings honor and glory to His children. In his second letter to the Corinthians, Paul makes this clear,

> For momentary, light affliction is producing for us an eternal weight of glory far beyond all comparison, while we look not at the things which are seen, but at the things which are not seen; for the things which are seen are temporal, but the things which are not seen are eternal.
>
> (2 COR. 4:17–18)

Adversity in this life, when handled properly, provides for the believer glory and honor in the life to come. In this passage Paul speaks of glory as if it were a tangible thing that could be progressively added to. It is as if each believer has an eternal account wherein glory is being applied in relation to personal suffering on this earth.

He closes this section by giving us the motivation we need to adopt this perspective. Simply put, our sufferings are temporary. But the rewards we are accumulating while in these temporary bodies are eternal. What an investment! What a system! God has allowed us to participate in a system by which the temporal can be used to gain what is eternal.

This truth is especially important as we focus on the end of the story of Lazarus. Many may be tempted to say, "Well, it always works out fine for people in the Bible, but my husband was not raised from the dead," or "My wife never came back to me," or "I have not seen God get any glory out of my situation." To which God would add one essential word: "Yet!" Remember, eventually Lazarus died for good. Christ's miracle was in that sense only temporary. The glory connected with Lazarus's being alive was short-lived. Any time God bails us out of adversity—as He often does—the glory connected with that is to some degree temporary. Yet God has established a means by which our suffering can result in eternal glory, glory that exalts not only Him, but also those who suffered.

"REMOVE THE STONE"

Jesus said, "Remove the stone." Martha, the sister of the deceased, said to Him, "Lord, by this time there will be a stench, for he has been dead four days." Jesus said to her, "Did I not say to you, that if you believe, you will see the glory of God?"

(JOHN 11:39–40)

Had they refused to remove the stone, they would have suffered for nothing. No good would have come from it. Mary and her sister would have missed the glory of God. I meet people all the time who are dealing with personal tragedy of the worst kind. Sometimes it is their own fault. At other times they are the victims. Oftentimes greater than the tragedy itself is their response. Because they see no immediate good, they assume that there is no good to be found, that God has abandoned them or perhaps was never interested in the first place. They refuse to remove the stone. They will not trust God with what they cannot see.

If God can gain glory for Himself from the unjustified murder of His Son, can we not trust Him to somehow glorify Himself in and through the things we struggle with on a daily basis? If God can find for Himself glory in the death of His Son's close friend, should we not trust Him to do the same through even the major tragedies in our lives? God specializes in taking tragedy and turning it into triumph. The greater the tragedy, the greater the potential for triumph.

There will always be things we cannot explain. In time some answers will become clear, while others will remain a mystery. One thing we do know: God is in the business of glorifying Himself. He wants the world's attention, and oftentimes adversity is His way of getting it. As Christians, we are His representatives. We are extensions of the ministry of Christ on the earth. We, then, are the tools through which God will attract the world's attention. He works through our conversations, our character, our preaching, and our adversity. His success in all of these areas depends in part upon our responses.

"IF YOU BELIEVE, YOU WILL SEE THE GLORY OF GOD"

Martha trusted Christ and removed the stone. I believe Jim too will trust God to gain glory for Himself through the tragedy of his wife's terminal illness. What about you? Are there stones in your life that are blocking the Lord's ability to gain for Himself the glory that is rightfully His? Have you cut your faith off at the point where things quit making sense? Have you attached your faith only to what can be seen? Have you refused to look beyond your loss? Have you allowed your pain to so consume you that you have forgotten that God may have something He wants to accomplish?

You have only two options. You can trust God to glorify Himself through your adversity. Or you can focus on your loss and spend your time searching for answers. In doing so, you may cause the means by which God was going to do something great to become a tragic end in itself.

An old saint contemplating his life summed up the point of this chapter perfectly:

> And I may return in faded armor
> Full of patches bent and aged.
> And I may face the heat of battle,
> To free the damned and free the slaves.
> And I may know both pain and rejection,
> The betrayal of my friends.
> But the glory that awaits me,
> Will make it worth it in the end—in the end.

Friend, regardless of the adversity you are facing, if you trust God, you, too, will one day say, "It was worth it all!"

FOURTEEN

ADVANCING THROUGH ADVERSITY

Biblical narratives such as those of Lazarus and Joseph make one point undeniably clear: *God uses adversity in the lives of His children.* Adversity, however, is not simply *a* tool. It is God's *most effective* tool for the advancement of our spiritual lives. The circumstances and events that we see as setbacks are oftentimes the very things that launch us into periods of intense spiritual growth. Once we begin to understand this, and accept it as a spiritual fact of life, adversity becomes easier to bear.

It is within the context of this principle that Paul was able to say,

> All things . . . work together for good to those who love God, to those who are called according to His purpose.
>
> (ROM. 8:28)

This is a conditional promise. For the person who does not love God and thus is not interested in knowing Him or growing spiritually, all things do not necessarily work for good because sometimes that "good" is the lesson or depth of character developed as a result of adversity. From God's perspective, it is good if we learn to be patient. It is good if we learn to love those who are unattractive. God values character far more than wealth, prominence, health, or many of the other things we hold dear.

WHOSE GOOD?

The "good" of Romans 8:28 is not necessarily the story of a man who loses his job and in the end gets a better one. It may be the story of a man who loses his job and comes to a greater understanding of what it means to trust God daily. The "good" of Romans 8:28 is not necessarily the story of a young woman who loses her love only to find a better catch later on. Instead it could be the story of a woman who through the tragedy of a lost love discovers God's call to enter full-time Christian service.

The reason so many of us struggle so intensely with adversity is that we have yet to adopt God's perspective and priorities. As you read about the lives of biblical characters, you will notice quickly that their stories do not end with, "And they lived happily ever after." Oftentimes their stories seem to end just the opposite way. Moses died in the desert just a few miles from the promised land. Paul, according to tradition, was beheaded by Nero. Many of the disciples were martyred.

Are we to conclude from these examples that God has no interest in His children being happy? No! We are told that heaven will be a place of great rejoicing and happiness. But God wants far more for us than simply living a life that is problem-free. The fact is, the people who have no problems as we usually think of them are some of the most unhappy people in the world. They are usually bored. After a while their boredom drives them to things that cause them problems. It is a mistake to think that a problem-free life is a happy life.

HAPPINESS DEFINED

Happiness, the way God defines it, "is a state of well-being that reaches deep into the soul of a man or woman." Its context is much broader than mere circumstance. Its effect on the emotions goes beyond momentary excitement. And the means by which one comes about it is not by the acquisition of more things. Neither is it the rearrangement of circumstances. The happiness God desires for His children comes only through the process of spiritual growth and maturity. Apart from that, there is no lasting happiness.

God does want us to be happy, but not the happiness advocated by the world. His desire for our happiness is expressed by His desire for us to "grow up" spiritually. The apostle Paul put it this way:

> As a result, we are no longer to be children, tossed here and there by waves and carried about by every wind of doctrine, by the trickery of men, by craftiness in deceitful scheming; but speaking the truth in love, *we are to grow up* in all aspects into Him, who is the head, even Christ.
>
> (EPH. 4:14–15, EMPHASIS ADDED)

To remain spiritually immature is to run the risk of eventually abandoning the faith. To adopt a worldview or life philosophy other than God's is to embrace a lie. No one has ever been "happy" for very long embracing a lie. Therefore, spiritual growth is imperative from God's point of view not only for our spiritual well-being, but for our general happiness as well. Continual spiritual growth, then, is the means by which God keeps us in tune with His purposes for our lives.

Since adversity is God's most effective tool, insofar as spiritual growth is concerned, the degree to which we desire to grow spiritually corresponds to our ability to handle adversity successfully. Men or women who are only marginally interested in maturing as Christians will have a difficult time with adversity. Their tendency will be to blame God and become bitter. Instead of seeing adversity as something God is trying to do *for* them, they will see it as something He is doing *to* them. It is all a matter of priority and perspective. If our priorities are ease, comfort, and pleasure, we will have little tolerance for adversity. We will see it as an interruption rather than a part of God's plan for us.

But when we allow God to shape our priorities, adversity takes on a whole new meaning. We see it as an integral part of what God is doing in our lives. We begin to understand that adversity is sometimes a means to greater joy and peace. We don't panic and assume God has forgotten about us. Rather, we can rejoice. Why? Because God is in the process of bringing about another good in our life.

Spiritual men and women emerge from adversity excited about what God has taught them. Carnal men and women often emerge bitter and angry with God for what He "put them through." They are quick to point out that "all things don't work together for good," conveniently ignoring the second half of the verse.

AN ANNUAL LESSON

It seems that I have to learn this same lesson at least once every year. I am an achievement-oriented person; I like to see projects begun and completed. I like to have several projects going at the same time. I enjoy setting goals. I am always writing out to-do lists. Because of my go-go-go personality and lifestyle, nothing is more frustrating to me than getting sick. What a waste of time! First I become angry. "Lord, do You know what all I have going on? I don't have time to be sick." Then I remember I am in the ministry and try to sound spiritual. "Lord, Your work is suffering! If I don't get well quick, what is going to happen to the ministry?"

I finally realize that God is not impressed with my commitment to His work and that He cannot be bribed or manipulated. Only then do I begin to ask the right questions: "Lord, what are You saying to me? What do You want me to learn? What about my lifestyle needs to be changed or eliminated?" For some reason, it is not until I am flat on my back that I am willing to take the time to ask these kinds of questions. The rest of the time I am too busy doing the "work of the Lord." But it is during these seasons that God has taught me some of the most exciting things I have ever learned.

THAT'S EASY FOR YOU TO SAY

I realize that the adversity you are facing in your life may be a far more serious ailment. And I am painfully aware of the tendency in literature and sermons to oversimplify when it comes to the subject of adversity. But the truth is, God wants to work through the adversity you are facing right now to advance your spiritual growth. The Bible gives us plenty of reason to believe that God could erase all adversity from our lives with just a word. But experience tells us He has chosen not to do that. Far more important than our ease, comfort, and pleasure is our spiritual growth.

If we are believers—that is, we have put our trust in Christ's death on the cross to be the payment for our sin—God has us in school. He is in the process of teaching us about Himself: His faithfulness, His goodness, His compassion, and His holiness. Just like any other school, some classes are more appealing than others. And if we are honest, Adversity 101 is not one of our favorite classes. But it is essential if we are to "grow up" in the Lord.

THE OLD STANDBY

The most-quoted verse in all the Bible when it comes to the topic of adversity is James 1:2. Unfortunately, verses like this one become so familiar that they lose their punch after a while. That being the case, I purposely waited until this chapter to bring it up.

As much as we may hate to admit it, the truth of James's words is foundational. It serves as the basis upon which our understanding of adversity rests. He wrote,

> Consider it all joy, my brethren, when you encounter various trials, knowing that the testing of your faith produces endurance. And let endurance have its perfect result, that you may be perfect and complete, lacking in nothing.
>
> (JAMES 1:2–4)

We need to take note of several things in these verses. First of all, our initial response to trials is to be joy. Upon first glance James seems to be demonstrating an incredible amount of insensitivity. When I am facing a crisis in my life, the last thing I want is some preacher telling me to *rejoice!* However, James is not telling us to be joyous because of the trial. There is nothing joyous about trials in and of themselves. We are only deceiving ourselves when we dutifully and unenthusiastically say, "Praise the Lord," every time something goes wrong.

James is very clear as to why we are to be joyous in the midst of adversity. He states it, however, in the form of an assumption rather than a reason. James assumes that his readers are so committed to spiritual growth that when they understand that trials lead to more spiritual growth, they will rejoice because of the end result—growth! The "testing" of our faith produces "endurance."

Endurance is a maturing factor. The term *perfect* carries with it the idea of maturity. Whenever persons are forced to endure hardship, they mature in some fashion. James says that endurance can bring about a great deal of maturity in individuals.

James warns that there is a way to interrupt this maturing process. He instructs his readers to "let endurance have its perfect result." The implication is that by reacting to adversity incorrectly, we short-circuit the maturing process. By resisting adversity, we rob ourselves of the work God desires to do in our lives. We put off the very thing God sent the adversity into our lives to accomplish.

I know of several people who are mad at God because of the adversity that has come their way. One particular fellow refuses to step foot inside the church because he did not get the promotion he thought he deserved. Another lady is mad because God did not stop her daughter from marrying an unbeliever. The tragedy in each case is that these people have put themselves on the sidelines spiritually. They cannot advance one more inch spiritually until they change their perspective on adversity. The very thing God allowed into their lives as an incentive to grow has put them into a spiritual coma. Why? Because they refused to "let endurance have its perfect (maturing) result."

Until we are committed to the process of spiritual maturity and growth, we will never be able to take James seriously. There will never be any joy in suffering. James assumed that when the majority of his readers learned that these tests of faith would produce endurance, they would be glowing with excitement.

REJOICE?

You may be thinking, *That is ridiculous. How could anyone be so enthusiastic about growing spiritually as to rejoice when confronted with adversity?* If that is your attitude, the next few verses of this passage are for you.

> But if any of you lacks wisdom, let him ask of God, who gives to all men generously and without reproach, and it will be given to him. But let him ask in faith without any doubting, for the one who doubts is like the surf of the sea,

driven and tossed by the wind. For let not that man expect that he will receive anything from the Lord, being a double-minded man, unstable in all his ways.

(JAMES 1:5–8)

James was not out of touch with the real world. He realized how strange it sounded to tell people to rejoice in the midst of trials. So he followed up by saying, "Hey, if you find that hard to accept, ask the Lord to make it clear to you." That is what he means by asking for wisdom. Wisdom is the ability to see things from God's perspective; it is usually a matter of getting the big picture. The big picture in this case is God's ultimate desire for His children—spiritual maturity.

For a long time I had trouble accepting this connection between adversity and growth. I could grasp the connection mentally, but emotionally it was difficult to take. I thought all this talk about God's using illness and tragedy and other forms of adversity to teach people things was just a way to cover for Him. People like to be able to explain things away, and I assumed this was just another means of dealing with what could not otherwise be explained.

My problem, when I got right down to it, was faith. It was hard for me to accept that God is so intent on bringing us to maturity that He is willing to let us suffer. In His economy, adversity is a small price to pay for the benefits of spiritual growth. As I studied passages such as the ones we have already examined, it became clear to me that the issue was not whether or not I thought adversity was a fair trade-off for spiritual growth. The issue was whether or not I was going to take God at His word and begin viewing adversity from that perspective.

I think my wavering back and forth is exactly what James was talking about when he said we must ask "in faith." That is, when God reveals the answer, we must accept it—not debate it, not simply consider it. We are to take God at His word and live by it. Until we are willing to do that, things will never be clear.

Strangely enough, it was not the adversity I was facing in my life that made this principle so difficult to accept. I could readily see the spiritual benefit that came through the adversity in my life. I was disturbed by the things I saw confronting other people: divorces, serious illnesses, the loss of friends, family, and possessions. I would look at their circumstances and think, *Lord, are You paying attention? These people did not deserve this! What are You doing?*

Over and over again, however, I would go to these people to comfort them and find that God was ministering to them in such a powerful way that they became an encouragement to me. Women whose husbands had walked off and left them were praising God for His mercy and provision. I talked to men who lost their jobs but in doing so rediscovered their families and praised God for what happened. I'll never forget a couple who had just lost everything they owned in a fire. After the initial shock wore off, they began to understand why God had allowed it to happen. Before long, they were giving testimony to God's faithfulness and rejoicing that they were able to better understand what really matters and what does not.

One day I was in a restaurant and noticed that the hostess was wearing a cross. I asked her if she was a Christian. Big tears welled up in her eyes. "You better believe it," she said. As we talked, she told me one of the saddest stories I have ever heard. It was just four days before Christmas, and her husband had walked out on her for another woman. To make matters worse, her daughter and son had turned on her and were planning to spend Christmas with her husband and his girlfriend, leaving this woman with no one to share her holiday. But what issued forth from her lips were not words of criticism and resentment. Instead she was praising God for His sustaining power. She went on to tell about the people to whom she had been able to witness. I sat there amazed.

Stories like these, along with the clear teaching of God's Word, finally convinced me that God could be trusted in the midst of adversity, that He really could work all things together for good if we would adopt His definition of good and accept His system of priorities. I realized that God knows exactly how much pressure each of us needs to advance in the spiritual life. It was hard for me to stand back and watch others suffer because I was not aware of all God was doing for them on the inside. My perspective was limited to what was taking place on the outside.

TAKING THE LONG LOOK

Dealing with adversity is like preparing for surgery. By putting our faith in what the doctor has said, we believe we will be better off if we have the surgery.

But that does not make it any less painful. By submitting to the hand of a surgeon, we are saying that our ultimate goal is health, even at the cost of pain. Adversity is the same way. It is a means to an end. It is God's tool for the advancement of our spiritual lives.

Perhaps you cannot bring yourself to adopt this attitude. In light of the adversity you or a loved one has faced, it may seem too much like a sugar pill, an excuse Christians use to keep God from looking bad. If that is where you are in your thinking, I want you to contemplate this question: If adversity is not a tool in the hand of God, what is it? What are your options?

You could adopt the philosophy of some who say God is fighting a cosmic battle with evil. In that way of thinking, adversity surfaces when God loses a round. Embracing that form of religion, however, means abandoning Christianity. There is no way the God of the Bible can be made to fit into that worldview. The two are mutually exclusive.

A person could argue that God does not care; therefore, He is unconcerned about the adversity we face. The problem there is that the question of God's love and concern was settled two thousand years ago when God sacrificed what was most precious to Him for the sake of man. The Cross puts to rest any question of love.

One may argue that there is no God. But simply because God does not behave the way *we might expect* Him to certainly does not disprove His existence. That would be like my determining the existence of my wife based upon how I think a wife should act.

The whole problem of injustice in the world kept C. S. Lewis from embracing Christianity. He assumed, like many, that there could not possibly be a good God in light of all the evil in the world. In *Mere Christianity* he describes his pilgrimage as he tried to cope with this perplexing question.

My argument against God was that the universe seemed so cruel and unjust. But how had I got this idea of just and unjust? A man does not call a line crooked unless he has some ideal of a straight line. What was I comparing this universe with when I called it unjust? If the whole show was bad and senseless from A to Z, so to speak, why did I who was supposed to be part of the show, find myself in such violent reaction against it? . . . Of course I could have given up my idea of justice by saying it was nothing but a private idea of my own. But if I did that, then my argument against God collapsed too—for the argument depended on saying that the world was really unjust, not simply that it did not happen to please my private fancies.[4]

To deny the existence of God based on the presence of adversity and pain is to say that in order to validate His existence God must conduct Himself according to my wishes. Clearly, there are multiple problems with that approach. There really are no good alternatives when it comes to the question of adversity. Adversity is God's tool to promote growth among His children. To resist this principle is to resist all God wants to do in your life; it is to say no to spiritual growth.

THE CROWN OF LIFE

James ends this section with an interesting promise:

> Blessed is a man who perseveres under trial; for once he has been approved, he will receive the crown of life which the Lord has promised to those who love Him.
>
> (JAMES 1:12)

Not only does adversity lead to spiritual maturity in this life, it purchases for us a crown of life in the next. God understands the trauma of dealing with adversity. He has not overlooked the sacrifices we are forced to make when adversity comes our way. Therefore, He has provided a special reward for those who "persevere under trial." Once again we are faced with a conditional promise. This reward is reserved for those who willingly accepted Christ in their lives. These are the ones who understood that God was up to something, that the adversity they faced was the means by which something good would come about in their lives.

Are you persevering? Are you enduring? Or are you resisting? Are you mad at God for what He is doing? My friend, God wants to advance you through the use of adversity. He wants to grow you up and mature you to the point that your character is a mirror image of Christ's. That is His goal for you. And adversity is the means by which He will accomplish it. Why not trust Him? It is futile to resist. Your sorrow will only be magnified, for there is nothing worse than a life filled with adversity from which nothing good ever comes.

Why not tell the Lord, "Lord, I don't like it, but by faith I rejoice that You are up to something good in my life"? Eventually you will begin to see the "good." You will begin to experience peace. You will begin to advance through your adversity.

FIFTEEN

THE POWER OF WEAKNESS

One of my favorite Old Testament narratives is the story of David and Goliath. From the way the writer describes this incident, an outsider would have found the whole thing somewhat comical. It seems that every morning the Israelites would line up on the hillside for battle. Just as they were ready to do battle with the Philistines, Goliath would stroll down into the valley. Standing there dressed for battle, with his shield bearer by his side, he would shout at the Israelite army and dare them to come and get him. At that point the entire Israelite army would turn around and run back to camp (1 Sam. 17:1–24).

Apparently this pattern of events had been going on for some time when David appeared on the scene. After a round or two with his brothers, he gathered five stones and went down into the valley to challenge Goliath. Again, to anyone watching from the hillside, this must have been amusing. Imagine—David and his sling going against the giant and his weapons of war. But to everyone's surprise (not the least of which was Goliath) David emerged the victor.

Many great lessons can be drawn from this familiar narrative. And many stirring sermons have been preached concerning David's faith and courage. But for just a moment let's look at this story from God's perspective. In doing so, we gain great insight into the mind of God and discover another way in which He uses adversity in our lives.

Why did God choose to use David in this encounter with Goliath? He was untrained, ill prepared, inexperienced, and young. Humanly speaking, he had nothing going for him. There were thousands of well-trained Israelite soldiers present who would have been far more likely candidates. Yet God chose David. Why?

WHAT IF . . . ?

Imagine for just a moment that you are the bystander I spoke of a couple of paragraphs ago. You are sitting on the hillside watching all this take place. You see Goliath coming down into the valley on his daily run. Then you notice a stirring among the Israelite soldiers. A cheer goes up from their ranks as one of their own takes up his sword and shield and charges down into the valley. Although this fellow is not as big as Goliath, he is certainly no wimp, either. As he positions himself to fight, it becomes apparent that this man has seen many battles and has probably faced great odds before.

Then suddenly the two warriors lunge at each other. For several minutes it looks as if this valiant Israelite warrior has met his match. But then, faster than you could bat an eye, our hero performs an incredible maneuver that catches Goliath off guard. As the giant struggles to regain his advantage, the Israelite thrusts his sword through the Philistine's breastplate and falls with him to the ground. For a minute the two men struggle together on the ground. But the blow proves to be fatal, and soon Goliath's body lies lifeless. The Israelite soldier slowly stands, picks up the giant's sword, and with one swoop separates the Philistine's head from the body. The men of the Israelite army cheer wildly as their enemies flee.

Exciting, huh? But not all that surprising. We have seen the underdog win before. Besides, Goliath made a tactical error, and the Israelite took advantage of it. No big deal. We could chalk the whole thing up to military skill and leave God out of the picture completely. God did not choose to send a soldier for that very reason. He chose a young shepherd instead. He looked for someone who seemed to have not even the slightest chance of success. Someone who would be completely dependent upon Him. An instrument through which He could demonstrate His mighty power in such a way as to get credit for it. When David slew Goliath that day, there was no doubt in his mind who delivered the giant into his hands (1 Sam. 17:37). And there was no doubt in anyone else's mind, either.

GOD'S CHOICE

The point is simply this: *The greater the odds, the better for God.* Our heavenly Father gets far more attention and thus more glory when He works through persons the world considers weak. The apostle Paul put it this way:

> But God has chosen the foolish things of the world to shame the wise, and God has chosen the weak things of the world to shame the things which are strong, and the base things of the world and the despised God has chosen, the things that are not, so that He might nullify the things that are, so that no man may boast before God.
>
> (1 COR. 1:27–29)

Look at that second phrase. God chooses to use the weak things of the world. He does not have to. That is His choice. When He uses what is weak, His power and might are that much more evident.

So how does all this fit into our discussion of adversity? One of the reasons God allows adversity into our lives is to cause us to rely on *His* strength instead of our own. In doing so, He perfects His power in us (2 Cor. 12:9). Relying on His power manifests His sufficiency to us and to all those who are familiar with our situation. David's victory was a source of rejoicing and encouragement to the entire nation of Israel. And so it is when God works through one of His children in spite of the individual's weakness.

HANDICAPS

Adversities always handicap us in some way. They either slow us down physically or drain us emotionally and mentally. Adversities keep us from functioning at 100 percent. Our minds get divided. Our energy level drops. And even the simplest tasks become major ordeals. Jobs that once took a couple of hours now take all day. Our tempers shorten. And the least little thing irritates us to no end.

I once had to deal with a sensitive family situation. My stepfather was blind and unable to care for himself any longer. This became a terrible strain on my mother. In spite of the pressure that having him at home was placing on her, she did not want me to put John in a nursing home. Back and forth we went. Finally, after much prayer and discussion, I put John in the nicest nursing home I could find. After visiting him on Saturday, my mother decided they were not taking care of him the way they should, so she packed his things and brought him back home. Poor John. For a while there he did not know from week to week where he would be living.

I can remember sitting down to study and struggling to concentrate on my work. My mind kept wandering; I would find myself staring out the window, thinking about my mom and John. It killed me to see her suffering. And yet I did not want to force her to do something against her will. The incident served to handicap me mentally and emotionally.

That is the nature of all adversity. It robs us of the resources we need to function properly. Areas of strength become our greatest weaknesses. Adversity is always unexpected and unwelcomed. It is an intruder and a thief. And yet in the hands of God, adversity becomes the means through which His supernatural power is demonstrated.

PERFECT POWER

The apostle Paul certainly understood this principle. After asking God three times to remove his thorn in the flesh, Paul finally received an answer. It was not what he expected. God told him flatly that He would not remove the thorn. He would, however, supply the extra strength Paul needed to carry out the work he had been called to do.

> And He has said to me, "My grace is sufficient for you, for power is perfected in weakness." Most gladly, therefore, I will rather boast about my weaknesses, so that the power of Christ may dwell in me . . . for when I am weak, then I am strong.
>
> (2 COR. 12:9–10)

Like all of us, Paul wanted his circumstances to be right. So that is how he prayed: "Lord, get rid of this thorn." But God wanted Paul to live with a handicap. It was His will that Paul remain weak. But not for weakness's sake. God's purpose was to weaken Paul's dependence on his own strength, his own wisdom, his own intellect. God wanted Paul to minister and live out of his weakness, not his strength. This is the idea behind the phrase "power is perfected in weakness."

The term *perfected* does not mean perfect in a moral sense, as in perfect versus imperfect; the idea here is that of being "completed" or "fulfilled." God was giving Paul a general principle. According to this principle, the weaker something is, the greater its need for strength. When what is weak is finally strengthened, the presence of renewed strength is more noticeable by comparison. One of the best ways for God to show forth His power is to manifest it through an otherwise weak or handicapped vessel. For this reason, God allows adversity to enter our experience: not for the purpose of making us weak and incapable of going on with our lives, but for the purpose of enabling us by His strength to do what otherwise would be impossible.

A PAINFUL PRIORITY

From God's perspective, it was more important for Paul to experience supernatural power than it was for him to live a pain-free, adversity-free life. The closer you look at Paul's life, the more difficult that is to accept. He was stoned and left for dead, shipwrecked, beaten, bitten by a snake, and finally imprisoned—all for Christ's sake. When all was said and done, Paul's response was this:

> Therefore I am well content with weaknesses, with insults, with distresses, with persecutions, with difficulties, for Christ's sake; for when I am weak, then I am strong.
>
> (2 COR. 12:10)

I have seen men and women emerge from far less strenuous circumstances than Paul's full of anger and hostility. They were mad at God for what He did *to* them. But not Paul. Why? Because he recognized that what God allowed to be done *to* him was simply preparation for what He wanted to do *for* him. As Paul grew more and more dependent upon the Lord for strength, it became second nature to him. His faith in Christ grew to the point that he could say with all sincerity, "I am well content with weaknesses."

The whole idea of being content with weakness contradicts the messages society sends us. In an age characterized by so many striving for power and control, it is unusual for people to get very excited about living in a state of weakness. But upon examining the life of the apostle Paul, one hardly gets the impression that he was a weak man. On the contrary, he debated against Christ's apostles over the question of Gentile salvation, and he won! He spent his life preaching in the most hostile of circumstances. He planted churches throughout the major cities of Asia Minor and in the port cities along the Aegean Sea. Paul trained the first pastors and elders of these early congregations. And to top it all off, he wrote half of the New Testament!

I don't know what you think, but that certainly doesn't sound like a weak man to me. If Paul had been a businessman, he would have been extremely successful. He knew how to set goals and accomplish them. He understood the principles involved in motivating people. He was a mover and a shaker.

So how do we reconcile Paul's claim to weakness with his amazing accomplishments? Simple. The answer is in the phrase "when I am weak, then I am strong." A paraphrase of his comment would go something like this: "When I, Paul, in and of my own strength, am weak, then I, Paul, relying on the power of Christ in me, become strong, capable of whatever the Lord requires of me, full of energy and zeal to accomplish His will."

IN SEARCH OF THE WEAK

God wants to work through our weaknesses in the same way He worked through the apostle Paul's. You may have been born with characteristics you consider weaknesses. Or you may have been born into a family that did not provide you with the things you think are necessary for success. Perhaps a recent tragedy or illness has left you wondering about your usefulness or self-worth.

If any of these situations sound familiar to you, rejoice! You are just the type of person God is looking for. He wants people through whom He can show off His mighty power, people who know their weaknesses and are willing to allow Him to control and direct their lives. God is looking for men and women who are willing to take on challenges too difficult for them to handle, trusting Him to carry the load. He wants people who understand from experience what Paul meant when he wrote, "My [God's] grace is sufficient for you." He wants believers who grow accustomed to weakness, but who draw daily upon the sufficiency and power of Christ!

More times than I can remember I have faced challenges that I knew were beyond my abilities to cope with them. I have suffered rejection from men I thought were my best friends. There have been occasions when I have hurt so deeply and cried so intensely that I told God I was ready to die. But in the midst of my pity parties, as I rehearsed for the heavenly Father what I could and could not do, He has always sent a gentle reminder: "Charles, I was not interested in your strength and your ability when I called you. And I am still not interested in them now. What I want to know is, are you available? If so, then let's go. For My grace is sufficient."

I want you to think about something at this point. Your biggest weakness is God's greatest opportunity. Instead of complaining and begging God to change your circumstances, why not ask Him to fill that void with His strength? God has allowed adversity into your life to loosen your dependence on your own strength. It is His desire that you learn to live in dependence on Him for those things you lack. As you grow more and more accustomed to this arrangement, you will actually begin to sense contentment. His power will be perfected in you. And as you make yourself available, His power will be demonstrated through you to the lives of others. And with the apostle Paul you will be able to boast in your weakness. For when you are weak, then *He* is strong!

SIXTEEN

FAITHFUL IS HE WHO CALLED YOU

You may have heard it said that a person does not really know who his friends are until the bottom drops out. I think there is great truth to that. All of us have experienced the pain of discovering that people we thought would be faithful—no matter what—were simply "fair-weather friends." You know, friends whose loyalty hinges upon the climate of the circumstances. As long as the relationship is enjoyable, they are with you all the way. But when it begins to demand some sacrifice on their part, they are hard to find. The ultimate measure of friends is where they stand in times of challenge and controversy. That being the case, apart from adversity of some kind, we would never know who our faithful friends really are.

In the same way, we will never know in a personal way the faithfulness of Christ apart from adversity. Without it, our faith in Him would never increase. It would remain static. One of the primary reasons God allows us to face adversity is so that He can demonstrate His faithfulness and in turn increase our faith. If you are a believer, you have made a decision to trust Christ with your eternal destiny. But you will not experience His faithfulness in that particular area until you die. God wants more from you and for you than simple intellectual acknowledgment of His faithfulness. It is His will that you *experience* it now.

If our lives are free from pain, turmoil, and sorrow, our knowledge of God will remain purely academic. Our relationship with Him could be compared to that of a great-great-grandfather about whom we have heard stories, yet never met personally. We would have great admiration, but no intimacy, no fellowship. There would always be a sense of distance and mystery.

That is not the kind of relationship God wants with His children. Through the death of Christ, God has opened the way for us to have direct access to Him. He went to great lengths to clear the way so that nothing stands between Him and His children. There is potential now for intimacy between us and our Creator. Christ went so far as to say that we are His friends (John 15:14–15).

God is in the process of engineering circumstances through which He can reveal Himself to each of us. And history as well as our personal testimonies bear witness to the fact that it is in times of adversity that we come to a greater realization of God's incredible faithfulness to us.

For Example . . .

Imagine how Noah's comprehension of God's faithfulness must have been increased after having been delivered through the Flood. Think about how David's faith was increased through his battle with the lion and the bear that came to steal his sheep. I can't imagine what must have been running through Gideon's mind when God told him he had too many soldiers and he had to get rid of most of them (Judges 7)! But after the victory, his faith soared. God used the Red Sea and Jericho to demonstrate His faithfulness to Israel. He used Lot's selfishness in Abraham's life. And on and on we could go. In every case, adversity was the means through which God revealed His faithfulness to His servants.

The psalmist expressed it this way:

> I sought the LORD, and He answered me,
> And delivered me from all my fears . . .
> This poor man cried and the LORD heard him,
> And saved him out of all his troubles.
> The angel of the LORD encamps around
> those who fear Him,
> And rescues them . . .

Many are the afflictions of the righteous;
But the LORD delivers him out of them all.

(PSALM 34:4, 6–7, 19)

Here is the description of someone who is experiencing the faithfulness of God. It is an experience that would be impossible apart from "fear," "troubles," and "afflictions." Notice that the writer is not depressed or angry with God. On the contrary, the mood of the psalm is very positive and upbeat. It is a psalm of praise and thanksgiving. Where there is adversity, there is always great potential for praise. The most elaborate celebrations described in the Scriptures always followed an event in which God demonstrated His faithfulness through adversity.

Think back to the last time you genuinely praised the Lord for something He had done. Were the events leading up to your excitement touched by adversity or conflict of some kind? More than likely they were. God's faithfulness through adversity is usually the catalyst for praise. And in the process, faith is stretched and strengthened.

A CAUSE FOR PRAISE

I recall a series of events in my life that led to an experience of praise but was initially full of adversity. For a week I had been involved in a continuing dialogue with a young lady who had made the decision to end her pregnancy through abortion. She knew it was wrong, but the thought of telling her family and friends was overwhelming. Besides, she had just started a new career, and a baby did not fit into her immediate plans. I met with her and her boyfriend for about an hour and got nowhere. The evening after we had talked, they told a mutual friend that they did not appreciate my trying to scare them.

After several days of not knowing which direction they were heading, I finally got word that the young woman decided to go ahead and have her baby. She called and apologized for her attitude and even thanked me for my help. I have been praising God for His faithfulness ever since. It is not that *He* was any less faithful before, but by allowing me to see and experience His faithfulness in action, *my* faith is increased.

IN THE REAL WORLD

Unfortunately, things do not always work out so well. Sometimes circumstances don't end up at all as we'd like. People we pray for die. Husbands leave their wives and never come back. Children wreck and ruin their lives in spite of the influence of godly parents. Businesses go bankrupt. Christians lose their jobs. And thousands of women *do* have abortions.

But God is no less faithful in these events than He is in the others. His faithfulness, however, takes a different form. Nevertheless, many Christians are quick to doubt God when adversities are not resolved the way they deem appropriate. Some become angry and turn their back on Him completely. I cannot tell you how many men and women I have counseled who lived for years in rebellion toward God over this very issue. God did not do things the way *they* thought He should, so they wrote Him off as unfaithful and walked away.

God is *always* faithful to His promises. Nowhere, however, did He promise to always work things out the way we think they should be. If that were the case, He would be no more than a magic genie. God's ways are not our ways. And in the same vein, His goals are oftentimes not our goals. But He is always faithful.

FAITHFUL JUST THE SAME

God's faithfulness does not always take the form of deliverance *from* adversity. Many times God demonstrates His faithfulness by sustaining us *through* adversity. Take, for instance, a man marooned on a deserted island. As he explores the island looking for food, he discovers a speedboat washed up on shore. Upon further examination he finds that the tank is full of gas. He cranks the engine, and away he goes. He is delivered from being stranded.

Let's take the same example again. Only this time he does not discover a boat; he discovers a deserted house and a fruit orchard. Inside the house he finds all the tools he will need to cultivate the orchard. Although he is still stranded on the island, he has what he needs to survive. He will be able to carry on.

No doubt we would all agree that the first set of circumstances sounds much better. Yet the man in the second scenario could have been much worse off. In both illustrations the man was provided what he needed to survive. God does not always change our painful circumstances, but He sustains us through them. This is what the writer of Hebrews was referring to when he wrote,

> Therefore let us draw near with confidence to the throne of grace, that we may receive mercy and may find grace to help in time of need.
>
> (HEB. 4:16)

The writer makes an interesting promise. When we are in need, God will provide us with mercy and grace. This verse does not promise us a change of circumstances, freedom from pain, or deliverance from our enemies. It simply states that when we have a need, God will shower us with mercy and grace. Granted, we would rather have God relieve us of pain than sustain us through it. But He is under no obligation to do so. And He is no less faithful either way.

Paul certainly did not lack confidence in God's faithfulness. Yet God opted not to remove his thorn in the flesh. He chose instead to sustain Paul through it. When Paul asked for relief, the answer he received was simply, "My grace is sufficient for you" (2 Cor. 12:9). In other words, "Paul, you will continue to suffer, but if you hang in there with Me, you will make it."

GRACE BEYOND MEASURE

In his fascinating book *A Shepherd's Look at Psalm 23,* Phillip Keller described God's wonderful faithfulness during his wife's illness and death. As much as Phillip must have desired to see his wife healed, she was not. Yet he wrote,

Again and again I remind myself, "O God, this seems terribly tough, but I know for a fact that in the end it will prove to be the easiest and gentlest way to get me to higher ground." Then when I thank Him for the difficult things, the dark days, I discover that He is there with me in my distress. At that point my panic, my fear, my misgivings give way to calm and quiet confidence in His care. Somehow, in a serene quiet way I am assured all will turn out for my best because He is with me in the valley and things are under His control.

To come to this conviction in the Christian life is to have entered into an attitude of quiet acceptance of every adversity. It is to have moved onto higher ground with God. Knowing Him in this new and intimate manner makes life much more bearable than before.

During my wife's illness and after her death I could not get over the strength, solace and serene outlook imparted to me virtually hour after hour by the presence of God's gracious Spirit Himself. It was as if I was repeatedly refreshed and restored despite the most desperate circumstance all around me.[5]

Could anyone deny God's faithfulness to Phillip? Though God elected not to heal his wife, He was recognizably faithful before, during, and after this painful ordeal. As He did for the apostle Paul, God chose to answer Phillip's cry for help with sustaining grace and mercy.

A PERSONAL NOTE

I am no different from most people in that I would much rather God deliver me from adversity than sustain me through it. The greatest lessons of my life, however, have been taught to me during times of prolonged adversity. There was a time in my life where one thing in particular was a burden on me for twelve years. I prayed, fasted, and at times literally cried out to God to remove the weight from my shoulders. But His answer every time was, "Charles, My grace is sufficient for you." And praise God, it was! Every moment of every day it still is.

There are times when I operate in my own strength. When I do, I go down under the pressure every time. Then I begin complaining again: "Lord, how do You expect me to be a good husband and father, prepare sermons, and keep everything at church going when I have this extra load to bear as well?" When I finally get quiet enough to listen, He reminds me through His Word or in the privacy of my heart that He does not expect me to do anything on my own. And if I will let Him, He will provide grace and strength in my time of need.

Through all of this I have emerged with a greater sense of who God is. I understand in a much deeper way His commitment to His children. I know beyond a shadow of a doubt that we serve a faithful God—the God who can be trusted in even the darkest valleys and whose grace is always sufficient and always on time.

Dear friend, I do not know the nature of the adversity you are facing at this time. But I do know that if you will allow Him to, God will use this trial to deepen your faith in His faithfulness. He will reveal Himself to you in ways that are afforded Him only in times of difficulty and heartache.

At no other times are we forced to depend so completely upon the mercy and grace of God. And it is only after we are driven to rely upon His sustaining power that we know it to be adequate; and it is only then that we know in our experience that He is faithful and we can absolutely trust Him.

Perhaps God has chosen to leave your circumstances the way they are. You may never feel any better. Your spouse may never return. You may never recover financially to the economic level you had previously attained. But God is no less faithful, for He will provide you with mercy and grace in time of need.

The Lord did not say to Paul, "My grace *will* be sufficient for you," or "My grace *has been* sufficient for you." He said, "My grace *is* sufficient for you." That's in the present tense; that means right now. And so it can be in your experience if you will choose to trust Him. Then you will be able to say with the apostle Paul,

Most gladly, therefore, I will rather boast about my weaknesses, that the power of Christ may dwell in me.

(2 COR. 12:9)

PART FIVE

GOD REVEALS A PLAN FOR YOUR LIFE

SEVENTEEN

A PERSONAL PROMISE

Does God have a purpose and a plan for my life? If so, can I know it?" Each time I hear these two questions, I answer the same way: yes, He does. In fact, His personal promise to you is that He does have a purpose and a plan for your life (Jer. 29:11). While you may not know or understand all the twists and turns of life, you can be sure of one thing: the same God who breathed life into you loves you enough to plan for your future. He has promised that if you will seek Him, you will find Him, and you also will discover His will for your life.

At times, He may reveal to us a portion of His will. We will know that God has brought us to a certain point but not know all that is connected with being there. Remember, Abraham did not wait for God's promise to be completely revealed to him before he obeyed the Lord. Instead, he left his home believing in the One who had called him.

David was anointed king over Israel. However, it was many years before he sat on the nation's throne. These were years of extreme danger and disappointment. He was forced to run for his life from an angry king whose sole existence was wrapped up in ending David's life. Before David could do God's will, he had to be trained by adversity, disappointment, and, at times, extreme difficulty. Was he outside the will of God? There were moments when he made decisions that were not the best, but David kept pace with God's will even when he could not see how he would make it through the next day.

Like David, you may be walking through a deep valley and wondering if you are in God's will. Remember, He has promised to guide you and lead you to a place where you will fulfill His will and purpose for your life. David wrote, "Even though I walk through the valley of the shadow of death, I fear no evil; for You are with me" (Ps. 23:4). David was walking through the valley and knew that he would emerge victorious on the other side of his problems. He did not become a sorrowful person. He became a man after God's own heart and learned to do God's will regardless of his circumstances, and we can do the same (Acts 13:22).

LEARN TO TRUST

David also was the author of a majority of the psalms, and in Psalm 40, he wrote, "I delight to do Your will, O my God" (v. 8). Then in Psalm 143:10, his words form a personal prayer, "Teach me to do Your will, for You are my God; let Your good Spirit lead me on level ground." God answered David's prayers and continued to lead him through a lifetime of trials and victories. The question we need to answer is, Are we willing for God to do the same thing in our lives?

He has a will for every single one of us, and the prayer of our hearts always should be, "Lord, teach me to do Your will." When we pray this way, we are praying the same way Jesus prayed before facing Calvary: "Not My will, but Yours be done" (Luke 22:42). This is a prayer of surrender—surrender to God's perfect will and not our human desires.

Even Jesus, God's Son, understood that God had a plan in mind for His life. While He did not know all the steps in that plan, He knew He could trust the One who was in control of His destiny.

TAKE THE FIRST STEP

You may be thinking, *Well, I would take the first step, if I only knew what the plan looked like.* Remember, David did not know. He just wanted to obey the Lord's call to him. God does not show us more than what we can handle. He only revealed a portion of His will to Moses. Then, like David, he was forced to live years in a wilderness situation that probably left him wondering if he would ever do what God had called him to do. The same was true of Abraham and Joseph. Both of these men were given glimpses of God's plan for their lives, but they had to trust in the Lord and wait for His appointed time for all of it to come to fruition.

Timing is everything to God. He knows the perfect moment to call to you and the perfect moment for you to answer Him. When we are willing to listen and wait for His will, God will begin to unfold His plan and purpose for us. We know the right steps to take because, with each move we make, we will sense Him saying, "Yes, this is what I have planned for your life."

Three Things We Need to Know Concerning Waiting on God's Direction

First, He will show us His will. He desires that we know it and assumes responsibility for telling us how to live each day in the center of His will. This is a part of His nature and character. It is, however, our responsibility to do what He leads us to do. If He says move forward, as He did with Abraham and David, then we need to put on our walking shoes and move forward by faith, trusting Him to set up the circumstances of our life and to provide for the needs we have.

Second, He is committed to our success. He wants us to live in the center of His will. This is why it is not a mystery that cannot be found or discovered. He tells us in Psalm 32, "I will instruct you and teach you in the way which you should go; I will counsel you with My eye upon you" (v. 8). From our birth, God has been working the circumstances of our lives together in order for us to fulfill His will. However, because we live in a fallen world, we often get off track. Yet God remains steadfast in His desire to teach us how to fulfill His purpose and plan for our lives. David knew God had a plan for his life, but he didn't know all the aspects of that plan. However, he realized if he would commit himself to follow wherever the Lord led him, he would discover it. It would unfold before him over time, and this is exactly what happened. There are times when God places a dream or a goal in our hearts, and we have to step forward with the intent of reaching that objective. If we say, "Lord, I don't want to move until I can see the whole picture laid out before me," then we will miss not only a great blessing, but we also will miss His will for our lives.

Third, He will correct and redirect us when we make a wrong turn. Many of the people that I talk with have made mistakes in their walk with the Lord. Maybe they made wrong choices that ended up devastating their families. Others have written to say that they felt God was leading them to a certain line of employment, and they ignored His call. Years later, they are fighting feelings of hopelessness as they wonder if it is too late for them to discover God's will for their lives, and the answer is no. His promise is the same as it was the day you were born. God doesn't change; we may, but He is the same yesterday, today, and forever.

No matter how badly you have messed up, He will take the broken pieces of your life and, with the glue of His unconditional love, put your life back together. Whenever you turn back to Him, seek His forgiveness, and ask Him to guide you from this point on, He is quick to embrace you with His unconditional love and forgiveness. He says, "I will take you, right where you are, and show you how to live out the rest of your life with My help and My strength."

How Do We Discover God's Promise, Which Is His Will and Purpose for Our Lives?

Through:

- reading His Word
- the circumstances of life
- godly counsel
- listening to your spirit-driven conscience

First, God reveals His will to us through His Word. The saints in the Bible learned to meditate on the truth of His Word. They studied His principles and considered how He had worked in the lives of others. As we pray and study Scripture, the Holy Spirit leads us to passages that demonstrate what God wants us to do or learn. The Bible is God's primary form of communication with us and, because of that, we cannot live the Christian life apart from it. Once we begin to read it, we will want to continue. As we study its message, we will see God's hand guiding, teaching, and spiritually nurturing us so we will find the right road to travel.

Second, God reveals His will and promises to us through the circumstances of life. There are times, from our natural perspective, that life may seem out of sorts. We may face a sudden tragedy or loss. Without warning, a husband or wife may come to us and say he or she is leaving. Maybe there were things that we should have done differently, but now it is too late. Our lives are shattered by our circumstances, and the stress feels unbelievable.

We wonder, *How can any good come out of such sorrow?* God never finds delight in our suffering. He is not glorified by evil or the brokenness of our world, but He certainly can do the impossible. What appears to be an ending is really a beginning to Him. Yes, He cares when we hurt. He cried at the tomb of His friend Lazarus, and His heart cries even now with us when we are hurting. However, just as Lazarus rose from the grave, God wants to resurrect our lives. We may go through a season of mourning, but it will not last forever (Ps. 30:5; 51:12). When we allow Him to move close to us, He will heal our hearts and shattered dreams and lead us on to a spacious place of blessing (Ps. 18:19).

God uses the circumstances of our lives to reveal His will to us. He also uses them to position us for a greater purpose and blessing. What seems to be a dead end to you today may be God's avenue of hope tomorrow. You need to be willing to stay on course and believe that He is using everything in your life to accomplish His will (Rom. 8:28). There may be times when we are tempted to wonder how we will reach the goals He has given us, but we will because He is guiding us through the circumstances of our lives. Every turn we take, every challenge we face, and every disappointment that works its way into our lives are opportunities for Him to demonstrate His faithfulness to us.

We may think that we are just going through a daily grind, but we are not. That so-called daily grind is leading us to a place and a position where God can bless us and use us in ways that we could never imagine. Every challenge we face is used by God to prepare us for the next step in life. We never stop growing, and He never stops working in our lives. Even to our dying day, God is working His will out through our lives. I've never lost sight of this fact, even when life became very difficult, and I wondered what in the world God was doing in my life. I knew that He had a plan, and my responsibility was to stay focused on Him, allow Him to guide me, and be willing to obey Him in every situation. If I did that, He would take care of the details, and the same is true for you.

The third way God reveals His promise for our life is through the godly counsel of others. Often, God speaks to us and reveals His will through the counsel of a godly friend, pastor, or counselor. In Proverbs, He reminds us, "Where there is no guidance the people fall, but in abundance of counselors there is victory" (11:14). However, we must always consider if what others say to us lines up with the Word of God.

Many well-meaning people have given counsel that is just not a part of God's plan. Regardless of the situation, the counsel we give and receive needs to be godly and something that we know is sanctioned by the Lord. If we are unsure about a matter, we need to stop and wait for Him to lead us to the next step. He will, and He always does. So be patient, and be committed to receiving the best He has to offer for your life. That way, you will never be disappointed.

God reveals His will to us through our conscience. How do we know what is best? We know He has a planned will, but how can we be sure that we have discovered it? When we ask God to make His will plain to us, He will do it. He has placed within our lives a conscience, an awareness of His presence (Rom. 1:20). He trains our conscience with the principles written in His Word. This is why the activities of reading, studying, meditating on, and even memorizing the Bible are so crucial to our daily walk with God. If we have taken time to hide His Word in our hearts, then we will have a clear and firm vision of hope for the future.

When tragedy comes, we will stumble and grope for hope. However, if we have the principles of God within our hearts, we will know that when trouble comes, we are not alone. We will remember that His Holy Spirit who lives within us will never leave us alone. We will also recall the places in God's Word where He has promised to guide us and give us the wisdom we need to meet every challenge (Prov. 2:6; 9:10; 14:33).

TWO ASPECTS TO GOD'S WILL

There are two major aspects to the will of God. First, God has a *determined will*. Second, He has a *desired will*. The determined will is God's sovereign, operational will in the world. It reflects how God operates as the Lord of the universe. The Bible tells us that He has established His throne in the heavens, and His sovereignty rules over all (Ps. 11:4). The problem is that some people do not believe that He is in control of all things; but if He is not, then who is? Satan is not in control. He has limited abilities that God has allowed to be operational in the world, but he is not sovereign and certainly not in control of God's creation. Likewise, we are not in control of our world or our destinies. God is the only One who has His hand on the controls.

This world did not create itself. Mankind did not begin life as a result of evolution from a single-celled animal. God created us in His image, and the light of His love lives within those who have placed their faith in His Son, the Lord Jesus Christ. What a marvelous gift we have been given by God—life and breath and enough joy to live each day without feelings of fear or anxiety. The reason? The One who created us watches over us and has promised never to leave us (John 14:16). That is sovereignty and absolute control.

God's determined will is what must be done in this world. It is not up for discussion, nor is it optional. This means that whatever falls within His determined will absolutely, inevitably will happen. His determined will is also immutable. This means it is not going to change. It is irresistible in the sense that no one can ignore it or decide that it will not take place. It also is unconditional. There are some things that God does and will do that only He understands.

His determined will is comprehensive and purposeful. For example, in Ephesians the apostle Paul wrote, "He predestined us to adoption as sons through Jesus Christ to Himself, according to the kind intention of His will, to the praise of the glory of His grace, which He freely bestowed on us in the Beloved" (1:5–6). In love, He predestined you to the adoption of His Son. This means He drew a circle around your life once you came to know Christ as your Lord and Savior. However, God's determined will is also unpredictable. We should never assume God will act in the way we think He should or that we can determine who Christ will or will not save (John 3:8).

However, what you can know for certain is that those who receive Jesus Christ as their personal Savior belong to Him forever. Once you have come to know the Lord as your Savior, you cannot lose your salvation. You may yield to temptation, fall into sin, and even walk away from God, but He never stops loving you. This does not mean that you will avoid His discipline or the consequences of sin. Often, He allows us to experience suffering so that He can gain our attention and motivate us to return to Him. David reminds us that we can never travel away from His presence. "Even before there is a word on my tongue, behold, O Lord, You know it all. You have enclosed me behind and before, and laid Your hand upon me. Such knowledge is too wonderful for me; it is too high, I cannot attain to it" (Ps. 139:4–6).

GOD MAKES KNOWN HIS WILL

The knowledge of God is too great for us ever to know fully. We may gain knowledge, but apart from God, we really know very little. He holds the world and all of us in His hands. We may think the government is in control of the future, but it is not. God is the One who places men and women in power. He also is the One who removes them. Without a doubt, He knows exactly what is going to take place and when it will happen. He is aware of the problems with terrorists and the unrest in the Middle East, but He is just as concerned about what is going on in your daily life. He is omniscient—all-knowing—and all-powerful. He cares when you are hurting or struggling with a decision and wants to guide you through your difficulty.

Paul tells us God has "made known to us the mystery of His will, according to His kind intention [that is according to His good pleasure] which He purposed in [Christ]" (Eph. 1:9). There are a lot of mysteries to God's will— events in the past and those to come that we will not fully understand. There will be some things that He shows us and other things that we will not know. Our minds cannot comprehend all the ways of God, but we can use the things

He has revealed to us to discern His purpose in many situations (Deut. 30:16; Acts 2:28).

There is a difference between God's determined will and His desired will. His *determined will* includes the things in this life that He is going to do regardless of how we respond. It is absolutely indisputable and irresistible. However, the same is not true of His *desired will*, which includes the things that He wants to do. His determined will happens outside our sphere of control. God says that a certain thing will happen, and it does. Period. This also includes the things that He will do regardless of our cooperation or not. His desired will includes the things that He wants to do. When it comes to His desired will, we have a choice. We can obey or disobey Him. Included in God's desired will are decisions that we make each day. They may be major or minor choices.

One of the reasons so many of God's people are not living in His will is because they do not understand it, and they get confused. They wobble through life, hoping that they are on the right pathway. His determined will is very clear-cut—Jesus came to save us from our sin. God's mercy and grace were demonstrated through His Son's life and death. Do we understand how Christ was conceived? We know it was by the power of the Holy Spirit, but God has not chosen to reveal every aspect to us.

THE STEP BEFORE US

When it comes to His desired will, He provides instruction so we will know what we need to do, but we must decide to follow His instruction. In Colossians, Paul wrote, "For this reason also, since the day we heard of it, we have not ceased to pray for you and to ask that you may be filled with the knowledge of His will in all spiritual wisdom and understanding" (1:9). This was Paul's prayer for the Colossian church, and it really is God's prayer for each one of us so that we might know and experience His personal will for our lives.

In her book *Candles in the Dark*, Amy Carmichael wrote, "If the next step is clear, then the one thing to do is to take it. . . . Once when I was climbing at night in the forest before there was a made path, I learned what the word meant in Psalm 119:105: 'Thy word is a light to my path.' I had a lantern and had to hold it very low or I should certainly have slipped on those rough rocks. We don't walk spiritually by electric light but by a hand lantern. And a lantern only shows the next step—not several ahead."[6] When we walk with our eyes set on Christ, then we will do His will.

A life that is focused on obedience is a life that is lived in the center of God's will. One of the first things that trainers teach their animals, especially dogs, is to watch them. The command of "watch" is given, and the dog learns to stay focused only on its master. Even if there is noise or other activity, the animal must hold its watch. The only person who can break this command is the owner or trainer. The purpose is simple. When the animal is watching its master, it is not distracted.

On a greater scale, if the focus of our hearts is set on Christ, then when we have to make a decision, we will do several things:

- We will turn to the Lord in prayer.
- We will be willing to wait for His answer.
- We will take time to seek His wisdom through reading His Word.
- We will obey Him.

TRUST GOD ABOVE ALL ELSE

It all boils down to a level of trust. Do we trust God with our lives regardless of what we see, or is there a shadow of doubt lurking in the back of our minds? One second of doubt can change the way we view God's presence in our lives. For example, many people believe the Bible contains the Word of God. Here is the error: The Bible does not just *contain* God's Word to us; it *is* the Word of God. Period. The moment you say, "Well, I don't know if every single word written within it is true," is the moment you discredit what God has spoken to us through His Word.

The Bible totally relates to your life and situation right now. It is the infallible Word of God—written by God Himself, through men who were His agents or scribes. They were His chosen vessels to record His principles and plan of redemption for a lost and desperate world. If you deny even a part of God's Word, you take a major step in the wrong direction—a direction that leads far from God's will and purpose for your life. It is also a direction that leads along a pathway of doubt, fear, and anxiety. The results of a single decision as this one can bring more heartache and sorrow than you can bear, because apart from faith in God and His Word, you will begin to drift spiritually. You will lose your sense of direction because you have tossed aside the very compass God has given you to keep you on course and in the center of His will.

However, when we choose to obey the Lord, we are telling Him that we believe He is who He says He is. We have a choice to believe or not to believe. If we choose to obey and believe, we will come out a winner every time. It is foolish not to obey God.

Still the question remains, Can we know the will of God? The answer is yes, but in a limited way. While on earth, even Jesus did not know all that His heavenly Father knew about the future. When questioned about the hour of His return, Christ told His disciples, "That day or hour no one knows, not even the angels in heaven, nor the Son, but the Father alone" (Mark 13:32). While on the earth, there was a limitation to what Jesus knew. He was God in the flesh, but He took on the limitations of humanity in order to be our perfect Representative and High Priest (Phil. 2:5–8; Heb. 2:17).

However, God has full knowledge, and when we ask for His guidance in a particular situation, He will provide it (Ps. 73:24; Matt. 7:7). Never lose sight of the fact that God's determined will is just that—what He has determined will happen. Nothing can change it. One day, He will return for those who have placed their faith in Him. This is an upcoming event, and we can rest assured that it will take place. His goal for us is to prepare us for the day of His coming by leading and guiding us through His Spirit into truth and godly understanding.

In Psalm 25, David prays a prayer that we can pray each day: "Make me know Your ways, O LORD; teach me Your paths. Lead me in Your truth and teach me, for You are the God of my salvation" (vv. 4–5). If you really want to catch God's attention, ask Him to "teach you more about His ways" as He guides you each day. He will not resist a heart that is fully submitted to Him.

EIGHTEEN

SUCCESS GOD'S WAY

Is it part of God's plan for your life for you to be successful? When I first met Kyle, he was the picture of dejection. He gave me a limp handshake and collapsed wearily in the chair opposite me. I thought perhaps he was ill. But then he said, "Pastor Stanley, I just don't get it. I'm trying to live a good Christian life out there in the business world, but I just don't think the honest guy can get ahead. Every time I turn around, I see a good person getting stabbed in the back, and lately I've been the one getting stabbed. It seems to me that those who care the least about God are the ones who are getting the promotions, raises, and all the perks. I don't see any evidence at all that God cares one bit about whether I or any other Christian succeeds."

If that is the way you feel today, let me assure you, as I assured Kyle, God is committed to your success. God *wants* you to succeed and stands ready to help you succeed beyond your greatest dreams.

How do I know this? I believe there are three main forms of evidence:

First, God has given us all of the principles for genuine success in His Word. He has made the knowledge of how to be successful available to every person.

Second, God has built into each person a desire for success.

And third, God has given each person talents and gifts that, when developed and employed, yield the benefits of success.

Let's take a closer look at each one.

251

THE BIBLE IS GOD'S SUCCESS MANUAL

Over the years, I've probably read two or three dozen books on the subject of success. Some of them have included God in their discussion, and a few have put God at the center of a successful life. But I discovered that, without exception, every genuine principle of success in these books can be found in the Bible.

The principles of success are not foreign to a godly life; rather, they are embedded in a godly life. The world may think it has discovered this idea or that idea about success, but in truth, God is the author of all success, and God's Word has presented success principles for human living for thousands of years.

The word best translated *success* appears in the Bible only seven times— twice in Joshua, and once each in Genesis, Nehemiah, Job, Ecclesiastes, and Daniel. No word directly translated *success* appears in the New Testament. We might be tempted to conclude from the lack of Bible references directly linked to success that God is disinterested in the success of His people. Such a conclusion, however, would be erroneous.

Rather than use the word for *success*, the Bible uses the word for *prosper*. To prosper in all you do is to succeed in all you do. To be prosperous is to be successful. Anytime we read about the Lord prospering His people, we can be assured that the Lord is helping His people to succeed in all ways. For example, John wrote, "Beloved, I pray that you may prosper in all things and be in health, just as your soul prospers" (3 John 2 NKJV).

WHOLE-PERSON PROSPERITY

The success or the prosperity that God has for you is always a whole-person prosperity. Note again in 3 John 2 that the prayer of John was that the people would prosper in all things—their material, social, natural, financial, outer lives—just as they would prosper in their personal health and their spiritual lives. The prosperity he desired for them covered their entire lives. It was prosperity that might be described as "wholeness in action."

Take inventory of your life today. Ask yourself:

- Where am I in my spiritual walk?
- Where am I in my finances?
- Where am I in my vocation?
- Where am I in my service to the Lord?
- Where am I in my health?
- Where am I in my relationship with other people, including my family, my friends, and those with whom I am involved at church and at work?

God desires for you a success that will touch every aspect of your life. He desires for you to become whole and, in wholeness, to prosper in all areas of your experience.

Notice also that John prayed that the Lord's followers would prosper outwardly as their souls prospered. How many of us truly want to prosper to the degree that our souls are prospering? Frankly, most people I encounter hope that the Lord will prosper them in their finances and material lives far more than their souls are prospering. If they were to prosper financially only to the degree they were prospering spiritually, they'd be living in poverty.

The Lord links outer and inner prosperity, and the clear implication is that the Lord is going to prosper us financially, in our work, in our relationships, and in our material lives only to the degree that we are prospering spiritually or in proportion to our spiritual prosperity.

Consider the person who desires to prosper financially but fails to obey God when it comes to giving his tithes and offerings to the work of the Lord. Is the Lord going to be committed to helping a person who is disobedient in the use of finances to prosper financially?

When the Lord sees slothfulness and sloppiness and laziness in our lives, He cannot be committed to prospering those character qualities.

When the Lord sees a misuse of resources or a failure to be good stewards of our income, including a failure to give what we are commanded to give, the Lord cannot be committed to prospering us financially.

Our success always has conditions on it, and the conditions are primarily spiritual.

Wholeness Is Independent of Circumstances

The Bible also teaches about prosperity that our wholeness—our inner and outer prosperity—depends not on outer circumstances but on our inner-faith relationship with the Lord.

Perhaps no person faced more difficult circumstances for his entire life than Daniel. Daniel was taken into captivity by the Babylonians as a young man. He was transported to Babylon and forced to live in an alien culture the rest of his life. He served under three heathen kings—Nebuchadnezzar, Cyrus, and Darius.

Not only did Daniel face death when the magicians of the king failed to interpret the king's dream—something Daniel later did after the Lord revealed the dream and its meaning to him—but he faced a den of lions for being faithful in his prayer life. Few of us have ever faced, or ever will face, ongoing circumstances as negative or as harsh as those faced by Daniel. And yet we read in Daniel 6:28, "So this Daniel prospered in the reign of Darius and in the reign of Cyrus the Persian." Daniel lived well and lived successfully in the midst of his circumstances. And that is precisely what we are called to do.

One of the principles at the foundation of Bible prosperity is faith. Every success book I've read states, in one form or another, that a person has to believe he can be successful. The principle of faith is a constant for success. The real question for Christians is this: Faith in what or in whom? It is only when we identify the object of our faith that we truly know the foundation for our success.

If you put your faith in yourself and your abilities, intellect, and dreams, then your foundation is only as strong as you are. And no matter how strong you may be, you are neither omnipotent nor omniscient.

If you put your faith in God, then your foundation is as strong as He is, which is all-powerful and all-knowing.

GOD'S CALL TO SUCCESS

Not only do we find God's desires for our success expressed in the Bible, but we find numerous examples of people whom God called to be successful.

God called Joshua to be successful. Not only was Joshua to be successful personally in his leadership role, but all the Israelites under his leadership were called to success. We read in the first chapter of the book of Joshua:

> After the death of Moses the servant of the LORD, it came to pass that the LORD spoke to Joshua the son of Nun, Moses' assistant, saying: "Moses My servant is dead. Now therefore, arise, go over this Jordan, you and all this people, to the land which I am giving to them—the children of Israel. Every place that the sole of your foot will tread upon I have given you, as I said to Moses. From the wilderness and this Lebanon as far as the great river, the River Euphrates, all the land of the Hittites, and to the Great Sea toward the going down of the sun, shall be your territory. No man shall be able to stand before you all the days of your life; as I was with Moses, so I will be with you. I will not leave you nor forsake you. Be strong and of good courage, for to this people you shall divide as an inheritance the land which I swore to their fathers to give them."
>
> [The LORD spoke to Joshua,] "Only be strong and very courageous, that you may observe to do according to all the law which Moses My servant commanded you; do not turn from it to the right hand or to the left, that you may prosper wherever you go. This Book of the Law shall not depart from your mouth, but you shall meditate in it day and night, that you may observe to do according to all that is written in it. For then you will make your way prosperous, and then you will have good success. Have I not commanded you? Be strong and of good courage; do not be afraid, nor be dismayed, for the LORD your God is with you wherever you go."
>
> (JOSH. 1:1–9 NKJV)

What a tremendous statement of God's desire for Joshua and the Israelites to be a success! What a tremendous statement of God's commitment to help Joshua and the Israelites achieve success!

At the opening of the book of Joshua, God told Joshua that He was giving him the awesome responsibility of leading a nation of more than two million people across the Jordan River into the land that God promised them. Twice in the opening chapter, God said, "This land will be yours—it will be your territory, your inheritance." Twice, God said to Joshua personally, "No man will be able to take over your position of leadership. You will be successful in the role to which I have called you."

The real question is not whether God has promised success to you if you are faithful in following His principles related to success. The real question is, Are you willing to accept and believe that God desires your success?

Nehemiah Believed in God's Commitment to Success

Nehemiah was a man in the Bible who believed and claimed God's success for himself. Nehemiah was a servant of the king, and when he heard news that the walls and gates of Jerusalem were in ruins, he fasted and prayed about the situation.

The king noticed the sorrow in Nehemiah's countenance, and he asked him why he was sad. Nehemiah explained the situation in his homeland, and the king offered to give Nehemiah everything he needed to go to Jerusalem and make repairs to the city, including an escort to ensure his safe passage to Jerusalem and back.

Once Nehemiah arrived on the scene, he faced opposition from those who did not want him to succeed in the task before him. We should never be surprised when we face opposition. Any person who is doing the will of God is going to face opposition from the devil and those whom the devil can influence. Read how Nehemiah responded to the opposition:

> I told them of the hand of my God which had been good upon me, and also of the king's words that he had spoken to me. So they said, "Let us rise up and build." Then they set their hands to this good work. But when Sanballat the Horonite, Tobiah the Ammonite official, and Geshem the Arab heard of it, they laughed at us and despised us, and said, "What is this thing that you are doing? Will you rebel against the king?" So I answered them, and said to them, "The God of heaven Himself will prosper us; therefore we His servants will arise and build, but you have no heritage or right or memorial in Jerusalem."
>
> (NEH. 2:18–20 NKJV)

The God of heaven Himself will prosper us. Is that your attitude today toward your success? Are you truly believing that God is on your side and that He is committed to your success?

SUCCESS IS A PROCESS

Too often we look at the people in the Bible and conclude, "But I'm not like that." The fact is, we *are* like the people in the Bible, and they were like us in their responses to life, their struggles, their successes and failures, and their personalities and desires. The human heart has not changed. Technology and places may change, but the human heart has not changed through the ages. What you feel, the people of the Bible felt. What you think, the people of the Bible thought.

Did Jesus' apostles have days that seemed mundane and drab? Of course!

Were all the days of Moses glorious? No!

Was every moment of every day a high point for any one hero or heroine of the Bible? Certainly not.

For most of our lives, and their lives, the days are marked by sheer obedience, persistence, endurance, and struggle. Most days are not ones of either glowing success or devastating failure.

The point is this: Achieving success does not mean that you are going to live on the top of the mountain with a big grin on your face and a blue ribbon attached to your lapel every moment of every day of your life. High points may come. They may be frequent at times and virtually nonexistent at other times.

Success is not based on how you feel or on the uplifting moments when you receive rewards, recognition, or overwhelmingly positive responses from others. Success is to be found in the way you live day in and day out. It is to be found as you *pursue* what God calls you to be and to do.

Success is not the end of a process. Success is *how we undertake the process* called life. God's Word is our guidebook for the journey.

A BUILT-IN DESIRE FOR SUCCESS

Not only has the Lord given you His Word to challenge, call, and compel you to success, but He has built into you a deep desire for success.

Every child comes into this world goal oriented. Take a look at a baby in a crib who begins to cry and is given a pacifier. He may suck on that pacifier for a little while, but the next thing you know, he is playing with it, and before long, he has pulled the pacifier out of his mouth and it has rolled just beyond his reach. The baby might squirm a little or raise his arm in hopes of reaching that pacifier, but when his efforts fail, what does that baby do? He begins screaming and crying again! He is goal oriented even in the crib, even for a pacifier. That child will do everything in his power to get his needs satisfied.

Every normal, healthy baby comes into this world with a desire to achieve and succeed in life—to do and have the things that will bring a sense of satisfaction and fulfillment and contentment. He has a desire to communicate and express himself, a desire to relate to others, and a desire for mobility—to scoot, to crawl, to walk.

God has given you an inbred desire for success so that you will *act*. He has given you the desire so that you will motivate yourself to discover your gifts and talents and use them. You have a built-in drive to get your needs met in a way that brings pleasure.

Some people seem to have been inbred with the idea that they should always be taken care of or that handouts from others are the way to live. To live with a reliance upon others is not God's design. Rather, it is a *choice* that people make, consciously or unconsciously.

Some people choose defeat, choose to fail, choose to be lazy, choose not to care, and choose to blame others continually for their own lack of success. To a certain degree, these people have made a choice to live by manipulating others, guilt-tripping others, or using others for their purposes. They don't have any less desire to live a good life—they have chosen ungodly means for attaining that good life. (Manipulating others, imposing guilt on others, and using others for selfish purposes are *not* in line with God's plan. They are methods of the enemy, not methods that God calls righteous.)

The drive that God builds into you is neutral. It can be directed into lust of the flesh, lust of the eyes, and the pride of life. Or it can be directed into a pursuit of the things of God and the success that God has planned for you. But the drive toward success, satisfaction, and fulfillment is present in you—it is a gift of God to you that He expects you to use in right ways.

GOD HAS EQUIPPED YOU FOR SUCCESS

In addition to the promises of God's Word and the desire for success God has built into you, God has equipped you with one or more natural talents and abilities as well as one or more spiritual gifts (which are also called motivational or ministry gifts). These gifts have been embedded in your unique personality for one reason—so that you might use these gifts to the best of your ability and produce quality work that has a potential for both earthly and eternal reward.

Let's take a closer look at the process involved in the use of your gifts. The first step is the discovery of your unique gifts. If you do not know what God has gifted you to do, study your life and abilities. You may benefit from taking certain aptitude or spiritual-gifts tests. Discover what God has built into you.

The second step is the development of your gifts. Gifts do not emerge full-blown and at peak perfection. Your talents, abilities, and spiritual gifts must be developed through practice, application, and exercise. You become better at your talents, whether they involve playing the piano or functioning in the spiritual gift of exhortation, the more you *employ* your gifts.

The third step is yielding your gifts to the Holy Spirit. At the time you trust in Jesus Christ as your personal Savior, God gives you the presence of His Holy Spirit in your life. One of the functions of the Holy Spirit in you is to empower what you do in the name of Jesus and to cause what you do in the Lord's name and for His glory to produce eternal fruit.

THE HOLY SPIRIT IN YOU ENABLES YOUR SUCCESS

The Holy Spirit functions in many ways to help you become successful as you practice and use your gifts. One way is to heighten your ability to discern right from wrong, good from evil, and to make choices among good alternatives. As you face decisions regarding when and where and how to employ your talents and spiritual gifts, ask the Holy Spirit to help you in the decision-making process. Ask Him to help you discern the way in which you are to go.

Another way in which the Holy Spirit helps you is to empower you to use your gifts to their maximum effectiveness. All work takes effort and energy. The Holy Spirit helps you by renewing your strength, sharpening your senses, and helping you to do the greatest amount of work in the least amount of time in the most efficient manner. What you think you can do well on your own strength and ability, you can do much better when you actively rely on the Holy Spirit's help.

Yet a third way the Holy Spirit helps you is to give you His comfort and reassurance that all things are working together for your good from God's perspective (Rom. 8:28). Too many people waste precious time and energy worrying about whether they did enough, did well enough, or did the right thing in the use of their talents and spiritual gifts. They second-guess virtually everything they have done or are about to do. The Holy Spirit assures you that when you use a talent or spiritual gift with a right motive of love toward God and toward others, He will take what you use and mold it and edit it and transform it into something that is effective, beneficial, and applicable.

A fourth way the Holy Spirit helps you is to nudge you in the direction you should go and toward the people you should touch with your talents or spiritual gifts. Some say the Holy Spirit *convicts* them about the direction they should take, the words they should say, the deeds they should do. Others say the Holy Spirit *moves* them to do certain things, and still others say the Holy Spirit *compels* them to act in certain ways. Whatever term you use to describe the guiding power of the Holy Spirit in your life, the fact is, the Holy Spirit seeks to guide you daily into the ways in which you should walk and the activities in which you should engage. Listen closely to how He leads you.

Now if I said to you that I was sending a person to help you make wise decisions for the greatest amount of success, to empower your work so that you will function at maximum capacity, to ensure that all of your efforts are effective and beneficial, and to motivate you continually, you would no doubt accept the help of that person eagerly and enthusiastically. Well, the Holy Spirit has been sent to do all of that in you and through you. When you ask the Holy Spirit to help you in the use of your talents and spiritual gifts, He *makes* you effective and successful.

It doesn't matter if you are a schoolteacher, a homemaker, a plumber, a carpenter, an attorney, a doctor, or a business executive—God wants you to succeed at the tasks ahead of you. He has built into you the abilities and talents and spiritual gifts necessary for you to do your job exceedingly well, consistently well, and effectively. And He has sent the Holy Spirit to ensure that your use of your talents and gifts will be successful.

NEVER DISCOUNT WHAT GOD HAS GIVEN YOU

Too many Christians do not move into the full success that God has for them because they discount the gifts of God.

Never underestimate or discount yourself or your abilities. If you have the Lord Jesus Christ as your Savior and the power of the Holy Spirit resident in you, you can do *all* things that the Lord leads you to do. To underestimate yourself or sell yourself short is to underestimate God in you and to sell His abilities short.

Never belittle yourself. In criticizing or saying negative things about yourself, you are also saying critical and negative things about Christ in you.

Never count yourself out. As long as you are alive and the Lord is resident in you, you are very much "in the game."

Never use your race, your color, your lack of education, or your background as an excuse. God knows all about your race and color and culture—He caused you to be born with that race and color and into that culture. What you don't know, God knows. What you don't have, God has.

Never use your age as an excuse for not pursuing success. God doesn't have a retirement age for you. You may change your vocation at age sixty-five or seventy or seventy-five, but you are still to live and minister to others and set goals as the Lord directs you to set them and then do what the Lord leads you to do. You are to bear fruit in your old age (Ps. 92:14).

Never use circumstances as an excuse for why you aren't pursuing God's goals for your life. Are you aware that most of the people who have accomplished anything truly worthy in life have come from difficult circumstances? The struggle and strain and stretching and refusing to give up in the face of difficult circumstances create the very qualities that make people successful. God knows all about your circumstances, and He will enable you to overcome them.

A young blind woman had enrolled in a college that was not particularly easy for any person to navigate, much less a person who was blind. A reporter for the college newspaper asked her if she found the campus a major challenge. She responded, "Every day of my life is a challenge. Every day I have to move about in spaces that are new to me. This college is just one more unknown space I must explore. I have trusted God all my life to help me move about safely, so I'll just continue to trust Him to help me move about safely here."

This young woman certainly didn't let the circumstance of blindness keep her from her goal. Her courage had been built up over the years—one day at a time—to handle the challenge ahead of her.

THE POWER OF PRAYER IS RELATED TO YOUR SUCCESS

Not only has the Lord given you the Holy Spirit to enable your success, but He has given you the powerful privilege of prayer. You have the privilege of bowing before God every single morning and saying, "Lord, I need You to guide me today. I need Your help. I need Your strength. Show me how to get along with this person. Show me how to rally the troops. Show me how to be motivated toward my family and toward my job in the balance that You desire."

The Lord delights in your prayers requesting His help. He delights in your prayers of faith and uses them to move aside the obstacles that stand before you. He uses your prayers to thwart the evil intentions of others against you, to destroy the works of those who seek to persecute you, and to demolish the devil's efforts to destroy you and steal from you. God has given you a very powerful tool in prayer—it is a tool that activates the forces of heaven on your behalf and builds a wall between you and the forces of hell.

INTENDED FOR USE!

God put His principles and promises for success in the Bible for one purpose: so that you might believe them, learn them, and use them.

God has built a desire for success into your life so that you will act.

God has built gifts and talents into your life, given you the Holy Spirit, and given you the tool of prayer so that you might use your gifts, follow the leading of the Spirit, and pray with faith that God's will for your success and the success of others will be accomplished.

God does not only want you to know how to be successful in theory; He has given you all you need to be successful in reality.

NINETEEN

A NEED FOR YOU TO MEET

Who *needs* you?

Who will be worse off if you don't show up in their lives today?

You may feel as if nobody needs you, nobody cares whether you are alive. But let me assure you of this: *somebody* on this earth needs you. There is someone out there who is part of God's plan for your life—someone to whom He created you to minister (Eph. 2:10). Someone to whom He will reveal Himself through you. You may not have met that person (or those people) yet, but somebody is desperate for your love, care, and talents.

I once met with a woman whose husband had died a few months earlier. She had been a Christian for quite some time, but she was devastated by her husband's death. He had done everything for her. She had virtually no skills to take care of herself. She didn't know how to write a check or drive a car. About the only things she knew how to do was to shop for groceries and fix meals. She said, "When my husband died, my world fell apart. Without him, there just isn't any life."

She began to sob. She admitted, "I've been having one of those pity parties you talk about ever since my husband died. My mother has talked to me about my getting on with my life, my friends have tried to encourage me, but nothing's working. I try to tell myself that things will get better, but they aren't getting better. I try to pray, but I feel as if the words are just echoing around the empty house. I feel helpless. I feel hopeless. I'm depressed."

I knew enough about her situation to know that her husband had left her with financial means so that she had no worries about meeting the basic needs in her life. But still, she felt she had no purpose, no direction, no meaning to her life.

She finally concluded, "I came to ask you, Do I have a reason for living?"

I let her talk and cry herself out, and then I said, "Let's think about this for a minute." She calmed a bit.

I asked her if she had accepted Jesus as her Savior. She said she had. I asked her when she had done that, and she told me that it had been a number of years ago. "Well," I asked, "are you still saved? Is Jesus still in your life?"

She said, "Yes . . . ," then proceeded to give me a number of "buts."

I said, "Now wait a minute. Is He in your life, or isn't He?"

She said, "Yes, He's in my life," and then she went right on with another "but" and continued with a description of how bad things had been for her in recent months.

I said, "Has Jesus changed?"

"No."

"Do you believe His promises? Are His promises still true?"

"Yes." Again, "But I feel so hopeless and so helpless. What am I supposed to do in my life?"

I said, "Here's the way I look at life. If you are going to enjoy life, you need someone to love and someone to feel loved by. You need something to live for, something that grabs your attention and is bigger than you are. You need to be able to laugh at something. You need somebody to lean on."

This time she didn't come back at me with any "buts." She listened intently. I continued, "You have God to lean on. He's there. He hasn't changed or moved away. You can count on Him. He loves you. So does your mother. So do your children and your friends. From what you've told me, you have some things in your life that are good for a laugh or two. Now what you need to start doing is to focus on someone to love, and something that is bigger than yourself to live for. You need to start reaching out beyond yourself and start giving something of yourself to someone else."

"Do you mean money?" she asked.

"No," I said. "I mean something of *you*. If you get committed to something that requires money or if the Lord leads you to get involved in a project that needs money, He'll show you what to give in that area. I'm talking primarily, however, about giving something of yourself to somebody in need."

"I don't feel as if I have anything to give," she said candidly.

"Sure you do," I encouraged her. "Everybody has something to give. You have time you can give—even if it is to sit with somebody in a rest home or a hospital. You have lots of talents to give. You may not have discovered all your talents because your husband did so many things for you and made so many of the decisions that related to your life, but you are an intelligent, educated, and talented woman. You have abilities you have never tapped into. The main thing is to make yourself available."

She agreed to give some thought to what she might be capable of giving to someone—a person or perhaps an organization in need of volunteers. I gave her the names of several people who could use a willing person to help out in tangible, important ways that were not overly demanding emotionally.

I said, "In choosing a place to give yourself away, you are also going to be putting yourself into a position to find somebody to love."

She quickly said, "I don't think I'll ever fall in love again. My husband was my only true love."

"That isn't what I mean," I said. "There are lots of lonely people in this world who need love—not romantic love, but the love of friendship or the divine *agape* love of God. Look around. There's somebody you know, or somebody you will meet in the course of your giving of your time and talents, whom you will recognize as being a person truly in need of love."

I could tell she was considering this carefully. Some of her "buts" still echoed in my mind—including her great need to feel loved. "You are feeling right now that *you* are the one who is in need of love," I said. "Isn't that right?"

She nodded.

"And you are," I said. "I'm not overlooking your need at all. The way you are going to have the need for love met in your own life is to give love. When we give, we open ourselves to receive. We always receive more from the Lord than we give away."

I opened my Bible to Luke 6:38 and handed it to her to read aloud: "Give, and it will be given to you: good measure, pressed down, shaken together, and running over will be put into your bosom. For with the same measure that you use, it will be measured back to you" (NKJV).

"I thought that was about money," she said after she had read the verse aloud.

"There's no mention of money in that verse," I said. "In fact, that verse is part of a longer passage of Jesus' teaching that is about loving other people and giving to them—a passage that is about doing good to others, even our enemies, and showing mercy and forgiveness to others. When you give love, you are in a position to receive overwhelming, abundant, generous, flowing-over-the-top love."

She said, "Where do I go to find somebody to love?"

I said, "First, find a place where you can serve others in the name of Jesus. Get involved in an outreach ministry of some kind that is helping other people who are in need. Since you are lonely right now, I suggest your going with other Christians in helping with a project that is bigger than what any person can do alone. Get involved."

"I don't know if I have the strength to do this," she said.

"In all likelihood, you don't," I said. Then I turned in my Bible to Philippians 4:13 and again handed my Bible to her so she could read this verse for herself: "I can do all things through Christ who strengthens me."

"You can trust Christ to help you," I said. "Even before you get out of bed in the morning, ask Him to give you the strength to get up, get dressed, and get moving. Ask Him to help you do just one thing every day that will be of help to just one other person. I'm not asking you to take on the world. I'm encouraging you to get involved in some way, every day, in helping to show love to just one other person who needs to know that God cares about him or her."

I paused for a moment, and when she didn't say anything, I added, "What do you have to lose? You're already miserable and without any hope. It doesn't seem to me that you can get any lower than you already are. You said you didn't want to go on this way. Why not give this a try? Trust God to help you, and then make an effort every day to do something to help or show love to another person."

I sensed that she was just about out of "buts." She said, "All right. I'll give it a try."

We had prayer together and she left. I didn't hear directly from her for several weeks. I did ask a couple of people about her and learned through the grapevine that she had volunteered to assist in the childcare center answering the phone and making sandwiches for the children's lunch. Then I heard that she had also volunteered to help with a feeding program for street people. My guess is that when she discovered that making sandwiches was a form of ministry she could do easily, she also volunteered to help make and distribute sandwiches at the early-morning food line.

A couple of months went by, and then I ran into her after a church service. The look on her face told me her story even before she opened her mouth. "It's gone," she said to me. "All that depression. The darkness lifted. I don't know exactly what happened, but I realized one morning that it was just gone."

"Have you found someone to whom you can give your love and care?" I asked.

"Oh, yes," she said, and then she added in a very serious tone of voice, almost as if she was telling me a secret, "Pastor, there are more people in this city who need love than anybody knows. There are some people with real *needs*. I may not be able to do a lot of the big jobs, but I've found that there are a great many little jobs that I can do—jobs that need doing and people who need helping."

"The more you give, the more you receive," I encouraged her, recalling our conversation.

She said, "That's certainly true. I don't think I've ever been this busy in my whole life. I don't have time to be depressed! But you know, I'm the one who is receiving so much. It's just as you said. The more you give, the more you receive."

She was beaming as she spoke. You could see the joy on her face. "And you have hope back in your life?" I asked.

"Oh, my, yes!" she said. "There's a lot that still needs to be done, and I'm convinced that I can help do it!"

YOUR NEED TO GIVE LOVE TO OTHERS

One of the great love stories in the Bible is found in Luke 15:11–24. It is perhaps the most famous of all Jesus' parables. Even if you know this story, I encourage you to read it again:

> A certain man had two sons. And the younger of them said to his father, "Father, give me the portion of goods that falls to me." So he divided to them his livelihood. And not many days after, the younger son gathered all together, journeyed to a far country, and there wasted his possessions with prodigal living. But when he had spent all, there arose a severe famine in that land, and he began to be in want. Then he went and joined himself to a citizen of that country, and he sent him into his fields to feed swine. And he would gladly have filled his stomach with the pods that the swine ate, and no one gave him anything. But when he came to himself, he said, "How many of my father's hired servants have bread enough and to spare, and I perish with hunger! I will arise and go to my father, and will say to him, 'Father, I have sinned against heaven and before you, and I am no longer worthy to be called your son. Make me like one of your hired servants.'" And he arose and came to his father. But when he was still a great way off, his father saw him and had compassion, and ran and fell on his neck and kissed him. And the son said to him, "Father, I have sinned against heaven and in your sight, and am no longer worthy to be called your son." But the father said to his servants, "Bring out the best robe and put it on him, and put a ring on his hand and sandals on his feet. And bring the fatted calf here and kill it, and let us eat and be merry; for this my son was dead and is alive again; he was lost and is found." And they began to be merry. (NKJV)

This parable of Jesus is often called the parable of the prodigal son. In my opinion, it should be called the parable of the loving father. The story is not so much about the son who turned his back on his father and fell into sin, but about the father who continued to love his son and fully accepted him back into his family.

This is the last of three stories and teachings that Jesus gave in Luke 15. In the first story, a man has a hundred sheep. He loses one of them and leaves the other ninety-nine sheep to go in search of the one he has lost until he finds it. He returns home rejoicing and calls upon his friends and neighbors to rejoice with him.

In the second story, Jesus told about a woman who has ten silver coins—very likely the coins of a headdress that was her dowry—and she loses one of the coins. She sweeps and searches her entire house until she finds it, and just like the shepherd who returns with the lost sheep, she calls her friends and neighbors and says, "Rejoice with me, for I have found the piece which I lost."

In both stories, Jesus said, "There is joy in the presence of the angels of God over one sinner who repents" (Luke 15:1–10 NKJV).

What do these three stories tell us about the love of God?

God Is Committed in His Love

God extends Himself to those He loves. He goes after those who turn away from Him.

People often seem to think that God has turned His back on them or given up on them. The very opposite is true. The shepherd goes after his one lost sheep. The woman searches for her one lost coin. The loving father is looking for his son; otherwise he wouldn't see him while he is still a great way off. He runs and falls on his son's neck and kisses him.

God's arms are always open wide, extended to those who have turned from Him. He is committed to love regardless of what happens.

God Desires Your Best

A sure sign of committed love is this: a person wants what is best for the loved one.

I heard recently about a young man who was very much in love with a young woman he had met in college. He had dated her for more than a year and had every intention of marrying her. Just a few months, however, before he had planned to present her with an engagement ring, she went on a short-term missions trip as part of one of her college classes. Her trip dramatically affected her life, and she decided that God might be calling her to be a missionary.

The young man said, "I don't feel the call she feels, and I hate the idea of giving her up, but I love her enough to say to her, 'I want God's best in your life.' If God's best is for her to be a missionary, then she needs to be a missionary."

Giving up his relationship with the young woman was the most difficult thing he has done in his life. At the same time, he had peace. He said not too long ago, "I know that whatever happens, God wants what is best for her *and* for me. I've got great hope that things are going to work out okay . . . maybe not in the way I had thought and hoped and dreamed about a few months ago, but things are going to work out for good. God is in charge of both of our lives, and He's not going to lead either one of us into something that is bad for us."

The loving father in Jesus' parable could have made his returning son a servant. That is what the son requested. That certainly would have been what the boy's older brother would have desired. It would have been what might be expected of the father by the community in which he lived. Nobody would have condemned the father for refusing to accept his son or for making his son a servant in his household. But that wasn't the position the father took. He wanted what was best for his boy—and nothing but the best. The best was to be a son, a full member of the family.

God's Love Is Always Affirming

God tells you repeatedly in His Word, "You belong. You are worthy. You are My child. I am your God. I believe in you, your talents, and your future." The loving father in Jesus' parable never ceased calling his son "son." He stated that his son "was dead and is alive again; he was lost and is found," but the father never stopped believing that his son was going to come home and be his son once again.

God Does Everything You Will Allow Him to Do to Build You Up

Throughout God's Word, we find the Lord giving to His people to build them up and make them great. *Their* turning away to other gods or discounting God or seeking to do things their own way results in their chastisement. God doesn't take from men and women; He doesn't draw His strength, power, or glory by stripping these things from His creation. No! The exact opposite is true. He gives His strength, power, and wisdom to humankind, freely and liberally. He gave His beloved Son to redeem humankind on the cross. He gives generously from the infinite storehouse of blessings in heaven to reward His people.

God asks only that we turn to Him, receive His forgiveness, and seek to obey Him. When we do, He opens the floodgates of blessing in our direction.

The prophet Malachi spoke to a generation of Hebrews who had turned away from God's commandments. They were no longer bringing their sacrifices and gifts to the temple. As a result, the entire nation was suffering, and so was the ongoing worship in the temple. Malachi called the people back to obedient giving with this word from the Lord:

> "Bring all the tithes into the storehouse,
> That there may be food in My house,
> And try Me now in this,"
> Says the LORD of hosts,
> "If I will not open for you the windows of heaven
> And pour out for you such blessing
> That there will not be room enough to receive it.
> And I will rebuke the devourer for your sakes,
> So that he will not destroy the fruit of your ground,
> Nor shall the vine fail to bear fruit for you in the field,"
> Says the LORD of hosts;
> "And all nations will call you blessed,
> For you will be a delightful land,"
> Says the LORD of hosts.
>
> (MAL. 3:10–13 NKJV)

What an amazing blessing is promised to those who obey! God asks them only to obey His commandments, to give one-tenth of their produce and earnings to Him. He gives back a blessing that is so great, they can't contain it. Their crops will produce in abundance. They will be a delightful nation, the envy of all other nations.

But that isn't all.

At the time of Malachi the people also were speaking harshly against God, saying, "It is useless to serve God" (Mal. 3:14 NKJV). The people were praising those who were disobedient and proud against God.

Malachi said that the Lord had a

Book of remembrance . . .
For those who fear the Lord
And who meditate on His name.

(MAL. 3:16 NKJV)

And read what he said of those in the book,

"They shall be Mine," says the LORD of hosts,
"On the day that I make them My jewels.
And I will spare them
As a man spares his own son who serves him. . . .
For behold, the day is coming,
Burning like an oven,
And all the proud, yes, all who do wickedly will
be stubble. . . .
That will leave them neither root nor branch.
But to you who fear My name
The Sun of Righteousness shall arise
With healing in His wings;
And you shall go out
And grow fat like stall-fed calves."

(MAL. 3:17, 4:1–2 NKJV)

God asks only that His people be obedient to His commandments. His blessings to them for obedience are life, healing, and prosperity of spirit. He calls the obedient ones His "jewels"—His special treasure.

You may think the Lord asks a lot of you, but in the context of all eternity and the infinity of the universe, He asks so little. In return for your halting, imperfect, sometimes wavering obedience, He gives you everything that you can ever count as vital or valuable.

God is the One who gives you health and who causes healing to occur in your body when it has been injured or attacked by disease. He alone can cause your body to function in the way He created it.

God is the One who puts you into a family and relationships that are for your benefit.

God is the One who gives you creative ideas for good and then imparts to you the courage to do them. He is the One who enables you by the power of His Holy Spirit to discern evil from good and to make wise choices.

God is the One who causes joy to well up in your spirit and who leads you into paths of righteousness.

God is the One who saves your soul and cleanses you from sin and promises you eternal life with Him.

The Bible tells us very little about God, apart from how generous God is to His people and how diligently He guards them, provides for them, and keeps them from being overwhelmed by evil.

What we know about the loving father in this parable of Jesus is primarily what he *did* for his son. We don't know what the father did for a living. We don't know what chores he gave his son to do. But we do know that he gave his younger son the inheritance that he requested, he greeted his son with open arms when he returned home, he gave him back all the marks of sonship—a robe, a ring, and sandals—and he ordered a celebration to be given in honor of his return. The father did everything within his power to build up his son and restore him fully to what he considered to be his rightful place.

THE PORTRAIT OF UNCONDITIONAL LOVE

In the parable of the loving father, we have a portrait of God and a definition of unconditional love:

- Unconditional love is committed.
- Unconditional love desires the best for others.
- Unconditional love is affirming.
- Unconditional love builds up others.

God desires that you give this brand of love to other people. The fact is, everybody needs this kind of love. And too few people give it.

In an article I read about world hunger, the statistics given regarding the amount of hunger in the world were staggering. In our nation of plenty, we can easily lose sight of the fact that the majority of people in the world will not have sufficient food today (this day and every day), or they have no storehouse of food to ensure that they will eat tomorrow. The majority of the world's people arc always hungry and are never far from the threat of starvation. Not only do tens of thousands of people die daily of starvation, but tens of thousands more are ill with diseases related to lack of food.

And yet, there is sufficient food production in the world to feed all of the people on the planet. World hunger is a matter not of food production, but of food distribution, and in most cases, effective distribution is hindered by the "politics of hate." In most of the places afflicted by starvation, one group of people (generally those in power) doesn't want another group of people to have sufficient food. At its root, hunger is a "heart matter." People don't care enough, don't love enough, and aren't committed enough in their love to feed their neighbors or allow them to be fed.

If every person on the planet awoke tomorrow morning and said, "I'm going to be committed to doing what I can to help others. I desire to see my neighbors fed. I believe my neighbors are valuable, worthy, and important to God and to my nation. And I'm going to do what I can to build them up rather than destroy them," world hunger would be eradicated within a matter of hours or days.

The same goes for wars—including disputes within the office, family, or church.

The same goes for problems that arise from racial tensions or disagreements among religious persuasions.

Unconditional love is never based upon a person's worthiness to receive love; rather, it is an act of the will.

In my opinion, we express unconditional love *only* when we acknowledge that we are the recipients of that brand of love from God. Freely we have received, and freely we must give. We must forget forever the word *deserve* in association with love.

MEETING NEEDS OUT OF A HEART THAT LOVES UNCONDITIONALLY

Why this concern for the nature of unconditional love? Because God desires for you to start giving of yourself with unconditional love to meet the needs of other people.

There are six hallmarks of the way you are to give love and care to others.

1. Acceptance

The loving father *ran* to his son on sight. The movement toward another person is a sign of acceptance. The father did not wait to see what his son looked like or what his son had to say. He ran to him regardless of his son's condition. His was an unconditional love expressed with unconditional acceptance.

God is always in a stance of acceptance toward His children. Anytime you are ready to turn to Him, He is ready to receive you. He accepts you as you are.

Surely, the desire of every parent is to see his child live up to his potential, love God, and do good in life. But the stance of the parent who loves unconditionally must be one of love without qualification. The parent can encourage the child to be and do his best, present the child with the gospel in both example and teaching, and train the child to do what is right. But no parent can control or determine the outcome of the child's life. That is a matter of the child's will and of the child's relationship with God. Encouraging is different from loving conditionally. The parent who loves conditionally says, "I will love you only if you do certain things." To encourage with unconditional love is to say, "I love you because you are my child. I encourage you to be and do your best for *your* sake, not mine."

277

The parent who puts conditions on love wants the child to do or be certain things so the parent will look good. The parent who loves unconditionally wants the child to be and do whatever God leads the child to be and do, so that the child will be blessed and God will receive the honor and praise for His work in the child's life. The motivations are very different.

Acceptance is manifested in many ways, mostly by your saying to another person, "Come be with me." Go with me on this errand, walk with me on our way to a place we both need to go, sit with me a while, or come over and visit. A person feels acceptance anytime you set another place at the table for her, are willing to include her in your plan, or invite her to be a part of your group.

I heard about a child who was adopted into a family when he was ten years old. He was having a little difficulty feeling truly accepted by his new family until the day came when his father said to him, "Here's your set of chores." He said, "When I knew that I had been given certain responsibilities, just like all the other kids, I knew I was on my way to being accepted." Then he added, "But I knew I was fully accepted when my dad disciplined me for failing to complete my chores. He disciplined me just the same as he did the other kids when they failed to do their chores—no dessert that night and no watching TV until the job was done the next day. That's when I knew I was really a part of the family." Acceptance means being included into a group, with the same status, same rules, same consequences, same treatment.

Showing acceptance means treating a person just as you would like to be treated.

Anytime you seek to give love and care to another person, you must examine your motives and ask, Am I willing to accept this person just as she is?

2. Touch

Upon reaching his son, the loving father in Jesus' parable embraced him and kissed him.

Consider the state of the boy. He had been traveling. But not only that, he had wasted all of his inheritance in "prodigal living." He had then experienced famine. And at his lowest point, he had gone to work feeding swine "and would gladly have filled his stomach with the pods that the swine ate." The boy no doubt looked and smelled like the hogs he had been tending. He was wasted away with sinful living and the hunger of famine. To the father, the boy no doubt looked like only a shadow of his former self. From a strict Jewish standpoint, the boy was unclean—a sinner. Of course, Jesus was telling the parable to the Pharisees and scribes, who had been very critical of Jesus' willingness to talk to and eat with sinners.

In the Jewish religious law, touching an unclean person made a person unclean also, and he was to be "separated" from the righteous until he went through certain rituals for cleansing.

The loving father was willing to become unclean. He was willing to touch his son even if it meant that he would be temporarily separated—perhaps even ridiculed or criticized—for his actions.

Our heavenly Father touched all of humankind in sending His Son, Jesus, to this earth. He mingled with sinners. He walked where we walk and did the things that we human beings do. He totally identified with our humanity. Jesus was fully human, even thought He was also fully divine.

The sense of touch is one of the most powerful senses related to emotional well-being and mental health. Children who don't receive sufficient hugs and loving attention have a greatly increased probability of developing psychological disorders in which they become detached from humanity and have an inability to make commitments or to enjoy satisfactory relationships with other people.

Touch has been linked to physical healing. Several research studies reported in recent years have shown that touching seems to be related to a patient's rate of progress after surgery or after an injury.

Taking a person's hand, giving a hug, putting a hand on a person's shoulder or arm can mean a great deal to a person in emotional pain. Touching a person affirms dignity and self-worth.

A woman described her work as a nurse in a rehabilitation hospital for those who had experienced neck and head injuries. Some of her patients were paraplegic or quadriplegic. She said, "Just because a person has been injured doesn't mean that he has any less need to be touched or held. One of our patients is a twenty-seven-year-old woman who was injured in an automobile accident. Her husband

and little girl drive more than forty miles one way, three times a week to visit her. Even though she can't feel anything from the neck down, and has very little control over her facial muscles, she somehow manages to kiss her little girl when her little girl leans over to hug and kiss her mother. She always has a much calmer demeanor after her husband gives her a long hug before he leaves. The sense of touch she has with them is her greatest link to the life she once knew."

So much is said today about unnatural or abusive forms of touching that many people have adopted an attitude, "Better not to touch at all than to be misunderstood or charged legally with a motive that wasn't intended." Even so, everybody I've talked to about touching knows intuitively when touching is good and welcome, and when it is bad and unwelcome. We all need "good touch." If you have a question about whether your touch will be welcomed by another person, ask the person. Don't make assumptions one way or the other. If you touch another person and that person pulls away or rejects your touch, don't force yourself upon the person.

If you have questions about what another person means or intends by touching you, ask the person. You may be reading into the touch a message that the person didn't intend. You can help the person become a better communicator by discussing the matter of physical touch. In the process, you might also become better informed about what others like and don't like about the way you relate to them physically.

Be sensitive to those around you who *need* an unsolicited show of your affection, concern, or compassion. Those who are grieving, who are in emotional pain, or who have just suffered a major disappointment or rejection nearly always appreciate a kind touch.

"But," you may say, "I wasn't raised to show affection in physical ways."

You may not have had a lot of experience in receiving or giving physical affection as a child. That doesn't mean you need to remain a cold, aloof person as an adult. You can change the way you relate to other people. Granted, it will take some courage for you to do so. It may take some practice. But if you choose to be a person who is warm and affectionate, you can become such a person. Ask God to help you show others how much you love them in ways that are appropriate and beneficial to you and the other person.

The key question to ask yourself is this: In giving my love and care to others, am I willing to touch them with the love of Christ?

3. Time

The loving father took time to listen to what his son had to say. Although we have no evidence that the father expected or required the confession his son made, the implication is that the father heard his son fully. Nothing else was as important to him in that hour as being with his son.

Furthermore, he immediately ordered that preparation begin for a celebration. Such celebrations in the culture at that time could last for days. The father made it clear he intended to spend some time with his son! He very well could have said to him, "Well, son, you get cleaned up for dinner, and we'll talk about this later." He could have said, "I've got lots of irons in the fire right now. I'll see you later when I have more time." He could have said, "Talk to my designated representative about getting together the things you need, and we'll touch base when the sun goes down." The loving father didn't take any of those approaches. He was present for his son when his son needed him most.

Our heavenly Father is available to us at all times. He is never too busy to hear our prayers. He is never preoccupied with other concerns to the point that He rejects our presence. Rather, He delights in having close, intimate communion with us. Whenever we are willing to spend time with Him, He is willing to spend time with us.

Some months ago I was feeling overwhelmed by some of the problems I was facing in my life, and I was feeling particularly lonely one night. I began to pour out my heart to God, telling Him how I felt and how miserable I was. Suddenly, it seemed as if the Lord Himself was standing at the end of the sofa on which I was sitting. I didn't see a vision of Him, but I had a very strong awareness of His presence. His presence was tangible to me, although unseen—a presence and power so strong that I really can't describe it accurately. I had no doubt He was there. Then it was as if the Lord spoke to my heart as He stood in my living room, conveying to me His message without any spoken words, *You have Me. Am I not enough for you?*

I responded, "Yes, Lord, You are." And I began to weep.

No matter how you may feel; no matter how you may have been rejected by others; no matter how much you may hurt or how lonely you may feel, you *always* have the Lord. He is all-sufficient.

Who could love you more than the Lord does?

Who other than the Lord can be there at all times for you?

Who can possibly understand you better or know more clearly exactly what you are feeling and what you need?

Who is better able to meet your needs and satisfy your longings?

Who other than the Lord is instantly with you the very moment that you call upon Him?

The Lord loves you with His presence. He is with you every moment of your life and for all eternity.

In giving your love and care to others, take time to listen to people—really listen. Hear them out. Don't cut them short. Let them tell you their whole story.

Take time to sit with those who are grieving or who have suffered loss or who are in the process of recovery. You don't need to say anything. Just be present.

A woman who was in a very serious accident said to me after her recovery, "There were times when I didn't know if I was going to make it, but then I'd turn my head and see that my daughter was sitting in the chair next to my bed. She might be knitting, reading, or even napping. She didn't have to say anything, and neither did I. Just her being there was all that needed to be said. I believe the hours my daughter spent by my bedside were just as important to my healing as the treatment and medications that the doctors and nurses gave to me. She gave me the most precious gift she could ever have given. She gave me her time."

Take time to show up at your child's game, recital, performance, or awards ceremony. Take time to play with your child and share meals with your child. Be there for your spouse when your presence is the best gift you can give. Sometimes a weekend away or a vacation is the greatest expression of love you can make. It says, "I just want to spend time with you."

Are you willing today to show your love in terms of time?

4. Gifts

The loving father gave gifts to his son upon his return: sandals, a ring, and a robe. Each was a special sign that the son was being restored to full family membership. Servants went barefoot. Sons wore sandals. Servants didn't own or wear jewelry. Sons could conduct family business with a family signet ring. Servants wore tunics only. Sons wore robes, including, in many families, ones that were finely embroidered and that were considered to be family heirlooms.

The heavenly Father gives good gifts: "Every good gift and every perfect gift is from above, and comes down from the Father of lights, with whom there is no variation or shadow of turning" (James 1:17 NKJV). God's motives in giving to you are never shadowy and never manipulative. His motive is always unconditional love. He gives you life itself. He meets your material needs. He gives you challenges, opportunities, and work to do. He puts you into a family and gives you people to love and be loved by. He redeems you from evil and calls you His own.

He gives you free will to choose to serve Him and freedom in your spirit to be totally yourself in His presence. He gives you the beauty of nature. He allows you to own works of art and to decorate your home with possessions whose sole purpose is beauty. Everything you can imagine as being good comes from God.

I knew as a boy what it meant to live with a person who gave me nothing. No compliments, no kind words, no tangible presents—I don't recall my stepfather ever giving me anything that could have been considered a gift of any kind. It would have been very difficult for anyone to convince me as a boy that my stepfather loved me. If you love others, you give to them.

Your gifts don't need to be expensive; in fact, they don't need to cost anything. They need to be gifts that come from the heart and show that you took the time and interest to give something that was appropriate and that you thought would be appreciated.

A little girl handed her mother a bright red-and-orange leaf that she had picked up from the yard. "It's a present to remind you that I love you," she said as her mother prepared to leave for work. "I looked through all the leaves that fell last night, and this one is the prettiest." Now, you can't tell me that wasn't a highly valuable gift! It was truly a gift from the heart, and it didn't cost a dime.

Love is giving. Your acceptance, touch, and time are gifts. So are words of encouragement and acts of service. But in a very important way, your tangible gifts are important expressions that you care enough to recognize a need or desire in the other person's life and are doing what you can to meet it.

A coat given to a person who is cold, a casserole given to a family in need or in grief, a bouquet of flowers from your garden to brighten the room of a person unable to leave the house, a telephone call to a friend far from home, a bill paid secretly for a person who is struggling to make ends meet, a card sent to a person who is lonely—all are gifts that convey love.

Do you care enough to give a gift today?

5. Words of Encouragement

Perhaps the greatest word of encouragement that the loving father gave to his son upon his return was: "son." He defined their relationship in terms that must have been highly encouraging to the boy. The father said, "This my son was dead and is alive again; he was lost and is found." The father called his boy alive and found. What comforting and wonderful music to his ears! He had a place, a role, a future, a position. He was wanted.

Your heavenly Father always speaks words of encouragement to you—He tells you that you are His child, His delight, His beloved one.

Your heavenly Father also believes that you can accomplish what He calls you to do. He trusts you to use the abilities He has given you.

Jesus told numerous parables and gave many teachings in which He expressed His belief that those who followed Him were capable of living in right relationship with God. He believed they could invest their God-given talents and multiply them. He believed they could withstand temptation, could discern evil from good, and could understand and apply the Word of God to their lives.

Your heavenly Father believes in you more than *you* believe in yourself. He calls you His child. He believes you are worthy and valuable beyond measure.

Are you willing to put your love into words of encouragement today?

6. Acts of Service

The loving father called for a celebration in honor of his son's return. He ordered the killing of the fatted calf—a calf that very likely had been fed for quite some time in anticipation of that very celebration. He said, "Let us eat and be merry." The celebration was complete with music and spontaneous, joyful dancing.

In what way was a party like that an act of service? The loving father was making a public statement to all in his community that he had fully and immediately accepted his son upon his return. There was no waiting period or proving time before the father publicly declared his full acceptance of his son *as his son*. The father's action was an act that reinstated his son's dignity and worthiness among the extended family and broader community.

Your heavenly Father extends to you the full privilege of being His child the moment that you turn to Him and receive His forgiveness. The person who accepted Christ sixty seconds ago is as much a Christian as the person who has loved and served Christ for the last seventy years.

Your heavenly Father continually helps you, prepares opportunities for you, gives you wisdom to make right choices, and strengthens you with courage. Each is an act of service to you.

Your acts of service to others may take any number of forms:

- Raking a sick neighbor's leaves.
- Dropping off a mother's children at school on a morning when she has a doctor's appointment.
- Doing a chore for a sibling so he can take part in a special event.
- Helping out around the house when you know Mom is tired.
- Babysitting for free so a couple with triplets can go out on a date.
- Bringing Dad his slippers when he collapses into an easy chair after a hard day at work.

To truly serve means to anticipate a need and then act to fill it without being asked. Service can mean volunteering to help in simple ways—answering phones, delivering packages or meals, ladling soup, gathering cans of food, sewing buttons onto used garments, ironing linens used for a church function, manning a booth, helping an adult learn to read, or fixing a sandwich for a hungry child.

Service can also be prayer. Are you willing to take time to visit a person and pray with him or her about a need? Are you willing to intercede on behalf of that person until God answers your prayer?

Are you willing to give legs and arms—energy, effort, and talent—to your love?

SERVICE EVEN AFTER FAILURE

God isn't through with you yet! You may have failed at something in your life. You may have given in to temptation. You may have experienced a divorce. You may have failed in your business or suffered a major setback in your career. You may not have done the things as a parent that you now know you should have done. You may not have obeyed God in the past, and you failed to do what you believed He called you to do.

Those feelings can lead a person to conclude, "God has given up on me." I once heard a woman say, "I feel as if God put me on a shelf and He hasn't even dusted me for a long time."

Let me assure you today, if you are breathing, God is working in you, and He is desiring to work through you.

His love for you hasn't changed one bit. Even if you don't feel His presence or love as you perhaps once did, He still loves you just as much as He ever did or ever will. His love for you has no bounds, no beginning or ending.

Let me also assure you that He still has a great plan and purpose for your life.

Have you ever tried to tell something to someone and he didn't seem to understand you, no matter how many different ways you tried to tell him? It's as if he had a blockage of some kind. That same thing can happen in your relationship with God. If you have no prior relationship with Him, if you have a faulty understanding of Him, or if you have a wrong attitude toward God, you aren't going to hear what the Lord wants to say to you. The fault is not His. It's yours.

My purpose is not to blame you or lay some kind of guilt trip on you about this. Rather, I want to point out to you that we sometimes believe that God is finished with us because we have been taught incorrectly in the past or we don't understand how God works. At times, we don't want to believe that He has more for us to do.

Much of what you believe God desires for you to do is based upon what you have come to believe about God through the years. What is your understanding of God today?

Do you see God as a loving father or a demanding judge?

Do you see God as an intimate friend or a distant acquaintance?

Do you see God as a patient and gentle teacher or an intolerant and angry guide?

Do you see God as a faithful companion or someone who comes and goes from your life?

Do you see Him as a generous provider or a stingy God who reluctantly metes out His blessings?

Do you see God as understanding you thoroughly and yet loving you completely, or do you see Him as removed and conditional in His acceptance of you?

The ways you regard God will determine to a great extent what you believe God desires to do in your life.

DISQUALIFICATION

Others believe that they have sinned in a certain area, and because of that sin, God can no longer use them. That is *not* the gospel of Jesus Christ.

While it is true that God will not use a person who remains or willfully chooses to abide in sin, it is equally true that God always desires to use a person who abides in Him and His forgiveness and who chooses *not* to sin.

Moses killed an Egyptian, but God made him the leader of the people of Israel.

Abraham and Sarah erred in Abraham's fathering of a child by Hagar, but God called Abraham His "friend" and rewarded his faith by giving a son to Sarah.

David once pretended to be a madman, deceiving a king who had given him refuge, but God made him king over Israel.

Jacob tricked his father, his brother, and his father-in-law, but God made him the father of the twelve tribes of Israel.

Mary Magdalene was once filled with demons, but Jesus trusted her to tell His disciples about His resurrection.

Saul was a vicious persecutor of the church, even consenting to the death of Stephen, yet God used him as the apostle Paul to take the gospel to the Gentiles.

The difference in these people's lives was this: when they had an encounter with God, they said yes to Him. They were willing to turn from doing things their way to doing things His way. They didn't remain the people they once were. They chose instead to order their lives after God and to follow His plan for them.

As long as you are in sin, your sin disqualifies you from being a leader in God's kingdom. If you were the commander in chief of an army, you wouldn't put a known spy and traitor in charge of a division of your troops. If you were the head of a company, you wouldn't knowingly put an acknowledged thief and embezzler in charge of all your company funds. If you are serving Satan, God can't make you responsible for completing a task that is intended to benefit His kingdom.

QUALIFICATION THROUGH FORGIVENESS

As much as sin disqualifies you, God's forgiveness qualifies you. There is only one unforgivable sin, and it doesn't apply to any person who still acknowledges that God is God. As long as you have any desire for God, you haven't committed the unforgivable sin.

The unforgivable sin is the sin of saying, "I don't need forgiveness. I don't need God. I don't want anything to do with God's love." As long as a person holds that position, God will not override the free will. He will not demand that the person love Him or receive His forgiveness. He will allow that person to remain in the sin because that is a willful choice. Therefore, a person with that attitude cannot be forgiven or saved from the sinful state. It has nothing to do with God's desire for that person. It has to do solely with the person's lack of desire for God.

If you have any desire whatsoever to know God or to receive God's wondrous love, or if you have ever accepted Jesus as your Savior, you have not committed an unpardonable sin.

Of course, some people set up false standards for behavior—standards that far exceed what the Bible requires. Jesus had trouble with such people in His day. The Pharisees insisted that a person follow every minute detail of the law in order to be considered righteous. The law they insisted be followed was a law largely of human creation—it was a law that went far beyond the Law of Moses in its detail and restrictions.

For example, the Law of Moses stated,

Remember the Sabbath day, to keep it holy. Six days you shall labor and do all your work, but the seventh day is the Sabbath of the LORD your God. In it you shall do no work: you, nor your son, nor your daughter, nor your male servant, nor your female servant, nor your cattle, nor your stranger who is within your gates.

(Ex. 20:8–10 NKJV)

The law that the Pharisees followed went far beyond this. Their law had dozens and dozens of restrictions about what specific activities could be done on the Sabbath and which were considered to be illegal. According to their code, Jesus couldn't heal on the Sabbath.

Jesus' response to those who attempted to supersede the law of God with their own laws was this:

They bind heavy burdens, hard to bear, and lay them on men's shoulders; but they themselves will not move them with one of their fingers. . . . Woe to you, scribes and Pharisees, hypocrites! For you shut up the kingdom of heaven against men; for you neither go in yourselves, nor do you allow those who are entering to go in.

(MATT. 23:4, 13 NKJV)

The message of God's Word is one of forgiveness and mercy. He freely and completely forgives, and He calls upon us to do the same for one another. Whenever God forgives, we must forgive.

The apostle Paul made a clear distinction between those who choose to remain in sin and those who have accepted God's forgiveness:

> Do you not know that the unrighteous will not inherit the kingdom of God? Do not be deceived. Neither fornicators, nor idolaters, nor adulterers, nor homosexuals, nor sodomites, nor thieves, nor covetous, nor drunkards, nor revilers, nor extortioners will inherit the kingdom of God. And such were some of you. But you were washed, but you were sanctified, but you were justified in the name of the Lord Jesus and by the Spirit of our God.
>
> (1 COR. 6:9–11)

Note that phrase "and such were some of you." Paul stated that there were those in the Corinthian church, whom he addressed as "those who are sanctified in Christ Jesus, called to be saints" (1 Cor. 1:2), who once engaged in the most vile sins. *And yet*, God forgave them when they turned to Him. They didn't remain in their disobedience or unrighteousness. They received the righteousness of Christ in their lives. And God then used them to be His witnesses in the city of Corinth.

God's forgiveness of you qualifies you not only to be in eternal relationship with Him, but also to offer service *now*.

LOVE IS IN THE GIVING—EVEN IF THERE IS NO RECEIVING

Your willingness to love must never depend upon another person's ability to give love back to you. Some people will never be satisfied with what you do for them. Some people will never feel worthy, no matter how much you encourage them or attempt to include them fully in your life. In risking love, you are also risking the possibility of being rejected or turned away. A person may even reject you while saying that he loves you!

The goal in loving is not to succeed in evoking the response you want from another person, but to do what you believe the Lord is pleased for you to do.

You must seek to give love in ways that others can accept your love, but if they cannot accept your love in spite of your best efforts, then you must ask yourself, Is God asking me to show love to this person? If so, then you can be assured that He accepts your efforts and values them. He will reward you by sending you someone who can receive your love, and who can return love to you in precisely the ways and in exactly the moments you need it most.

Also ask yourself, Can I accept the forms of love that others are showing to me? Be open to receiving the love of others.

Because your challenge as a Christian is to love others *even if they don't love you back*, you are never without somebody to love. Reciprocity is not required for this kind of love. The only thing that is required is your willingness, your desire, your commitment to open up and give to others something of who you are and what you have.

If you don't have somebody who needs you today or who counts on your love, find somebody! You only need to open your eyes and look around, and you'll find dozens of people within immediate range who greatly need to know that somebody cares for them.

Volunteer your time to an organization or group that needs an extra pair of hands or perhaps a particular skill that you have.

Join a group that shares your interests. Do so not with an eye toward what you can get from the group, but with an intent to give something to the group. Your gift of love may be baking cookies for refreshment time once a quarter, typing up minutes of the group meetings, offering your living room for meetings, or picking up members who no longer drive so they might attend the group's meetings.

Get involved with a church group actively engaged in ministry to others. It may be a group of ushers who assist with church services. It may be a group that goes door-to-door to deliver information about the church. It may be a group that prepares boxes of clothing and bedding to send to mission stations.

You'll find more opportunities to give than you ever dreamed possible. You'll find more people in need of love and compassionate care than you ever anticipated.

THE LINK BETWEEN LOVE AND HOPE

To love others is the greatest purpose you can know.

When you know that someone is counting on your help, when you know that you're making a difference in someone else's life, when you can see that your gifts of time and talent are greatly valued, when your loving touches are accepted and returned, when your words of encouragement fall on appreciative ears, and when your acceptance of another person creates a friendship or establishes a good relationship, you automatically have a sense of purpose and meaning for your life. You have a desire to love more, to give more, to extend yourself further.

And in that, there is hope. You want tomorrow to dawn because there is still a lot of loving that you have to do tomorrow. You want next week to roll around because there's still a lot of giving that you want to do next week.

On the other hand, if you isolate yourself and turn inward, refusing to acknowledge the hands that are reaching out to you and refusing to believe the encouragement that others attempt to offer, you will become increasingly depressed and have a growing feeling that you are worth nothing and that life is over. Loving others is the most hope-filled thing you can do.

TWENTY

PROMISES TO EXPERIENCE

A young man walked down the aisle of our church, and to my surprise, he announced to me, "I just got out of prison." He had been in prison for several years and had actually anticipated spending a much longer time in prison. He had been paroled earlier than he expected.

He said, "When I went to prison, I thought my life had ended. I lost all hope." In his cell block, however, there was a television set, and he began to watch our *In Touch* program. At first he sneered and didn't pay much attention, but as the weeks went by, he became more interested. He said, "I kept hearing you talk about how God loves us and how God is good. I thought, *Well, if God is good, why am I in here? Why have so many bad things happened to me?* But week after week you kept telling me that God loved me. Finally, I said to myself, *Maybe this is true.* I was so hopeless, I figured this was better than the way I was feeling. I didn't see anything I had to lose."

The young man began talking to another man in prison—a Christian—and the man led him to Christ. He said, "For the first time in my life, I began to think that I might have a future. I had never thought about having a future before. I never thought I could have one. But when Christ came into my life, I began to think in terms of my future." He then said that he wanted to join the church so he could soak up everything he could about God and what God might have for him to be and to do. He said, "I do believe that God can use me now."

GOD'S CONDITIONAL PROMISES

Part of what God has for you to experience in your life—a part of your equipment for being who He wants you to be and doing what He wants you to do—are His many promises. Some of these are conditional promises, in which God says, "If you will do thus and so, I will do thus and so." You can keep yourself from receiving the fulfillment of God's conditional promises if you fail to do your part.

Other promises are ones that God says He is going to fulfill regardless of what you may do—these are the promises that relate to all of humanity or to His people as a whole. These promises were made possible by what Jesus did or according to what God has said. You cannot make them happen or keep them from happening.

Perhaps no place in the Bible are the conditional blessings of God spelled out in greater detail than in Deuteronomy 28–30. Read these words of potential blessing that God gave to His people:

> Now it shall come to pass, if you diligently obey the voice of the LORD your God, to observe carefully all His commandments which I command you today, that the LORD your God will set you high above all nations of the earth. And all these blessings shall come upon you and overtake you, because you obey the voice of the LORD your God: Blessed shall you be in the city, and blessed shall you be in the country. Blessed shall be the fruit of your body, the produce of your ground and the increase of your herds, the increase of your cattle and the offspring of your flocks. Blessed shall be your basket and your kneading bowl. Blessed shall you be when you come in, and blessed shall you be when you go out. The LORD will cause your enemies who rise against you to be defeated before your face; they shall come out against you one way and flee before you seven ways. The LORD will command the blessing on you in your storehouses and in all to which you set your hand, and He will bless you in the land which the LORD your God is giving you. The LORD will establish you as a holy people to Himself, just as He has sworn to you, if you keep the commandments of the LORD your God and walk in His

ways. Then all peoples of the earth shall see that you are called by the name of the LORD, and they shall be afraid of you. And the LORD will grant you plenty of goods, in the fruit of your body, in the increase of your livestock, and in the produce of your ground, in the land of which the LORD swore to your fathers to give you. The LORD will open to you His good treasure, the heavens, to give the rain to your land in its season, and to bless all the work of your hand. You shall lend to many nations, but you shall not borrow. And the LORD will make you the head and not the tail; you shall be above only, and not be beneath, if you heed the commandments of the LORD your God, which I command you today, and are careful to observe them. So you shall not turn aside from any of the words which I command you this day, to the right or the left, to go after other gods to serve them.

(DEUT. 28:1–14 NKJV)

Is there anything that a man or woman could desire that isn't covered in this conditional promise of God's blessing?

God tells His people that He will provide them with these things:

- Peace in both the city and the countryside (so that there will be no need for armed fortresses)
- Children who are a blessing
- Plenty of food and material goods
- Success in their work
- The accomplishment of everything they set their hands and minds to do
- Victory over their enemies
- An ongoing and lasting prosperity, not merely a temporary or seasonal one
- A firm relationship with God as His holy people
- An excellent reputation with other people
- The opportunity to be a blessing to others
- Leadership opportunities for the good of all

If you were to define what it means to be fulfilled in your life's work and to have all that truly matters in this life, you'd probably list these very things!

What do you need to do to avail yourself of this blessing?

- Diligently obey the voice of the Lord
- Carefully observe all His commandments
- Do not follow after other gods

God went on in the following verses of Deuteronomy 28 to identify what would happen if His people did not obey Him or keep His commandments. Deuteronomy 28:20 summarizes the condition: "The LORD will send on you cursing, confusion, and rebuke in all that you set your hand to do, until you are destroyed and until you perish quickly."

WE MUST DO OUR PART

I heard about a college professor who had a student complain that he had been unfair in giving the student a failing grade. The professor called for a conference with the young man and the chairman of his department to confront the student with the accusations that he was making against him.

The young man said, "Your course is too difficult. You expect too much of us students."

The teacher replied, "Out of forty students in your class, thirty-eight passed the course."

The young man sputtered, "Well, I think your tests are unfair. They aren't clear."

The professor asked, "How much did you study for each of the four tests in this course?"

The young man refused to reply but instead said, "You've had it in for me since the first day of class. You wouldn't answer my questions in class."

The professor said, "What was my frequent question to you when you asked questions in class?" The student sat in sullen silence. The professor said, "Didn't I ask you, 'Have you read the assignment in the text?'"

The professor then got out his class attendance book and said, "You were absent from class fourteen times out of fifty-one class and lab sessions. That's about 30 percent of the time. You failed eight out of ten multiple-choice quizzes that were directly related to textbook readings and that were graded by other students during class hours. I can't help concluding from those scores that you didn't read the text. You scored 40 percent on two of the exams and less than 30 percent on the other two."

The young man then asked belligerently, "Do you know who my father is? Do you know the size of the contributions he has made to this school and what is at stake if you fail me?"

The professor said, "I believe I would be failing to do the right thing by you if I gave you a passing grade."

The department chairman had heard enough at that point. He said, "This professor didn't give you a failing grade, young man. You earned a failing grade by what you didn't do. I'd be happy to have a conference with your father in attendance if that's what you want."

The young man stormed out of the professor's office in a rage.

Before you get mad at God for not blessing you enough, or become angry with Him for certain situations in your life, you need to ask yourself honestly, Have I been listening intently to what God has to say to me? Have I been reading His Word so I will know His commandments? Have I been heeding His commandments and observing them carefully in my life? Have I allowed myself to begin to worship idols—to hold some material possessions or relationships in my life with greater regard and devotion of time and service than I hold my relationship with God?

Many of God's promises of blessing are ones that are contingent on what you do or don't do.

Another of God's conditional promises to His children is found in Exodus:

If you diligently heed the voice of the LORD your God and do what is right in His sight, give ear to His commandments and keep all His statutes, I will put none of the diseases on you which I have brought on the Egyptians. For I am the LORD who heals you.

(15:26 NKJV)

Again, your part is to listen to God and keep His commandments to you. His part is to keep you free of the diseases of the Egyptians, which to a great extent were diseases caused by infected water, plants, and animals, as well as rampant sexually transmitted diseases.

God is a God of healing, but you must do your part.

A LIFESTYLE OF BLESSING

The Cross is God's designated entryway to a lifestyle of blessing. The Cross is the means by which you become God's person, a part of the greater family or people of God. A lifestyle of grace is something God desires for all His children. It is a lifestyle marked by these qualities:

- Acceptance—God's acceptance of you and your acceptance of Christ
- Availability—of yourself to God and God to you
- Abundance—for total prosperity and wholeness
- Abiding—Christ in you and you in Christ so that you might bear much fruit
- Accountability—facing up to your faults and sins so that you might repent of them and thereby remove the obstacles that limit blessing

A LIFESTYLE MARKED BY ACCEPTANCE

The Cross assures you of God's acceptance. When you believe in Jesus, God considers all barriers between you and Him to be removed. Full reconciliation and intimacy of relationship are possible.

God's acceptance and forgiveness of you, and God's acceptance and blessing of you, are related to your acceptance of God. Accepting God's forgiveness is not a matter of works. It's a matter of opening your heart, mind, and hands to *receive*. There is no earning or striving involved.

I want you to read me very closely on this point because the promises related to God's blessing are very closely tied to this matter of acceptance.

Many people question whether they can ever be accepted by God. They say, "I've committed too many sins," or "I've committed a sin that is too big," or "I've sinned after God forgave me, so how could He forgive me again?"

The Cross is God's plan to assure you that you can never sin too many times or commit a sin that's too big or too terrible. You simply cannot "out-sin" God's desire and ability to forgive you.

Later in Deuteronomy we read these words,

> Now it shall come to pass, when all these things come upon you, the blessing and the curse which I have set before you, and you call them to mind among all the nations where the LORD your God drives you, and you return to the LORD your God and obey His voice, according to all that I command you today, you and your children, with all your heart and with all your soul, that the LORD your God will bring you back from captivity, and have compassion on you, and gather you again from all the nations where the LORD your God has scattered you. If any of you are driven out to the farthest parts under heaven, from there the LORD your God will gather you, and from there He will bring you. Then the LORD your God will bring you to the land which your fathers possessed, and you shall possess it. He will prosper you and multiply you more than your fathers. And the LORD your God will circumcise your heart and the heart of your descendants, to love the LORD your God with all your heart and with all your soul, that you may live.
>
> (DEUT. 30:1–6 NKJV)

God told His people that even if they disobeyed Him and suffered the consequences of being scattered to the ends of the earth, if they repented—turned their hearts back to Him and followed what He commanded them—He would restore them fully to all that He promised.

Your acceptance of God and His commandments is all that is required for you to be in right relationship with God. There are no works that you must accomplish before He extends His promises of soul-satisfying, life-giving blessings.

Your relationship with God is not based upon your good deeds. It is not based upon your offering of a blood sacrifice at a designated shrine, your doing a series of charitable acts of kindness, or your belonging to a particular denomination. It is not based upon anything that you produce, achieve, or earn.

Rather, your relationship with God is based upon belief—your believing that Jesus Christ is God's Son come in the flesh and that Jesus Christ is Lord.

Behavior is the substance of religion. Belief is the substance of relationship.

You don't have to wonder if you have done enough to get good enough for God. You can say, "I believe in You, God, as the Giver of life. I believe in what Jesus did on the cross to give me life abundant and life forever. I accept Your plan!"

So many people I know live under a terrible cloud of "I hope I've done enough to please God." They hope they've read enough of the Bible and prayed enough. They hope God will forgive them. They hope they'll be considered worthy of heaven.

Such hope isn't true hope.

True hope lies in saying, "Thank You, God, for saving me! Thank You for loving me! Thank You for Jesus Christ and what He did for me on the cross! Thank You for giving me Your Holy Spirit to guide me and comfort me!"

Be very clear in your spirit on this point: your behavior and the state of your soul are two distinct things in God's eyes. Once you have accepted Jesus Christ as your Savior and have accepted God's love and forgiveness, you are His eternally. There is nothing that can separate you from Him (Rom. 8:38–39).

The mistakes you make and the sins you commit after you have accepted Christ Jesus do not separate you from God. He will convict you of these sins so you can confess them, be forgiven, repent of them, and make a change in your future behavior—for your sake, for your good. But these sins do not separate you again from God. God told His people that even if they disobeyed Him and experienced all the negative consequences, He would still be there when they turned to Him. He continually called Himself "the LORD your God." They never ceased being His people.

Suppose you say, "Oh, God, I've really messed up. I know You're going to wipe me out today." Believe me when I tell you that God isn't going to pay any attention to what you say! Your behavior—including what you think and say—doesn't bring you into a state of condemnation.

Your relationship with God is based upon what Jesus has done, not what you have done, do now, or will do. It's solely based upon what Jesus did on the cross. You may make mistakes, but Jesus does not. You may be imperfect, but He is perfect. God's forgiveness is based upon His plan that has been fulfilled through Christ Jesus.

Ephesians 2:8 clearly states, "For by grace you have been saved through faith, and that not of yourselves; it is the gift of God." Receive His gift with your faith. Be assured that you have been saved and are in right relationship with Him.

God's plan for you is that you have assurance of your salvation and that you are loved by God.

ACCEPTANCE AND BLESSING

How does this relate to your receiving the fulfillment of God's promises of blessing in your life?

First, you must accept the fact that God desires to bless you. You must stop accusing God and blaming God for the lack of substance or the troubles you experience. In many cases, you have brought upon yourself the consequences that you are experiencing. God makes it very clear in His Word that His desire is to bring about good things in your life, in the present and for all eternity.

Second, you must accept the fact that your sins are related to your blessings. But, you may be saying, I thought you said that behavior had nothing to do with my relationship with God.

I did. Your good deeds can't earn you God's salvation, forgiveness, or love. Salvation is a free gift of God extended to you. You must only believe and receive in order to be saved and born again in your spirit.

As long as you continue in sin and refuse to accept God's offer of forgiveness, there's nothing God will do. He will not override your free will.

After you have accepted God's forgiveness, there is no amount of sin that can separate you from God's love. You have entered into a relationship with Him that is irreversible. At the same time, your behavior does influence the degree to which God can trust you with His blessings and to which He will reveal Himself to you. If you continue to ignore God, He will not force Himself upon you. If you continue to choose sinful behaviors over righteous behaviors, He will not ignore the consequences of sin and pour out to you a blessing.

Your behavior doesn't determine your relationship with God, but it does determine to a great extent the degree to which God can bless you.

I heard about a young woman who was very angry that a bank had not given her a loan that she desired. "I need that money to pay my bills," she said. "If I go into default on my house and car, it's the bank's fault."

She refused to accept the fact that she had terrible credit and was too great a risk for the bank. Her lack of funds wasn't the bank's fault. It was the fault of her overspending in the past.

When you face up to your sins and accept responsibility for your behavior and its related consequences, you then can turn to God and accept again His forgiveness for your sins. You can say to God, "Please help me not to do that again. Show me the way in which You want me to walk, and give me the courage and strength to walk in Your path." You can accept again the plan and purpose that God has for you.

If you fail to heed God's voice, you can turn to God, receive forgiveness, and begin again to listen to Him and to obey Him.

If you fail to keep His commandments, you can turn to God, receive forgiveness, and begin again to observe and keep His commandments.

If you have served false gods and given your time, talent, devotion, and respect to things or people above God, you can turn to God, receive forgiveness, and begin again to worship and serve God as your first priority.

The acceptance of God's way is your responsibility. When you accept Him, His acceptance of you is both certain and firm. You can always count on God to forgive you every time you ask Him for forgiveness.

A LIFESTYLE MARKED BY AVAILABILITY

Through the cross, God has made Himself totally available to you—sixty minutes an hour, twenty-four hours a day, every day of every year of your life.

Jesus invites you to come boldly into the throne room of God and to find grace and mercy for help in your times of need. He makes God completely accessible.

Anytime you have a need, problem, difficult question, doubt, or lack of substance in your life, you can turn to God immediately, make your request known, and receive His wisdom and His provision.

God's provision for you may come about in stages or steps. You may not receive immediately all that you request from Him, but the tide is turned the moment you turn to Him. Whenever you cast all of your care and concern upon Him and rely upon Him totally to supply your need and to show you how you are to live, He is quick to respond.

The woman I mentioned who had asked for and been denied a bank loan experienced this. A friend confronted her by saying, "It isn't the bank's fault you are in financial trouble. It's your own fault. If you want real help, you need to see a financial counselor."

The woman agreed to accept this form of help. She went with her friend to see a financial counselor, who had volunteered his services at her friend's church. The woman made a budget for the first time in her life. She faced her mountain of bills and mapped out a plan for paying them.

In the process, she allowed her car to be repossessed, and she used public transportation for six months while she could save for the purchase of a used car—one she later called a real "clunker." She gave up her home and moved into an apartment she could afford. Slowly but surely, she began to chip away at her debt. One of her favorite pastimes had been shopping. She decided that the best way to avoid overspending was to avoid shopping. She took on a part-time evening job as a diversion. She later said, "This took my eyes off all of the commercials on TV, which really caused me to focus on material things, and it took me out of the mall." To her benefit, of course, was added income to pay against her debt. It took her two years of very diligent saving, paying bills, and working an extra fifteen hours a week to pay off all her bills.

Then she found that what she had been paying on her bills was money freed up to spend on a better car. After she had her car paid off, she began to save for a house. In all, it took her almost five years to completely turn around her financial situation to one where she had no indebtedness other than her mortgage and enough monthly income to pay her bills.

Was God at work in this? Most assuredly. The woman began to attend the church where she had received the free financial counseling, and she learned about God's plan for prospering her life. She began to tithe regularly and to get involved in outreach ministries at the church. She said about her activities in the church, "One day I realized that the things I enjoyed doing the most were things related to the church. And you know what? Most of those things were *free*. I had spent thousands of dollars a year on entertainment—on going places and doing things to try to have a good time and make friends. Now I was having a good time and making friends, and it wasn't costing me a dime!"

Was God available when this woman turned to Him for help? Absolutely.

Was His desire to bless her and bring her into greater prosperity and wholeness in every area of her life? Absolutely.

Did He begin to work immediately when she turned to Him for help? Absolutely.

Was her problem solved in a day? No. Was her problem solved in a way that brought glory to God and was of lasting and eternal benefit to her? Absolutely.

God is available to you whenever you turn to Him.

Stop to consider what Jesus did with His disciples and those who loved Him. He traveled with them. He watched them fish. He fixed breakfast for them by the side of the lake. He walked the dusty roads of the land with them. He had picnics with them on the hillsides of Galilee. He had supper with them. He washed their feet. He laughed with them and cried with them. Jesus made Himself totally accessible to His disciples while still maintaining His need for prayer and time alone with His heavenly Father. He even said about the little children who were brought to Him, "Don't stop them from coming to Me." Jesus had time for people.

Jesus didn't demand or require that His disciples bow to Him and give

Him homage. He said to His disciples, "You aren't My servants. You are My friends!" (John 15:15).

Many people I've met assign these labels to God: *severe, condemning, stern, perfection-demanding taskmaster.* These words make God seem untouchable.

How about these words instead? *Tender, warm, loving.* That's the way we think of Jesus as He held little children and touched the sick and raised them to wholeness. Jesus said He was just like the Father. In fact, He said to His disciples, "If you've seen Me, you've seen the Father!" (John 14:9).

God is accessible to you today. So are the blessings He has for you. You may not receive them in an instant, but you can count on receiving them ultimately.

Make yourself accessible to God. Open up the areas of your life that you have tried to keep from Him. Let Him have all of you. As you make yourself accessible to God, He is able to pour more and more of Himself into you.

A LIFESTYLE MARKED BY ABUNDANCE

Jesus said that He came to give us an abundant life (John 10:10). When we think of abundance today, many people use the word *prosperity.*

One of the foremost concepts you need to understand about prosperity is this: biblical prosperity relates to your entire life. A person can be rich in money and still not be prosperous. When you think of blessing and prosperity, you must think in terms of life's whole—a harmony that has spiritual, mental, emotional, physical, financial, and relational dimensions.

Many people have the mind-set that "my spiritual life is my spiritual life" and "my business life is my business life." They separate the two in their thinking and in their behavior. God, however, does not. From His perspective, the two are virtually and intricately connected. It is not possible to be fully prosperous in life if your spiritual life is lacking, just as it is not possible to be fully prosperous if you have a material or financial lack.

God is not opposed to your having money. Rather, He is opposed to anything that you make an idol or a false god in your life. He is opposed to your worship or love of money. Paul wrote to Timothy, "For the love of money is a root of all kinds of evil, for which some have strayed from the faith in their greediness, and pierced themselves through with many sorrows" (1 Tim. 6:10).

Conversely, God is for your having your needs met. He receives no glory from His people suffering from lack of provision. Some people have misinterpreted the Word of God to believe that God condones poverty and has a special blessing for the poor. There is no blessing attached with poverty in the Scriptures. Jesus wants His followers to care for the poor, give to the poor, and recognize that the poor are with us, but His greater desire is that all men and women be blessed and made whole, including having financial needs met.

God has placed a number of rules regarding prosperity in His Word; among them are these:

- We are not to covet the wealth or possessions of others (Ex. 20:17).
- We are to stay away from greed (Prov. 1:16–19; 15:27).
- We are to shun laziness and work diligently (Prov. 20:4; Eccles. 9:10).
- We are to give generously to those in need (Luke 6:38; 1 Tim. 6:17–19).
- We are to avoid debt (Prov. 22:7; Rom. 13:8).
- We are to trust God fully for our provision and our prosperity (Prov. 11:28; 16:20).
- We are to recognize always that God is the Source of our total supply of provision (Ps. 34:8–10; James 1:17).

Prosperity is far from a matter of receiving only. It is related to your giving, your trust of God, and your attitude toward possessions.

THE BLESSING OF WORK

Part of God's blessing to us is work. Each of us has been given specific talents and abilities that God expects us to use in labor for His kingdom. Some of us are required to labor in full-time ministry. Some are called to be God's witnesses in the workplace, in the medical world, in the school systems, or in a wide variety of other careers. We are to use our talents fully and to trust God to multiply the fruit of our labor for His purposes.

Your place of employment, your employer, your supervisor, your clients, your patients, your students—all are blessings from God to you. They are His tools of provision for your life and also the ones to whom God desires to give *through you*. Again, they are part of God's plan for wholeness and total prosperity in your life— just as you are a part of His plan for wholeness and total prosperity in their lives.

One of the prayers I believe we are all wise to pray is that God will enlarge our usefulness—our capacity and ability to work. We do well to heed this proverb:

> A man will be satisfied with good by the fruit of his mouth,
> And the recompense of a man's hands will be rendered to him.
>
> (PROV. 12:14 NKJV)

God desires that we be rewarded fully for the work that we do.

The Lord also desires that we "increase more and more." Paul wrote to the Thessalonians,

> We urge you, brethren, that you increase more and more; that you also aspire
> to lead a quiet life, to mind your own business, and to work with your own
> hands, as we commanded you, that you may walk properly toward those who
> are outside, and that you may lack nothing.
>
> (1 THESS. 4:10–12 NKJV)

Part of increasing lies in your learning how to work smarter, faster, and more productively and efficiently. I firmly believe that God imparts His wisdom to you regarding your work whenever you ask Him.

WITHHOLDING FROM GOD

Many people miss out on the blessing of God's abundance because they withhold their substance from God. They refuse to give Him any of their material goods—their money, financial resources, or possessions. Some do this out of ignorance; others out of rebellion; others out of a lack of trust that God will meet their needs.

If you truly want to be blessed financially and to loosen the grip that money, or the lack of it, has over your life, you must be generous in your finances toward God. As in all other areas, the degree to which you open yourself to God in giving is the degree to which you open yourself to God for receiving. Jesus taught, "Freely you have received, freely give" (Matt. 10:8 NKJV). And in 2 Corinthians 9:6, we read, "He who sows sparingly will also reap sparingly, and he who sows bountifully will also reap bountifully."

Why does God ask us to give our money to His work? I believe that it is because, to a great extent, our money is a reflection of ourselves. Our giving is a reflection of the degree to which we trust God to supply what we need materially.

Malachi 3:8–12 is one of the clearest Bible passages about what God expects from us. It holds a conditional promise related to our financial and material well-being.

> "Will a man rob God?
> Yet you have robbed Me!
> But you say,
> 'In what way have we robbed You?'
> In tithes and offerings.
> You are cursed with a curse,
> For you have robbed Me,
> Even this whole nation.
> Bring all the tithes into the storehouse,
> That there may be food in My house,
> And try Me now in this,"
> Says the LORD of hosts,
> "If I will not open for you the windows of heaven
> And pour out for you such blessing
> That there will not be room enough to receive it.
> And I will rebuke the devourer for your sakes,

So that he will not destroy the fruit of your ground,
Nor shall the vine fail to bear fruit for you in the field,"
Says the LORD of hosts;
"And all nations will call you blessed,
For you will be a delightful land,"
Says the LORD of hosts. (NKJV)

The heartfelt desire of God is that He might be allowed to bless His people and rebuke the devourer. His very specific method toward this end is the tithe. The tithe, the first tenth of what you receive, is to be from your increase and for your increase. It is the way you open the door of your finances to give and then to receive God's blessing.

When you give the tithe to God, you must always remember, the tithe was never really yours in the first place! All things come from God, including this amount called the tithe. As 1 Chronicles 29:14 declares, "All things come from You, And of Your own we have given You" (NKJV). When you give the first tenth of your earnings back to God, you simply are returning to Him what was His in the first place, and you are asking Him to use your gift for your increase.

The tithe is a sign of your trust in God. It is a tangible sign that you are accepting what God has put forth as a commandment. You are obeying what God has said to do. The tithe, therefore, becomes something of a trigger that brings forth even more blessing. And what a blessing it is!

God will open the windows of heaven and pour out a blessing on you that is so great, you can't contain it all. Certainly, that blessing comes to you in the form of

- an abundance of innovative, creative ideas and insights.
- a fullness of joy and a positive attitude.
- an enhanced ability to communicate with others.
- an abundance of strength, energy, and physical vitality and health.
- new opportunities for work and investment.
- provision from unexpected sources.

Not only that, but God says He will rebuke the devourer. Your work will come to fruition. You will be spared many of the attacks of the enemy against your life and finances. In very practical ways this can mean the following:

- Less illness, and therefore fewer hours of lost productivity and less expense
- Fewer breakdowns in equipment, machinery, or vehicles
- Fewer obstacles or problems
- Fewer accidents or mishaps
- Fewer interruption or delays

Along with this personal blessing, tithes bring a blessing to God's people. The work of the Lord is accomplished more speedily and effectively. Honor comes to God's people. The witness about God's goodness is expanded. The four blessings in this passage of Malachi may be summarized:

- The promise of prosperity
- The promise of plenty
- The promise of protection
- The promise of personal testimony

With God's blessing, of course, you always receive an increased awareness of God's presence. Your relationship with Him grows richer, deeper, more intimate, and more meaningful. God's blessings are bestowed upon you not only so that God might prove Himself faithful to you, but also so that He might draw you even nearer to Himself. That is the greatest form of abundance the human heart can fathom.

I have seen God's principle of abundance work in my life in numerous practical ways. This lesson about giving to God and receiving God's blessing was one of the first lessons I learned as a young man.

In my first job as a young teenager, I worked as a newspaper boy making $4 a week. I gave $1 a week to God's storehouse. I never would have dreamed of limiting myself to a mere forty cents. I was so grateful for the job and so pleased to be earning $4, it never crossed my mind to give back to God less than $1.

Shortly thereafter, I got a job—still as a newspaper boy—for $20 a week. That was a fivefold increase. Talk about the windows of heaven opening! Again, I gave back far more than 10 percent.

While I was working part-time in that job and going to high school, a man offered to help me attend college. I went to college with $75, and I left college not owing a cent. God richly and abundantly met my need. Once I had only a dime in my pocket, but I was never completely without money. And I never gave only 10 percent to God's work. I was in relationship with a God of abundance. My giving was born of gratitude, joy, and thanksgiving. My only regret was that I couldn't give more.

A LIFESTYLE MARKED BY ABIDING IN HIM

Have you noticed a pattern in the receipt of God's blessings?

The more you accept what Jesus has done for you and what the Holy Spirit desires to do in you, the more you experience the loving and full acceptance of God.

The more you make yourself accessible to doing God's will, the more you experience the always accessible presence of God in your life.

The more you give to God with a cheerful heart and a willing hand, the more you experience God's abundance in every area of your life.

This opening of your entire life to God, and your receiving the fullness of God's life imparted to you, is a concept that Jesus called "abiding."

Jesus taught,

I am the true vine, and My Father is the vinedresser. Every branch in me that does not bear fruit He takes away; and every branch that bears fruit He prunes, that it may bear more fruit. You are already clean because of the word which I have spoken to you. Abide in Me, and I in you. As the branch cannot bear fruit of itself, unless it abides in the vine, neither can you, unless you abide in Me. I am the vine, you are the branches. He who abides in Me, and I in him, bears much fruit; for without Me you can do nothing. If anyone does not abide in me, he is cast out as a branch and is withered; and they gather them and throw them into the fire, and they are burned. If you abide in Me, and My words abide in you, you will ask what you desire, and it shall be done for you. By this My Father is glorified, that you bear much fruit; so you will be My disciples.

(JOHN 15:1–8 NKJV)

I want you to notice several things about the abiding process.

You Are to Abide in Christ

Your total identity is in Him. You don't presume to have any gifts, talents, or abilities apart from what God has given you. You don't presume to have any spiritual gift apart from what the Holy Spirit imparts to you. You don't presume to have any goodness in yourself or any righteousness. Your life is totally and completely embedded within Christ and what He has accomplished and is accomplishing on your behalf. Jesus clearly says that apart from Him you can do nothing.

Abiding in Christ means that your total trust is in Him. You don't trust a college degree, a relationship with the boss, appearance, acquisition of material goods, family reputation, "connections," or any other thing to bring you success and fulfillment in Christ. Your total trust is in Christ and in His ability and desire to bring you to the place of success and fulfillment according to His definition and His plan.

You Are Subject to Pruning

Notice here the reason for being pruned—that you might bear "much fruit." God's desire is for your good. He loves you enough to prune you. And he does so in order that you might increase and come to greater prosperity and wholeness.

This passage in John echoes what Jesus said earlier: "Unless a grain of wheat falls into the ground and dies, it remains alone; but if it dies, it produces much grain" (John 12:24 NKJV). Many seeds, much fruit. God's desire is to bless you more and more and more and more until you come to the place where you are into a spilling-over abundance of blessing that is beyond your ability to contain it.

The Fruit That You Bear Is His Fruit, the Result of Your Abiding

God is doing a work of refinement and perfection in you. He is the One who decides which blessing you need at which time. He is the One who directs you to give to others so you might be a blessing to them.

Abiding Is a Matter of Trust

Much of the theology we hear today is self-centered and self-seeking: "God, I want You to heal me, prosper me, bless me, protect me. God, do this, this, this, and thus and so for me."

The truth is that we are not at the center of the universe. But God is, and He requires that we serve Him. We are highly presumptuous when we demand that He do our bidding as if He is our errand boy. The proper relationship with God is one in which we put ourselves into a position to do *His* bidding. He is the Lord God almighty!

When we look to God in any other way, we are into idolatry. When we do not seek the presence of God in us as much as we desire the things that we want God to do for us, we are not worshiping God nearly as much as we are worshiping the provision of God. We are worshiping the blessing instead of the Blessing Giver.

I cannot emphasize to you enough how subtle and insidious idolatry can be. I feel certain that if I asked you, "Do you want to be idolatrous?" you would answer with a resounding, "No!" Most of us, however, are wise to search our souls diligently. As we do, we very often discover that we have placed too much value on certain possessions or relationships, sometimes elevating them above our relationship with God.

A number of years ago, the church was facing a financial challenge, and I felt impressed that I should sell my camera equipment and give the money toward the pledge drive. Through the years, I had invested in top-quality cameras and various pieces of photographic equipment. Since I love to take photographs, I worked to become good at photography, and I took a certain amount of pride in the photographic equipment I purchased. My personal gift involved the one possession that I cherished the most.

To my surprise, I felt a certain amount of pain in making my gift. As much as I wanted to make the gift in my mind, the actual giving of the gift—the day I took the cameras down to the camera store and turned them in for cash—was a tough experience. I hadn't been aware that it was going to be one of God's pruning experiences in my life.

I had to face the fact that I valued the cameras too much. Once I gave the cameras—not only in a literal sense but in my spirit—I felt a great release. He was going to use my gift to help resolve the need in the church, and He was going to use my gift to resolve a need in *me*. He was going to strip away from me my grip on this tangible, material substance that I held to be important.

As it turned out, once I had truly given my cameras to God in my heart and had surrendered myself anew in this area of my life, He dealt in a sovereign way to restore my cameras and equipment to me. They then became to me a gift from God—they were no longer solely something that I had purchased and owned as the result of my own planning and effort; God had turned them into a gift from *Him*.

I have seen this same principle work in the lives of countless people. When God prunes away something in our lives, He causes us to experience or to receive something far more valuable or beneficial. Even more important, spiritual fruit is produced in us. We gain more of the nature of Christ, more of the power of the Holy Spirit, more of the qualities of character that are eternal. Nothing is more valuable to us than our obedience to God, and our trust in Him. When we yield ourselves fully to Him, He pours Himself fully into us.

God will not allow you to abide in anything other than Himself, or allow anything other than His Holy Spirit to abide in you, because God will not allow you to place your trust in anything but Him. He will prune away at you until you come to total submission to His will and total reliance upon His presence and power flowing in you.

Abiding Is Subject to Conditional Consequences

Jesus taught that if you don't abide, you will be separated from His flow of blessings. If you do abide, you can ask for what you desire and receive it. The fact is, if you truly are abiding in God's Word—listening to God, reading and obeying His commandments, giving up idols—then your desires are going to be God's desires. They will be desires that are totally in keeping with God's plan for you. Your desires will reflect the very character of the Holy Spirit in you.

Pruning brings you to the place of desiring only things that are of God.

Once again, the more you abide in Christ, the more He abides in you.

A LIFESTYLE MARKED BY ACCOUNTABILITY

A life of blessing is marked by accountability for your actions. God desires that you be His witness in your sphere of influence. You are responsible for knowing God, experiencing Him, and reflecting Him.

How can you know God? You know Him primarily by reading His Word and communicating with Him in prayer—not only talking to God but listening to Him.

How can you experience God? You can wait on the Holy Spirit to assure you that the words you speak, the decisions you make, and the actions you undertake are right in His sight. He will make Himself known to you if you put yourself in a position before Him to listen to Him and wait for His guidance.

The more you seek to know God and to rely upon God, the more He reveals Himself to you. And the more He reveals Himself to you, the more you automatically reflect Him to others. You don't have to work up a spiritual resumé or strive to perform good works on God's behalf. You can trust God to bring to you the people to whom He wants you to speak and on whose behalf He wants you to take specific actions or to lead you to them.

Your witness is your life. It is reflected in everything you say and do. It is a normal part of your life. Your conversations are naturally sprinkled with the name of Jesus. In fact, you don't even have to think about bringing up His name. Your relationship with Him is something that you are totally at ease in sharing with others. His life becomes your life.

One of the things that the Holy Spirit does in you is to convict you about habits that you need to change so that you might reflect greater glory to God. The Holy Spirit points out to you the things you have done about which you need to apologize or seek to make amends with others. The Holy Spirit calls you continually to accountability—to a full recognition of and responsibility for what you say and do.

Each of us is called to self-judgment. God asks us to evaluate ourselves against the standard of His Word and the life of Jesus Christ. We are called to aim the searchlight onto our souls.

Every time we come to an area of our lives about which we must confess, "This is not what Jesus would do," we are to ask God to help us repent of our old ways and to adopt the behavior that He desires for us to manifest.

This is a lifelong process. No one ever arrives at full perfection. We will always find something more within us that needs to be cleansed and refined.

A number of years ago, I found myself going through an intense personal struggle. I had to confront a number of things in my life—things that I had tended to ignore over the years and things that turned out to be very painful for me to face. We all like to think we're on the road to being perfect, and I believe it's always painful when we realize just how imperfect we are.

Some of what I had to face were experiences and painful memories associated with my childhood. I had excess baggage that I needed to release to God in order to experience a genuine healing and a greater understanding of God's love.

In addition, I have had to face my frustration that life has not gone the way I desired it to go. I have had to deal with circumstances and situations that have been beyond my ability to control or to determine their outcome. Each time one of these situations has arisen, I have found myself in a position of having to choose—either to let God do things His way or to struggle to make things happen my way. I know that letting God do things His way is the course to take, but that doesn't make it any easier. There has been a pruning away of many dead branches in my life.

All of this is a process of accountability. God expects me to face the reality of my life so that I might truly experience and enjoy the reality of His life—a life of unlimited power, wisdom, love, and presence. He is everlasting and unchanging.

Our accountability is for ourselves before God and also an accountability to others in the body of Christ. God calls upon us to be vulnerable to others, to be in a giving and receiving relationship with them: "Confess your trespasses to one another, and pray for one another, that you may be healed" (James 5:16 NKJV).

God loves you too much to allow you to live in an isolation chamber, a state that can quickly lead to your living at one of two extremes. Either you will have a tendency to feel great loneliness and to suffer from feelings of rejection, or you will have a tendency to become self-righteous and highly critical of others. Instead, God desires that you know the blessing of human love—that you be willing to extend love to others and to receive love from others. As you confess your faults and weaknesses to others, and pray for and with others, you are healed.

Your accountability to others requires you

- to be honest with yourself and then with others.
- to value yourself and to value others.
- to tell the truth to yourself so that you might tell the truth in love to others.
- to pursue the excellence of Christ's nature so that you might help others to experience His presence more fully in their lives.

Accountability insists that you face your faults, and face them *first* before confronting the faults of others. Jesus taught, "Why do you look at the speck in your brother's eye, but do not consider the plank in your own eye?" (Matt. 7:3).

Accountability requires that you forgive others so that you might receive forgiveness from God and be able to forgive yourself (Luke 6:37).

What does accountability have to do with experiencing God's blessings? Everything! Unless you are willing to face up to the things in your life that keep you from accepting God's forgiveness, keep you from obeying God's commandments, keep you from making yourself accessible to God, hinder you from abiding in Christ, and cause you to remain outside the flow of God's abundance, you will not take the steps you need to take in order to experience the fullness of God's outpoured blessing.

Unless you are willing to face your sin, you won't repent of it and know an increase of God's power and presence flowing in you.

Unless you are willing to yield to God's pruning, you won't bear much fruit.

And until you are willing to face up to your faults and to submit them to prayer, you cannot be healed and made whole.

The good news is that the more you seek to be accountable for your life, the more the Lord blesses your relationship with Him and your relationships with others.

HOPE FOR A BLESSED FUTURE

What does all of this have to do with hope?

If you are in a state of expectation that God still has good things to pour into your life and through your life to others, you are going to have a hope that you can hardly contain! You are going to envision a bright future that's worthy of your anticipation.

When you know with certainty in your spirit that God is totally accepting of you because you are forgiven and in right relationship with Him, you live without the heaviness of guilt or self-condemnation. You have the freedom to explore all of God's creation and all of the opportunities that He sends your way.

When you make yourself accessible to God and know with certainty that He is always accessible to you, you have greater freedom and boldness to talk to God about what He desires for you.

When you know that God has abundance for you, you are more eager to live in such a way that you qualify fully for all of God's blessings.

When you are abiding in Christ, you have a wonderful sense of security.

When you hold yourself accountable, you are open to the changes that God desires to make in your life for your good. In all these ways, you put yourself into a position to receive more of God's presence and power at work in your life.

CONCLUSION

Walking with God

The Bible frequently uses the example of walking as a description of believers' behavior. For example, we are told to walk as children of light, walk in the truth, walk according to the Spirit, and walk in love. Colossians 2:6 uses this expression to give us an important command: "As you have received Christ Jesus the Lord, so walk in Him."

Many people walk by sight and feelings, but allowing our physical senses to guide us spiritually does not work because the Lord simply will not provide all the information we would like to have. Instead, He wants us to trust Him daily for whatever we require. That is why followers of Jesus Christ are commanded to "walk by faith, not by sight" (2 Cor. 5:7). We must take the first step by faith, and then another, not knowing exactly where He will lead us, but trusting that our omniscient, omnipotent, and loving God has our best interest in mind. Walking in faith means having a personal relationship with God through Jesus Christ that results in fixing our eyes on Him regardless of the circumstances, and believing He will do what is right and what benefits us every time, without exception.

And when you walk with the Lord and have your eyes fixed on Jesus, what do you do when facing a challenge that seems insurmountable? Exactly as Proverbs 3:5–6 instructs you to do, "Trust in the LORD with all your heart and do not lean on your own understanding. In all your ways acknowledge Him, and He will make your paths straight."

So we end this book where we began: Do you believe God can be trusted?

My hope is that after reading this book your faith has been strengthened and your confidence in the future He's planned for you has been made sure. I also pray that after discovering the many blessings that come when you trust God with your life, you will choose to walk with Him with full trust in His plans for you.

Of course, you may still wonder if you are worthy of His love because you've messed up. You've spent so much time doubting and questioning Him, that you're uncertain He truly wants you back.

But rest assured that God created you and knows you completely. He understands your weaknesses, your limitations, and the wounds that hinder you from trusting Him completely. But even when you feel as though you have failed Him, He is quick to receive you and demonstrate His love to you. The question isn't whether or not the Lord will accept you—He absolutely will.

After the Crucifixion, the disciples returned to their former ways of life. Instead of living by faith and doing what God had called them to do, they went back out on the Sea of Galilee to fish (Matt. 4:18; John 21:3–4).

However, after the Resurrection, it is noteworthy that Jesus made a point of going to Peter, reassuring him of His eternal love, and reminding the disciple of his calling. God's plan for Peter's life had not changed. Therefore, Jesus encouraged His disciple not to give up.

Take heart in that. God never gave up on Peter and He will never give up on you either. Even though you may stumble in your faith like the disciples did, it is certain that Jesus will never condemn you once you know Him as your Savior and Lord (Rom. 8:1).

You may falter and fail, but it is not the Lord's desire for you to focus on your shortcomings. Instead, He wants you to set your focus on Him. God evaluates your life not according to *your* ability to remain faithful, but according to *His* faithfulness and the work that was accomplished at Calvary (2 Tim. 2:13). You will always remain the beneficiary of His endless grace and eternal love.

So I challenge you to live as the disciples did. After they saw the risen Jesus, the disciples realized that God always keeps His promises. As their Creator, Savior, and Lord, they acknowledged that He was worthy of all their devotion, honor, obedience, and adoration. So they made the decision to live for Him and walk with Him regardless of what might happen.

I hope you will too. But to do so, you must make the decision they did.

Whatever trials you face, the truth you hold on to with all your heart is this: *God can be trusted.* Even when the world falls apart and it looks like you're in it alone, you can be absolutely assured of the fact that the Lord God is with you. He loves you. He defends you. He provides for you. And when you place your trust in Him and obey Him, it doesn't matter what your circumstances appear to be—brighter days are ahead and many blessings will be yours.

So continue to obey the Lord and trust that He will lead you well—He will not allow you to stray from the paths He has chosen for you. Yes, you may experience times of failure. Life may not always turn out the way you planned, but God is by your side on your journey. Ultimately, He will be glorified, and you will be blessed.

Every challenge presents an opportunity for God to display His faithfulness and love. That's what happens when you decide to believe God can be trusted, even when you do not know what the next day will bring. You can face any circumstance with confidence and hope because it is not your strength, wisdom, energy, or power that is the ultimate source of victory. It is God's ability, and when you trust Him, you tap into an eternal force that cannot be harnessed or hindered by any human constraints.

NOTES

1. J. I. Packer, *Knowing God* (Downers Grove, IL: InterVarsity Press, 1993).
2. Oswald Chambers, *My Utmost for His Highest* (Grand Rapids, MI: Discovery House Publishers, 2017 Classic Edition).
3. Attributed to Donald Grey Barnhouse (1895–1960). Source unknown.
4. C. S. Lewis, *Mere Christianity* (New York: HarperCollins, 1952).
5. Philip Keller, *A Shepherd's Look at Psalm 23* (Grand Rapids, MI: Zondervan, 1970).
6. Amy Carmichael, *Candles in the Dark* (Fort Washington, PA: CLC Publications, 1982).

SOURCES

Text adapted and excerpted from the following sources:

Introduction: Trusting God: *Living the Extraordinary Life*—Principle 4

Part 1: God Meets Your Every Need
1. The Promise Maker: *God Has an Answer for Our Unmet Needs*—Chapter 6
2. Unlimited Supply: *God Has an Answer for Our Unmet Needs*—Chapter 7
3. A Way Out: *God Has an Answer for Our Unmet Needs*—Chapter 8
4. His Presence: *God Has an Answer for Our Unmet Needs*—Chapter 9

Part 2: God Communicates with You
5. Ask, Seek, and Knock: *Living the Extraordinary Life*—Principle 8
6. A Message Precisely for You: *Discover Your Destiny*—Chapter 5
7. Are You Listening?: *How to Listen to God*—Chapter 6
8. Sitting Before the Lord: *How to Listen to God*—Chapter 7

Part 3: God Frees You from Fear and Anxiety
9. Why We Lose Our Peace: *Finding Peace*—Chapter 4
10. Overcoming Fear: *Finding Peace*—Chapter 12
11. Giving Up Anxiety: *Finding Peace*—Chapter 8
12. Dealing with the Causes of Anxiety: *Finding Peace*—Chapter 9

Part 4: God Provides a Way Through Pain and Suffering
13. The Power of Perspective: *How to Handle Adversity*—Chapter 2
14. Advancing Through Adversity: *How to Handle Adversity*—Chapter 5

ABOUT THE AUTHOR

Dr. Charles F. Stanley is the founder of In Touch Ministries and Pastor Emeritus of First Baptist Church of Atlanta, Georgia, where he served more than fifty years. He is also a *New York Times* bestselling author who has written more than seventy books, with sales of more than 10 million copies.

Dr. Stanley's greatest desire is to get the gospel to "as many people as possible, as quickly as possible, as clearly as possible, as irresistibly as possible, through the power of the Holy Spirit to the glory of God." Because of this goal, Dr. Stanley's teachings are transmitted as widely and effectively as possible. He can be heard daily on *In Touch with Dr. Charles Stanley* radio and television broadcasts on more than twenty-eight hundred stations around the world, on the internet at intouch.org, and through the In Touch Messenger Lab. Dr. Stanley's inspiring messages are also published in the award-winning *In Touch* monthly devotional magazine.

Finally Alive in Christ

Disappointment. Disobedience. Despair. When Debbie Gonzalez was on the brink of suicide, her sister knew one thing—only Jesus can save a soul. And His truth cuts through the darkness like a bright light.

She read to Debbie from *When the Enemy Strikes: The Keys to Winning Your Spiritual Battles*. This book by Dr. Stanley helps us recognize when evil is trying to tear us apart.

And Debbie listened. Jesus was reaching out for her! Step by step, she found the courage to say yes to the Savior.

Today, Debbie is a new person. Born again in Christ. Following Him. And enjoying everything she can become in the light of His love. If you know someone who's hurting, share the truth. It could save a life—forever.

THE ENEMY MAY BE STRONG, BUT GOD WILL ALWAYS BE STRONGER.

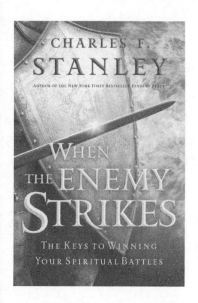

In *When the Enemy Strikes*, bestselling author Dr. Charles Stanley explores how to respond to spiritual warfare—the tactics used by Satan to taunt, confuse, slander, and harm God's followers. The most important component of warfare, says Dr. Stanley, is God's sovereignty and His power. Our world is one of conflict between good and evil, of powers beyond the merely human. You cannot avoid the battle, but do not lose heart—God has given you the strength to stand.

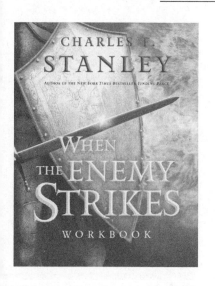

The *When the Enemy Strikes Workbook* includes

- questions for in-depth study,
- guided prayers, and
- quotes from *When the Enemy Strikes*.

This study is ideal for individual or group settings and will help heighten your awareness of spiritual warfare and strenghten your dependence on God.

Pick up a copy today wherever you love to buy books!